D0946354

302.2308 T892
Tucker, Linda G
Lockstep and dance : images
of black men in popular
culture
64885

WITHDRAWN

WITHDRAWN

LOCKSTEP AND DANCE

302.2308
T892
$45.00 1/11/08
064885

LOCKSTEP AND *DANCE*

Images of Black Men
in Popular Culture

Linda G. Tucker

UNIVERSITY PRESS OF MISSISSIPPI

JACKSON

Margaret Walker Alexander Series in African American Studies

www.upress.state.ms.us

The University Press of Mississippi is a member of the Association of American University Presses.

Copyright © 2007 by University Press of Mississippi
All rights reserved
Manufactured in the United States of America

Parts of chapter 2, "The Legacy of Type: Minstrelsy, Lynching, and White Lore Cycles" were published as "Not Without Sanctuary: The Politics and Perils of Teaching Students about Lynching," *Transformations: Teaching Through Testimony* 16.2 (2005): 270–86. Parts of chapter 3, "Court Gestures: Cultural Gerrymandering and the Games That Black Men Play," were published as "Black Balled: Basketball and Representations of the Black Male Athlete," *American Behavioral Scientist* 47.3 (2003): 306–28. Parts of chapter 5, " 'Holler If Ya Hear Me': Black Men, (Bad) Rap(s), and the Return of the Black Brute," were published as "Holler If Ya Hear Me: Black Men, (Bad) Raps, and Resistance," *Canadian Review of American Studies* 31.2 (2001): 57–88.

First edition 2007
∞
Library of Congress Cataloging-in-Publication Data
Tucker, Linda G.
    Lockstep and dance: images of black men in popular culture / Linda G. Tucker—1st ed.
        p. cm.—(Margaret Walker Alexander series in African American studies)
    Includes bibliographical references and index.
    ISBN-13: 978-1-57806-906-4 (cloth: alk. paper)
    ISBN-10: 1-57806-906-8 (cloth: alk. paper)
1. African Americans in popular culture. 2. African Americans—Race identity. 3. African American men—Public opinion. 4. African American men—Social conditions. 5. Stereotype (Psychology)—United States. 6. Racism in popular culture—United States. 7. Popular culture—United States. 8. United States—Race relations. 9. Public opinion—United States. I. Title. II. Series.
    E185.625.T83 2007
    305.896'073—dc22
                                                                                2006011829

British Library Cataloging-in-Publication Data available

For Russ
Who suggested I should,
insisted I could,
and put up with me while I did

CONTENTS

ACKNOWLEDGMENTS

This book would not have been started, let alone finished, were it not for the extraordinary people who gave of their time, energy, minds, and support before and during its gestation. Bouquets of gratitude to Professor Russell E. Chace Jr. for introducing me to Zora Neale Hurston and the richness of the African American literary tradition. Thanks also for suggesting that I scrap my plan to become a physical education teacher and instead pursue graduate studies in African American literature. Little did I know where a course that I took to fill a general education requirement would lead. My heartfelt thanks to Winston Smith, who tolerated the cockiest undergraduate ever and pushed me to "jump at de sun" in more ways than he knows.

I reaped the benefits of an incredible graduate committee at the University of Alberta. For her unwavering intellectual, professional, and personal guidance and support over the past decade, I thank my Ph.D. supervisor, Heather Zwicker. Likewise, a big thank you to Gamal Abdel-Shehid, Adam Krim, Mark Simpson, and Teresa Zackodnik for their generous and astute readings of this manuscript at various stages of its development. Special thanks to Teresa for her kind encouragement and support in the final stages of revision.

Robin D. G. Kelley, although surely one of the busiest people on the planet, is a magician about making time to mentor young scholars. For serving as the adviser of my postdoctoral fellowship and for many other acts of generosity, I am deeply appreciative.

Special thanks to my New York hosts, Jennie Tichenor and Wesley Sutton, for taking me under their wings and including me in their lives during my time there. I would surely have been on the first plane home were it not for the wild and crazy evenings we spent sipping tea, crocheting, and listening to Wesley read James Herriot stories out loud. This book would not have been written had I not had the opportunity to take a postdoctoral fellowship at New York University, but as a country person at heart, I would not have survived living in New York without Jennie and Wesley's kindness.

My warmth and affection go out to Rinaldo Walcott for reading chapters of the manuscript and for his friendship, encouragement, and advice over the years. Thanks to Diana Cooper-Clark for her eleventh-hour reading of the film chapter and to Aaron Blandon, whose friendship and perspective as a reader I value immensely. My gratitude to Mike Borshuk, my partner in time. The most critical career milestones of the past decade have been sweetened by his friendship, his empathy, and his support.

I gratefully acknowledge the financial support of the Social Science and Humanities Research Council of Canada, the University of Alberta, and Southern Arkansas University. Thanks to the librarians at the Schomburg Center for Research in Black Culture and the New York Public Library for their research assistance. It has been an absolute pleasure to work with my editor, Seetha Srinivasan. I thank her for her patience during the writing process and for the clarity with which she saw and articulated what the manuscript needed at various stages. Thanks also to Walter Biggins for his efficient assistance along the way and to Ellen Goldlust-Gingrich for her expert copyediting. I extend my appreciation to David Roediger for his helpful suggestions for revision of the original manuscript and the final draft.

Thanks to Donika Ross for her research assistance, to Shannin Schroeder and Micah Hicks for helping me find a wayward reference, to Michael Counter for sharing his ideas about representation and surveillance, and to all of my students for constantly asking when the book would be done. A special thanks to my colleagues at SAU, especially Lynne Belcher, Stacy Clanton, and Shannin Schroeder, for wisely not asking that question too often but for sharing my excitement when it was completed.

A big shout out to all my friends in the horsey set, especially my trainers, Maggie Johnston and Alan Shaw; my friend Nicky Young (aka Sarge); the amateurs with whom I compete on the American Paint Horse show circuit; and of course my dream horse, Te Lightful Sensation, aka Andy. Our collective escapes to a world where all that matters are boots and chaps and cowboy hats bring a balance to my life for which I am truly grateful.

As a fortune cookie once told me, my family is one of nature's great masterpieces. Bundles of love to my mom, Sharon Tucker; my brother, Gary; and my sisters, Susan and Janet, for their interest in and support of my academic endeavors.

I would be remiss if I did not make loving mention of Hurston and Conjure (1992–2005), who embarked on this journey with me and stayed the course until their times came to cross over across the rainbow bridge.

Finally, thanks to Russ for always showing up, for enabling me to turn my own lockstep to dance, and for epitomizing what it means to be a partner. His never-ending support, intellectual rigor, patience, cooking, and truly unconditional love are but a few of the gifts that he bestows on me each day of our life together. I could not ask for more.

LOCKSTEP AND DANCE

INTRODUCTION

From the point of view of the Afro-American experience, imprisonment is first of all the loss of a *people's* freedom. The questions of individual freedom, class freedom, and even of human freedom derive from that social imprisonment. From this point of view, American society as a whole constitutes the primary prison.

–H. BRUCE FRANKLIN

Scholars of African American literature and culture frequently quote the poignant lines with which W. E. B. Du Bois opens the second chapter of *The Souls of Black Folk*: "The problem of the twentieth century is the problem of the color-line,—the relation of the darker to the lighter races of men in Asia and Africa, in America and the islands of the sea" (16). The frequency with which African Americanists have employed and continue to employ Du Bois's words to capture the importance of race suggests that the problem of the color line continues to shape the social, cultural, and political landscapes of the United States in ways that remain disturbingly unchanged. I began this project during the final decade of the twentieth century, which was marked by the Los Angeles Police Department's beating of Rodney King; revelations of racially motivated corruption and acts of brutality in police departments in New York and Philadelphia; the political exploitation of Willie Horton; O. J. Simpson's fall from grace; the murder of James Byrd in Jasper, Texas; hostility toward and efforts to censor rap music; worsening economic and social conditions in inner-city neighborhoods; and unprecedented levels of unemployment, underemployment, and rates of incarceration for black men. Such events and changes provide evidence that racial hierarchies in the United States and the multiple forms of violence they enable remain central to the nation's organization and identity. Indeed, they are so central that more than one hundred years after Du Bois wrote those prophetic words, there remain critical, political, and social justifications for a book that argues that life for many black men in the United States is akin to living in a prison writ large. Given all that has been done to, done by, said about, and said by African Americans since

The Souls of Black of Folk was published, it is shameful that there remain grounds on which to argue not only that the problem of the color line still existed at the end of the twentieth century but also that it remains one of the major problems of the twenty-first century. *Lockstep and Dance* argues that the continuing problem of the color line is perpetuated through representations that circulate within popular culture and map onto black men the image of the criminal or a hybrid image of the criminal/clown. Such representations function as sites of containment in and further the development of the United States as a prison writ large. The ongoing criminalization of black men through representation is apparent in the images that circulate in advertising, in film, and in the arenas of professional basketball and hip-hop. Images from all of these realms make visible white America's ways of seeing and managing its fear of and fascination with black men. At the same time, images from these realms reveal the myriad ways that black men respond to and often resist the containment wrought by efforts to perpetuate notions that they constitute a class of criminals.

A glance backward provides a lens through which to view and consider contemporary representations that criminalize the images of black men. In the absence of slavery and Jim Crow, which produced, controlled, and exploited a subordinate population and protected the place of white Americans in the social, economic, and political strata, other, more subtle ways of controlling and containing blacks arose. During slavery, slaveholders controlled slaves through punishments that emphasized whites' control over black bodies. Punishments included whipping, poor diet, and hard work. After emancipation, whites found other ways to manage the social, economic, political, and ideological blows that ensued. The Black Codes, for example, circumscribed the mobility of black people in literal and economic terms, and spectacularly violent lynchings of black men reminded both blacks and whites that the theoretical effect of emancipation—racial equality—would be actively resisted in practice.[1] Such methods of containment and discipline constituted precursors to the more subtle but nonetheless related disciplinary method with which this book is concerned: the ongoing criminalization of the black male image through representations that circulate within popular culture.

H. Bruce Franklin, in *Prison Literature in America: The Victim as Criminal and Artist* (1989), traces the criminalization of black men to the U.S. Constitution, which abolished what he calls the "old form of slavery." The Thirteenth Amendment reads "Neither slavery nor involuntary servitude, except as punishment for crime whereof the party shall have been duly convicted, shall exist within the United States, or any place subject to their jurisdiction" (qtd. in Franklin 102). As a consequence of this amendment, as of December 1865 a person could legally become a slave in the United States if one of the states or the federal government defined him/her as a criminal. Accordingly, for all intents and purposes, emancipation did not end slavery in the United States: its form, but not its function, changed (Franklin 101–2). Dylan Rodríguez identifies the form through which the function was mobilized in the late twentieth century as a prison regime, which he defines as a "dynamic state-mediated practice of domination and control" (40). This is not to suggest that the institution of slavery, the penal system, and the representational practices that structure a contemporary system of containment are fundamentally the same in form or function. But it is to say that the language of the Thirteenth Amendment was prophetic, forging explicit connections among the condition of the slave, the condition of the prisoner, and what has over time become the ideological redefinition of black men as a race of criminals. What Rodríguez calls the "post-1960s White Reconstruction" period turns on the pairing of crime with race in the discourse of law and order and relies on "an indelible linkage between the . . . prison and the corresponding world of a consolidated and coherent—though always endangered—normative white civil society" (24).

The persistent and ongoing practices that make it seem as though black men are a race of criminals yield a racialized system of containment in the United States in the form of what Michel Foucault calls a "carceral network" and what I refer to in this book as a prison writ large. A carceral network is a complex ensemble in which incarceration within a prison is but one of many methods of depriving people of their liberty. Within a carceral network, the institution of the prison signifies a society's power to discipline its citizens. Convincing the citizenry of the need for the prison produces a base of support for its use as a disciplinary mechanism and achieves popular acquiescence to its centrality and power. Such support is achieved in part when the conditions that contribute to criminal behavior are introduced, exaggerated, and/or ignored within a society. It is also achieved, as is the case with black men in the United States, when a citizenry becomes convinced that a particular group is innately inclined toward criminal behavior and thus deserving of control via disproportionate levels of incarceration and surveillance. These techniques reproduce the perceived need and necessary justification for the prison as a means of controlling and containing a portion of the population (Foucault, *Discipline* 271).

In the United States, representational practices in popular culture perpetuate the image of black men as a group predisposed to criminal behavior. However, such representational practices have not arisen in a vacuum. Rather, contemporary representations of black men as criminals constitute the legacy of ideas and beliefs that have historically generated a large base of support for violent methods of controlling, containing, and annihilating black men. Such a base of support exists today, although it is solicited and manifests itself in more subtle ways. Nonetheless, these methods reinforce the structure of the prison writ large that limits the freedom and agency of many black men. The ideological effects and material forms of such constructions, representations, and reproductions reinforce racial hierarchies and perpetuate racial oppression. That is, central to the structure of the United States as a prison writ large are the ideological lenses that condition how and what white America sees when it looks at black men and the ways in which black men are implicated in these ways of seeing.[2] *Lockstep and Dance* explores the nature and function of such ideological lenses by analyzing representations of black men in a variety of contexts. In turn, these representations make apparent the peculiar constitution of white America's anxieties about black men. In particular, the complex relationship between white America's fear, envy, and desire vis-à-vis black men and the ideologies that inform these responses shape my discussion of the criminalization of black men. I argue that representational practices that foster the criminalization of black men function as a system of surveillance within popular culture.

On occasions when skeptical students and nonacademics have asked me what this book is about, my response is often followed by doubt and dismissals. "There are a lot of black men in prison," I am told over and over again, "because they commit a lot of crimes." One can see why people might offer this reductive explanation. Jerome Miller, in *Search and Destroy: African American Males in the Criminal Justice System* (1996), cites a 1991 study that showed that "nearly one-third of all the young black men (ages 20–29) living in Los Angeles County had already been jailed at least once in that same year" (5). Such figures suggest that the majority of young black males in Los Angeles will find themselves in some form of carceral institution between adolescence and age thirty (Jerome Miller 5). These statistics tell a story that is not confined to the West Coast. The 1990 Sentencing Project, based in Washington, D.C., revealed that "on an average day in the United States, one in every four African American men ages 20–29 was either in prison, jail, or on probation/parole" (Jerome Miller 7). The Sentencing Project's 1995 report, *Young Black Americans and the Criminal Justice System: Five Years Later*, shows that 32.2 percent of young black men, as compared to 6.7 percent of young white men, are entangled at some level with the penal system. According to the same report, 827,440 young black males are being supervised by the criminal justice system—that is, in prison or jail, on probation, or on parole—to the tune of $6 billion per year (Mauer and Huling 1). On the basis of these and other studies, Miller concludes that nearly three-quarters of eighteen-year-old black men in Washington,

D.C., can anticipate being arrested and jailed at least once before they turn thirty-five; over their lifetimes, that number likely rises to between 80 and 90 percent (7). In 1994, the U.S. Department of Justice reported that nearly six times more blacks than whites were incarcerated and that racial or ethnic minorities constituted 65 percent of the prison population, an increase of 5 percent since 1986 (Jacobson-Hardy 10–11). Such statistics make explicit the extent to which the U.S. penal system functions as a means of controlling and containing black men. The statistics also suggest the presence of a penitentiary rationality that generates overwhelming public support for the extraordinary expenditures required to maintain such high levels of incarceration. Indeed, in 2000 the penal industry was estimated to cost in excess of $40 billion a year (Davis 268). In light of these numbers, one can understand why the smugly articulated cliché "If you do the crime, you do the time" is often used to justify or explain away the disparities.

Many people seem to show little concern that the moral of the motto is upheld disproportionately when black men are involved. Indeed, pointing this out usually elicits the explanation that black men are inherently predisposed to criminal activity. More often than not, the people who have made such remarks to me are utterly unfamiliar with and/or are in denial about the residual effects of the histories that have brought us where we are today. Ignorance of such things notwithstanding, although the common perception that black men are disproportionately involved in the criminal justice system is relatively accurate, the understanding of what accounts for the disparities is usually not. Therein lies the problem, for the product of such ignorance is the penitentiary rationality to which I have already alluded. A penitentiary rationality, or base of public support, is a critical component of the prison writ large that operates in the United States today. This base of support is attributable to public blindness with respect to racist, social, cultural, and ideological maneuvers that make efforts to control and contain black men seem like logical and rational responses to what is perceived as their innate criminality. Such blindness results from the ways that race and the operation of racism distort how white America sees black men to the extent that its behavior, policies, and practices seem both moral and just. Such blindness makes it possible—easy, even—to ignore or deny the devastating consequences of such ways of seeing in black men's lives (Lubiano vii). Ignoring the structural character of racism makes it possible to elide the subject of race when discussing crime and criminality. This elision leaves intact the illusion of a black monopoly on crime, normalizes the disproportionate rates of incarceration, and obviates the need to investigate what underlies both. The legacies of the Thirteenth Amendment, then, are the political and social climates of the late twentieth and twenty-first centuries that demand conformity to politically correct postures and discourage only the most overt expressions of racism (Davis 265).

These legacies compel the development of increasingly subtle means of achieving historically familiar, oppressive ends. For example, the prison regime creates and maintains a disciplined society via both technologies of violence and national discourses that generate consent for the regime's operations. In particular, the regime mobilizes the symbolic realm in ways that yield discourses of "respectability and 'authority' through the mediating material of the prisoner" and criminality (Rodríguez 44–45). In lieu of overt discussions of race, which have been all but completely excised from contemporary political debates, one of the most significant methods of criminalizing black males is through the use of crime as a metaphor for race. John Edgar Wideman is among those who note that although hard-core racism has never been absent from the United States, racial fears have been recoded as fears of crime and criminals ("Doing Time" 16). This recoding enables the project of containing and controlling black men through representations that capitalize on historical fears of black men. The use of crime as a metaphor for race reinforces the penitentiary rationality as it furthers the project of constructing black men as a delinquent, pathological, or criminal class by representing them as dangerous and ubiquitous.

Such representations perpetuate the notion that black men exist as criminal before and after individual crimes. The criminalization of a group relies on the formation of a juncture between penal and psychiatric discourses. This connection posits that psychological causes for criminal behavior may exist (Foucault, *Discipline* 252). Although this may be the case in individual instances, to assume such a connection about an entire class of people is damaging. The notion that black men are predisposed to criminal behavior makes it seem plausible, possible, and wise to exploit their life experiences and cultural productions for political, ideological, and economic ends. Individuals who are members of a criminalized group and who commit crimes are therefore represented differently from non-criminalized offenders whose actions are viewed singularly rather than within a context of innate criminality. In the United States, the white offender is considered to be the "author of his acts," whereas the black male delinquent is seen as being connected to the criminal act by a series of innate traits and tendencies (Foucault, *Discipline* 253). One of the most striking uses of a black man's image to criminalize black men collectively occurred during the 1988 presidential campaign, when Willie Horton, a black man who raped and beat a white woman while on prison furlough, was exploited as a collective symbol of black male criminality (Reed 189–90). Such uses of black men's images perpetuate the view that, as

Toni Morrison puts it, "a nigger is not a person so much as a form of behavior" ("Official Story" xi). The recoding of crime as blackness enables the word *crime* to function as what Miller calls a "rhetorical wink": politicians can use it to advocate and to garner support for aggressive, anticrime agendas without having to openly acknowledge the racist assumptions that underscore them (149). The "rhetorical wink" articulates an otherwise unspeakable desire to manage both white America's fear of black men and black men themselves through such agendas and policies.

The effects of "rhetorical winks" are apparent in anticrime agendas and policies that rely on images of black men as criminals to acquire public support for actions undertaken to ensure safer communities. Although the goal of making communities safer is certainly legitimate, black communities are rarely among those in which such goals are realized. Indeed, more often than not, the opposite has been and continues to be true. The problems of crime, unemployment, lack of education, housing shortages, and debilitating poverty that plague many black communities distinguish them from the white, middle-class communities designated as worthy beneficiaries of crime-reduction efforts. Worse yet, the structural effects of segregation position the residents of black communities as scapegoats for politicians who covertly perpetuate white fears of black men as they mobilize support for anticrime measures. In this respect, such policies fail because they incarcerate black offenders in various kinds of disciplinary institutions that foster a culture of violence. This culture produces, teaches, and thrives on strategies that are necessary for survival within those institutions. The culture of violence then transfers to the streets, where the ethic of the street takes on the character of the rules by which one survives in a maximum-security correctional institution (Jerome Miller 91). In other words, incarceration is an important means by which a society fabricates and reproduces the conditions necessary for the successful construction of a delinquent class. Although the purported function of the penal system is to eliminate crimes and to discipline the behavior of those who commit them, the system in fact reproduces delinquents in ways that detract attention from crimes that a society prefers to hide, accommodate, or supervise through other means (Foucault, *Discipline* 277). For example, prisons offering inmates jobs that are unlikely to lead to gainful employment on the outside set the stage for inmates to commit crimes after their release in an effort to provide food, clothing, and shelter for themselves and often their families. Second, inmates subjected to violent constraints and arbitrary abuses of power within prisons come to view laws and authority figures such as judges and police officers with a deep sense of distrust. Third, prisons that allow inmates to have some degree of contact with one another enable—indeed, encourage—the formation of groups whose members are loyal to one another and are willing to participate together in future criminal acts. Finally, prisons produce future pools of delinquents by indirectly forcing offenders' families into destitution. In these ways, prisons produce delinquents by schooling offenders to regard society as their enemy, thus shaping a peculiar "morality" that drives inmates to devise clever and often violent ways to "escape the rigours of the law" and the abuse that often accompanies its enforcement (Foucault, *Discipline* 268). By creating consensus regarding the criminality of a particular group and by reproducing the conditions necessary to maintain that consensus, a society acquires a base of support for any means by which it attempts to exploit, to control, and/or to annihilate the group in question (Foucault, *Discipline* 266–68).

Further, the penal system serves an important political function by rendering certain types of crimes and transgressions hypervisible and scapegoating the people who (allegedly) commit them. In the United States, the sorts of crimes that receive this type of attention include drug (particularly crack cocaine) possession and trafficking, gang violence, and other forms of street crime. An overwhelming focus on street crime in black communities aids in the criminalization of black men. In contrast, crimes that take place beyond the media's gaze and crimes purportedly committed for the "social good" seem at best less violent and less damaging to the general health of the nation and at worst necessary parts of making communities safer. The sorts of crimes to which I am referring here include insider trading, bank fraud, antitrust offenses, and in black communities police surveillance, harassment, and brutality and other violations of civil rights supposedly undertaken in the interest of law and order. George Lipsitz, in "The Greatest Story Ever Sold: Marketing and the O. J. Simpson Trial," identifies a good example of this pattern in the ironic public response to Los Angeles Police Department Detective Mark Fuhrman's testimony during the trial:

> Rather than expressing anger that a police officer had compromised an important murder case by lying in court and by boasting about breaking the law, media outlets and callers to talk shows largely adopted the prosecution's line of argument, treating Fuhrman like an unsuccessful character whose part had to be written out of the show. They admitted that Fuhrman was a "racist," but contended that his racism was personal and had nothing to do with the widespread practices of the Los Angeles Police Department (witness Chief Gates) or the prosecutor's office. (22)

In contrast, the late Johnnie Cochran was publicly maligned for playing the so-called race card, and his strategy was used as evidence of the general "propensity of Black people to 'blame' their problems on racism." In this trial, Fuhrman was at best seen as an offender, whereas Simpson, his lawyers, and even the black members of the jury that acquitted him were represented as delinquents whose actions and strategies were compelled by a supposedly innate biological propensity to respond to stimuli on the basis of emotions and instincts rather than logic or intellectual reasoning (Lipsitz 23–25). In cases where invasive and violent crimes fail to generate public outrage when the victims are primarily black men, it is more difficult to discount racial prejudice as a factor that shapes public responses. If middle-class white people were subjected to the same routine violations of civil rights and liberties, police harassment, and brutality as black men, we would see considerably more outrage and disgust about such violations than we do now. However, thanks to politicians, the media, the tone and execution of the war on crime and drugs in black urban communities, the drastic deterioration of conditions and opportunities in the postindustrial inner city, and no doubt some black men's actions and cultural productions, the causes and effects of these crimes have been mapped onto the image of the black male.

Lockstep and Dance identifies and analyzes representative examples of images and texts that make apparent the subtle ways in which contemporary popular culture continues the historical practice of criminalizing black men. As the analyses in subsequent chapters reveal, contemporary representations constitute the legacy of stereotypes and beliefs about black men that underscored blackface minstrelsy and the ritualized lynchings that took place during the Jim Crow era. I also call attention to compelling efforts on the parts of black male writers, athletes, filmmakers, and rappers to identify, critique, and resist the ideologies, policies, and practices that structure the United States as a prison writ large for black men. My emphasis shifts gradually from forms of lockstep (containment) toward forms of dance (resistance, play, performance) that take place within such confines. Examples of the latter reside in sites or forms where they are often overlooked or misread. Integral to *Lockstep and Dance*, then, is my commitment to close, textual analysis of images, literary works, and other forms of cultural texts. Although I find the work of many European theorists enabling, I remain dedicated to the practice of drawing theory out of African American literary and cultural productions. My commitment to close reading stems from my appreciation that, as Barbara Christian put it, theorizing by African Americans has long taken place through the use of figurative language, stories, riddles, proverbs, and wordplay. Such are the means through which African Americans have engaged dynamically with questions about "the nature of life" and the "power relations of the world" (Christian 349). I subscribe to the deceptively simple definition that Hortense Spillers offers when she claims that a theory is a method of reading texts for living and dying through their diverse mediations (459). To understand theory as such is to acknowledge that those woven into the texts to which I direct my attention in this project are every bit as sophisticated as those of figures who are more readily recognized and accepted as theorists within the academy. The theorizing that takes place in the forms and forums that Christian and others privilege grows out of the spirited use of a rhetorical practice that is "both sensual and abstract, beautiful and communicative" (Christian 349). Such language is woven into narratives of pain and pleasure, life and death, remembrance and survival, celebration and critique.

I discuss four realms of representation in which the criminalization of black men takes place today and in which they respond to and resist the ways in which this occurs: advertising, film, professional basketball, and rap. The figures and texts on whom and which I focus share in common a place in the U.S. carceral network, which I discuss in chapter 1. This prison writ large is both shaped and upheld by white America's views and treatment of its black male citizens. Most of the men who figure in this project seem to thrive on—indeed, rely on—their ability to represent themselves and other black men as enigmatic texts. Accordingly, I undertake the task of reading what figures such as John Edgar Wideman, Dennis Rodman, Spike Lee, and Tupac Shakur have to say about the prisonlike structures that define so much of life for black men as well as how and why it is necessary and possible to break out of or learn to function more freely within those structures.

The representations to which I direct attention throughout this book reflect the peculiar combination of fear, envy, and desire that underlies white America's views of and responses to black men. Evidence of the persistence and pervasiveness of this combination of emotions is embedded in contemporary popular culture, where representations of black men constitute one of and contribute to the various forms of containment that define the prison writ large. The resultant criminalization of black men's images shapes a form of containment that is as real as and integral to that produced by actual prisons. Yet many of the representations reveal how black men use language, music, their bodies, sport, film, and the media to respond to the criminalization of the black male image. As I discuss in chapter 2, W. T. Lhamon Jr.'s notion of a lore cycle allows us to better understand the complex systems and processes of representation that shape the texts and contexts and the stories and images through which white America and black men alike understand, construct, reconstruct, negotiate, change, and represent themselves and their relationships to one another. In this regard, I focus particularly on the legacies of lore about black men that circulated through two of the methods by which white America has traditionally managed its fear of, fascination with, and desire for black men: blackface minstrelsy and lynching.

The texts and figures on which and whom I focus invite and sometimes force audiences to rethink the unidimensional images of black men that structure the prison writ large. Chapter 3 examines three very different black-focused films: independent filmmaker Aaron Blandon's *The Last Blackface* (2002), Spike Lee's *Bamboozled* (2000), and Cube Vision production *Barbershop* (2002) vis-à-vis Ed Guerrero's claim that an empty space of representation exists in film. Guerrero contends that cultural critics must direct their attention to evidence that there is wisdom and profit in "'loving' black men while simultaneously 'hating' them." Guerrero makes the point that "to fully comprehend society's love-hate bond to its fetish, the black male image must be framed in the broader parameters of the media paradox and the cruel social contradiction inflicted on black men daily." Each of the three films makes a foray into the empty space in representation and, with varying degrees of success, transcends "Hollywood's formulaic narratives" and "channeling [of] most black talent and film production into the genres of comedy or the ghetto-action-adventure" (Guerrero, "Black Man" 182–85). Chapter 4 examines the ways in which white America manages its fearful and voyeuristic responses to black male athletes in ways that are representative of how it has managed and continues to manage its relationships to black men generally. Here I link the game of basketball to the broader "games" in which black men are implicated and in which many are masters when it comes to finding ways to incorporate the pleasure of undisciplined sites into the closely curtailed and regimented structure of the prison writ large.

The texts and figures on which each chapter focuses differ markedly in the ways that they speak to the criminalization of black men's images. Some of these texts and figures reveal a peculiar tension between complicity and resistance. Chapter 5 examines the ways in which criticism of rap and calls for its censorship reflect the fear and loathing of black male agency, sexuality, and autonomy that have always existed at the root of American race relations. We see how the return of the black brute in the spectacular and audible form of the black male rapper haunts white America and compels the calls for censorship and cessation of production that have plagued rap since the 1990s. Such debates indicate a lingering desire to circumscribe the physical, social, and economic mobility of black men whose refusal to be "scene" and not heard, as Houston A. Baker Jr. puts it ("Scene" 39), is articulated so audibly in rap. The single biggest threat posed by the most controversial rap narratives is that they worry the historically consistent supporting logic of American racism.

Although I gesture toward and address the tension between complicity and resistance, for the most part I focus less on contradictions and complicity and more on coherence, consciousness, and resistance in black men's representations of themselves and others. I focus primarily on these areas to avoid perpetuating what Toni Morrison identifies as a historical tendency to assume from the outset that "[i]llogic, contradiction, [and] deception are understood to be fundamental characteristics of blacks." This tendency, as Morrison points out in her reading of the role of race in the O. J. Simpson trial, has the unfortunate effect of situating blacks "outside 'reason' in a world of phenomena in which motive or its absence is sheltered from debate." This tendency also is often played out in public and critical responses to controversial figures such as Tupac Shakur and Dennis Rodman. Yet critical attention to black men's involvement in popular culture reveals that what is dismissed as chaos can often be excavated in ways that reveal its underlying coherence (Morrison, "Official Story" x–xi).

James Baldwin, in *The Evidence of Things Not Seen* (1985) and *The Fire Next Time* (1963), captures the relationships among oppression, resistance, and culture in ways that guide my approach to this project. Baldwin acknowledges the weight of racial terror and contends that African Americans have coped with such terror by approaching its sources with "ruthless cunning, an impenetrable style, and an ability to carry death, like a bluebird, on the shoulder" (*Evidence* 78–79). In Baldwin's view, black people have always risen to the demands imposed by white racism by making "bricks without straw," which is another way of saying that they have found ways to inscribe their humanity on the face of white American culture in spite of and to some extent because of white America's efforts to dehumanize them (*Evidence* 104). Baldwin acknowledges that black people may never be able to usurp white power. Nonetheless, in *The Fire Next Time* he encourages African Americans to generate chaos within the social order because progressive change stands to emerge when chaos is generated within public as well as private realms. As he puts it so eloquently, the "Negroes of this country may never be able to rise to power, but they are very well placed indeed to precipitate chaos and ring down the curtain on the American dream" (*Fire* 88). Baldwin equates change with renewal and suggests that the most significant changes are likely to occur below the surface in what Ellison would term the "lower frequencies" of culture. As Baldwin puts it, "To accept one's past . . . is not the same thing as drowning in it; it is learning how to use it" (81). The images and texts that black men have created and in which they have been implicated indicate some of the ways in which they have learned and are learning to use their past with an eye toward emancipatory ends. My analyses have been directed by Robin D. G. Kelley's reminder that the evaluation of how visionaries use the past to imagine the future ought not to be based on whether the underlying visions were realized but rather "on the merits or power of the visions themselves" (*Freedom* ix).

To excavate the ways in which a past has been or is being used entails certain critical risks to which Ellison points in "The World and the Jug" (1964). In his well-known essay, Ellison takes Irving Howe to task for reducing black people and black writers to mere objects of oppression. Ellison criticizes the notion that unrelieved suffering is the experience with which they are most familiar and therefore the subject with which they are most consumed. Ellison also admonishes Howe for failing to see that African American life is not always a burden but rather a discipline and that black people are more than products of the sociopolitical predicaments that characterize the American experience. As Ellison reminds us, "[B]lacks are products of the interaction between their racial predicament, their individual wills, and the broader American cultural freedom in which they find their ambiguous existence" ("World" 113). He stresses, therefore, that critics must remember that people with black skins retain their humanity, forge values unique to their experiences, and work toward freedom in a multitude of ways and must respond with such pluralities in mind.

Although the United States functions as a prison writ large for black men, resistance has played a critical role in shaping African American cultural and literary traditions. The tension between complicity and resistance leads me to locate resistance on a continuum ranging from the most direct, overt, audible, legible, intelligible, and visible to the least so. The points on such a continuum do not correlate to the efficacy of a resistant act. Indeed, I am uncertain how or even if it is wise to compare the effects of the most elusive forms of resistance with those of the most overt. To evaluate such efficacy would require us to articulate the outcomes with which we associate resistance. It would require us to answer questions such as How many people need to benefit before an act of resistance is deemed effective? How long do the benefits, perceived or real, need to last? How can we know when or in what ways "change" has taken place? The continuum itself cannot answer these questions. But the notion of a continuum of resistance can remind us that there are many ways of understanding and engaging the world as political subjects and direct us to the contradictions, consistencies, continuities, heartbreak, anger, hate, and love that inform the ways that black men negotiate the often fine lines between containment, freedom, complicity, and resistance that shape their and in fact all of our lives.

One of the most recursive images throughout Wideman's fictional and non-fictional work alludes to the complex character of resistance. Wideman repeatedly refers to the sound of ice cracking. In *Brothers and Keepers*, for example, he writes, "Heartbreak is the sound of ice cracking. Deep. Layers and layers muffling the sound" (97). I became cognizant of the significance of that image vis-à-vis the nature of resistance generally and black men's resistance specifically on a November 1997 trip through the Canadian Rockies. We stopped on the outskirts of Banff at a park framed by a stunning view of the mountains and adorned by a small centerpiece of lake. It was a cold, crisp, sunny day with a sky as clear as any that I can recall seeing. Although the ground was bare, the mountains were snowcapped and the lake was frozen. As we stood admiring the scene, we became aware of what sounded like gunshots in the distance. Startled, we listened more carefully and soon discerned that the sounds that we were hearing were not gunshots but rather the sound of the deepest layers of ice on the lake cracking. We stood, mesmerized by nature's ventriloquism, marveling at how the lake's smooth, opaque surface muffled the chaos and noise beneath its frozen veneer. The sound resonated for me because of the extent to which Wideman invokes it throughout his work. He does so, as I realized that day, because the sound—deceptive in its violence, oblique in its location, startling in its effect—captures the nature and function of the social, cultural, and political layers that give rise to as they distort the varying ways in which black men respond to containment within the U.S. prison writ large. In short, this project is motivated by a desire to better understand the nature and function of the lenses through which white America is conditioned to see black men. It is equally motivated by a desire to better understand how and why, despite the ubiquitous presence of the prison and its official and unofficial keepers in their daily lives, black men from all walks of life have been and continue to be nothing short of brilliant, as Greg Tate puts it, when it comes to resisting and making use of "the myriad ways [they've] been fucked with" ("He" 113).

The scope of this book means that it focuses primarily on the experiences and representations of black men in the final decade of the twentieth century and early twenty-first century. As I discussed earlier, this era is of particular importance because the deindustrialization of America's cities and social policies and practices related to the so-called wars on crimes and drugs have had an enormously damaging impact on the material conditions of African American men's lives and the ways in which the media and popular culture have interpreted and represented those conditions.

Lockstep and Dance ultimately gestures toward a critical space where studies of black men's cultural productions benefit from our knowledge, appreciation, and consideration of what Alice Walker calls "contrary instincts" ("In Search" 235). Within such a critical space, I argue, the tendency should not be to dismiss and to discredit black men's representations of themselves and their cultural productions on the basis of their contradictions. On the contrary, the tendency ought to be to explore those cultural productions and their contradictions with a critical view clarified by hindsight concerning past responses to African American literary and cultural productions. To do otherwise, I suggest, is to risk one day discovering, as did Walker of her "mothers' gardens," that the objects of scorn were precisely those that fed the "muzzled and often mutilated, but vibrant creative spirit[s]" of black men who persist in their efforts to make the signs of their resistance and their roars of battle both seen and heard in spaces that seem most "wild and unlikely" (Walker, "In Search" 239).

1

WRITING HOME
Whiteness, Blackness, and the Showdown in the Big House

The journey home beginning and ending with the first word.
JOHN EDGAR WIDEMAN, *REUBEN*

Black men function within a prison writ large structured by various technologies of containment ranging from actual prisons to representational practices. Black men are subject to techniques of containment that criminalize their images and render them silent and, depending on the context, either threatening or comic, hypervisible or invisible. Despite their heterogeneity and pervasive presence, however, such technologies do not function absolutely, as they are constantly subjected to equally heterogeneous and pervasive responses, reversals, and forms of resistance enacted by black men. A clearer view of the systems of containment that shape the prison writ large becomes possible when we understand how white America's ways of seeing black men are implicated and how many black men resist the effects of the containment. The theory of containment, response, and resistance that John Edgar Wideman develops in his nonfictional narrative *Brothers and Keepers* (1984) helps us to see and hear the myriad forms through which African American males express themselves within the U.S. prison writ large. It is important in our efforts to hear the voices that articulate social truths and expose dangerous illusions to which we become attuned, even those that come to us from the most unexpected places.

Illusions about American freedom and justice detract attention from the cleverly disguised racism that motivates and mobilizes regimes of discipline and control in the United States. I have already discussed the extent to which black men are subject to containment within actual prisons at a rate disproportionate to black men's percentage of the U.S. population. This book seeks to make apparent other components of the U.S. carceral network that contain and discipline black men within cell-like compartments. That is, beyond the walls of actual prisons, various forms of cultural compartmentalization function in a manner akin to cells. The effects of such compartmentalization take both ideological and material forms and include, among many others, the criminalization of black men, the sanction of some activities but not others for black males, and surveillance and overzealous policing of black communities. The compartmentalization that structures the prison writ large thereby reproduces the conditions of heterogeneity and isolation that make it possible to surveil, to discipline, and to control black men beyond the walls of prisons.

Caught within such a carceral network, black men are subject to punishments and techniques of discipline and control that are difficult to verify yet every bit as pervasive, as constant, and in some cases, as violent as those employed in prisons. The technologies that discipline and contain black men within the prison writ large condition people to see black males as criminals and thus produce a system of surveillance that operates through representational practices. The prison writ large is produced and reproduced through ideologies of whiteness that inform how popular culture sees and represents black men. When I distinguish between actual prisons and other forms of compartmentalization, I avoid using the terms *literal* and *metaphoric* because the notion of a metaphoric prison suggests that the containment experienced therein is somehow less real than that produced by actual prisons. I do not deny that black men who are compartmentalized by the ways that they are represented as actors or athletes have more appealing lives than those of prisoners in penitentiaries. However, the effects of containment within the various sectors of the prison writ large are in their own ways damaging to black men's public images and psyches.

John Fiske, in "Surveilling the City: Whiteness, the Black Man, and Democratic Totalitarianism," describes the conditions that enable a nation such as the United States to develop and to maintain a racialized system of containment such as the prison writ large. He identifies those conditions collectively as democratic totalitarianism and elaborates on their nature and function. First, Fiske employs Anthony Giddens's definition of *totalitarian(ism)* as a method of rule within states as opposed to the nature of the states themselves (*Media Matters* 240). He lists surveillance, terror, intensified policing, and moral totalism as examples of disciplinary mechanisms that operate especially effectively within U.S. democratic structures by masking their totalitarian undercurrents ("Surveilling" 69). As I discuss in chapter 2 in relation to racial violence during the Jim Crow era, such methods defined the nature and function of lynching as a means of racial control. In environments characterized by democratic totalitarianism, disciplinary regimes disguise the presence and operation of racism in what are represented as democratic environments. The strange combination of democracy and totalitarianism is possible, Fiske claims, because racism is itself inherently totalitarian ("Surveil-ling" 70). The methods by which a democratic society hides racism enable a para-doxical situation in which democracy and totalitarianism coexist.

The masks that disguise the totalitarian undercurrents of U.S. democracy function collectively as the instruments of nonracist racism. These instruments are the systems and practices that have "been developed by white-powered nations that avow themselves to be non-, or even anti-, racist. It is a racism recoded into apparently race-neutral discourses, such as those of the law, of economics, of IQ and education, of health, of housing, or of capital accumulation: each of the social domains within which these discourses operate has racially differentiated effects for which the causes can always be made to appear non-racial" (Fiske, "Surveil-ling" 70). Such methods enable the coexistence of democracy and totalitarianism by making it relatively easy to hide and to distort and difficult to expose and to make people acknowledge the places wherein racism's damaging effects are pro-duced. That is, for those who have the luxury of choice, sidestepping the ques-tion of racism and its draconian effects makes it possible to ignore the totalitarian undercurrents of democracy in the United States while providing people with ali-bis for their blindness (Fiske, "Surveilling" 70).

The most violent aspect of a society that operates under a regime of democratic totalitarianism may well be the duplicitous manner in which it masks its contra-dictory nature and the violence of its effects. The plurality of methods that arise within this regime in the United States are important in the context of this book insofar as black men disproportionately feel democratic totalitarianism's violent material effects. Actual prisons are indisputably violent and frightening places. Yet the rapidity of their mutation into a carceral network that contains black men without walls and disciplines black men in ways that do not require uniformed guards produces another form of containment that may ultimately be even more violent and frightening precisely because its origins are so difficult to discern, its forms are so deceptively innocent, and its effects are so far-reaching.

Surveillance technologies represent one of the best examples of the instruments that mask racism and its effects in the United States. The supportability of the claim that surveillance technologies operate for a generalized public good enables them to effectively hide their oppressive, exclusionary, and racist operations. Further, surveillance is a technology of whiteness that enables different races to be policed differently. Indeed, surveillance is among the most significant of the technologies that enable totalitarian tendencies to hide and work within democratic structures. In part, the significance and effects of surveillance of space and people are so great because it is often viewed as having positive effects. However, Fiske cautions, beneath the assumed beneficence of surveillance technologies lurks a malevolence that often goes undetected. The presumed beneficence disguises the fact that "the law-abiding citizens who are most subject to it have no say in its operation and no ability to influence its impact upon their daily lives" ("Surveilling" 69–70). Furthermore, the supposed beneficence and objectivity of surveillance technologies mask its racialized applications. That is, what goes unrecognized and/or unacknowledged are the ways in which surveillance technologies produce and reproduce the racialized norms and standards according to which individuals and behaviors are seen as threatening or nonthreatening. As Fiske explains, "Coding normality is . . . crucial to surveillance, for the function of surveillance is to maintain the normal by disciplining what has been abnormalized. The racialized other . . . is one of the most urgent objects of abnormalization, for his or her visibility is a formative factor in the constant normalization of whiteness" ("Surveilling" 69–72).

The establishment and reinforcement of notions of the "normal" and "abnormal" are integral to the establishment and reproduction of any social order, and the United States is no exception. Such is the case because norms and the ideologies that give rise to them function as the lenses through which people are trained to recognize what fits, what does not fit, and/or where things fit within a particular order. Whiteness marks the place from which we are conditioned to see what is normal in the racialized social order of the United States. That location is itself marked by the power and the privilege that attend the angle of vision that encodes what is seen as normal and abnormal and thus determines what must be seen and who shall oversee it. In the United States, for example, surveillance technologies enable this kind of identification by coding all that is characteristic of white people and the dominant culture as normal and all that is not as abnormal. As Fiske asserts, "Black behavior is seen, white behavior is not, and the difference is solely one of color: blackness is that which must be made visible, just as invisibility is necessary for whiteness to position itself as where we look from, not what we look at" ("Surveilling" 71).

In significant ways, surveillance technologies include representational practices within popular culture. Surveillance technologies grow out of the notion that the power to see is conjoined with the power to correct—that is, to normalize—behavior that has been deemed abnormal. When behavior coheres with notions of normal behavior, individuals are trusted to go about their daily business in a normal fashion. This methodology is limited, however, by the fact that it is reactive rather than proactive. It does nothing to prevent the abnormal behavior from happening. In contrast, proactive disciplinary technologies such as representational practices at work within the prison writ large seek to predict and prevent abnormal behaviors by identifying those who are believed most likely to be the agents of such behaviors. Proactive disciplinary technologies construct ways of seeing those agents as the embodiment of the behavior that has been coded as abnormal and thus undesirable. One particularly effective way of identifying the abnormal involves criminalizing the figure who is seen and represented as the likely embodiment of an undesirable behavior as opposed to simply labeling as criminal the behavior itself ("Surveilling" 83). In the United States, the consequence of such identification has been the inscription of criminality onto the figure of the black male, who has become the primary signifier of that which white America fears and who is seen as a threat to the social order. Accordingly, black men must be watched (Fiske, "Surveilling" 71). In the United States, black men are watched through various kinds of representations that produce and reproduce the images and ideas by which white America has controlled black men. In keeping with practices common in disciplined societies generally, and as we shall see in my discussions of advertising, film, sport, and rap particularly, black men often are rewarded for representing themselves as criminals, as criminally inclined, or in ways that ameliorate the threat implicit in such images by performing the role of politically neutered, happy-go-lucky figures who like to dance, rap, or play sports.

The overwhelming presence of surveillance technologies today, including representational practices that criminalize black men, is indicative of the dynamic of fear and desire that underwrites the structure of the prison writ large. This dynamic is closely tied to the history of white America's ways of seeing black people generally and black men in particular. As bell hooks argues in "Representations of Whiteness in the Black Imagination," many white people like to think that black people cannot see them, that blacks do not observe whites and their behavior, and that blacks have no concept of whiteness and its role in structuring their relationships with whites and their positions in the social order. In short, hooks argues, whites' belief that black folks see whites as whites wish to be seen and as they see themselves underscores "the rhetoric of white supremacy [that] supplies a fantasy of whiteness" (42). The fantasy is that whites are free to see when, how, and what they choose without ever being seen. That fantasy directs us to the relationship between the surveillance of black men through representations that control how and in what contexts they are seen and their containment within the prison writ large. The fantasy, as David R. Roediger argues, "constitutes a white illusion at once durable, powerful, and fragile. It exists alongside a profound fear of actually being seen by people of color" (6). This is critical because the misguided notion that people of color do not understand the nature and function of whiteness and how it informs the behavior of white people is both "a byproduct of white supremacy" and "an imperative of racial domination" (6). So too, the prison writ large relies to a certain extent on the illusion that the power of surveillance technologies flows in only one direction. The notion that black men can see through, respond to, manipulate, resist, and profit from the effects wrought by representations of them threatens the social order. As I discuss in chapter 5, much of the hysteria around rap constitutes a reaction to black men's appropriation of the black brute persona and the voice that articulates views of white America that do not accord with how white America sees itself.

Accordingly, black men are frequently represented in ways that seem designed to ameliorate the threats that their knowledge of whiteness and their potential agency pose to the illusions that uphold white power and privilege. Cheryl Harris argues that whiteness is both "an ideological proposition imposed through subordination" and a form of property to which only some can lay claim and thus assert entitlement to the benefits and advantages that come with its possession. Furthermore, whiteness creates, reflects, and reproduces relationships between people. Such relationships embody whiteness, which is property "over which continued control was—and is—expected" (Harris 107). The representations of black men that I discuss in the following chapters also embody whiteness and are thus objects over which control continues to be repeatedly contested. Such representations of black men function as resources that are used in the United States to define real black men's relationships to whites and to enable the latter to maintain social, political, economic, and institutional control. The methods through which and the seemingly benevolent contexts in which such representations are used mask how whiteness works through them to affirm black men's subordinate position in the prison writ large. However, although acts of subordination reify ideologies of whiteness, black men's responses and resistance to such ideologies work also to deny their validity, if not their effects (Harris 107).

As distressingly absolute as containment within the prison writ large may seem, then, the potential for resistance is written into the technologies that operate therein. To a certain extent, the participation of those who are contained is integral to the system's efficacy. Yet the necessity for such complicity introduces an ironic variable that poses a potential threat to the absolute control supposedly wrought by the power arrangement generally and to the sovereignty of the white gaze specifically. Although various technologies of surveillance may encourage and/or compel behavior that accords with the dominant order, they cannot entirely prevent transgressions; surveillance technologies can only punish transgressions if they are committed and/or redefine them if they are seen. Thus, however unwillingly or unwittingly black men reproduce the conditions of their own containment, the notion that their complicity is at all important to the system's efficacy implies a risk associated with their recognition of and/or resistance to the ways that the system contains and subordinates them. There exists a dynamic of containment, performance, and resistance that shapes as it is shaped by whiteness and its role in producing the prison writ large.

In the heterogeneous compartments to which the U.S. prison writ large gives rise, power both produces and is produced by the incessant, murmuring voices of those whom it contains. Foucault draws attention to the often ignored, resistant noise characteristic of societies in which technologies of discipline and punishment are at work. He calls for people to attune themselves to the "distant roar of battle" emanating from various loci within the carceral networks of modern societies (*Discipline* 308). The racialized nature of the U.S. prison writ large and the range of forms through which black men respond to and resist their containment make theirs an especially noisy system. As we will see in later discussions of athletes such as Dennis Rodman and Latrell Sprewell, filmmakers Aaron Blandon and Spike Lee, and rappers such as Ice Cube and Tupac, some of these murmuring voices are complicit. Some are resistant. But the sounds of all keep the power arrangement that structures the prison writ large in a state of constant flux. Resistant noise threatens the absolute control that theoretically exists within the prison writ large. The heterogeneity, double-voiced forms, and evasive nature of resistant noise give it a disordered quality. The nature of resistant noise introduces additional disorder into the power arrangement, thus enabling individuals to hide from, to evade, to expose, to distort, and sometimes even to escape the oppressive effects of containment (Foucault, *Discipline* 202). The containment that is wrought within such a disorderly system is therefore considerably less absolute than its structure seems to guarantee. The state of flux within the prison writ large is the product of a perpetual battle in which the stakes include the power made visible through myriad performances, cultural rituals, and cultural products and sought through resistant sounds.

Such performances have the potential to reconfigure the directions in which and the strength with which power flows and operates. This is so because all performances—some more than others—are vulnerable to misuses and challenges, successes and failures. Reimagining power as a dynamic of containment, response, and resistance makes it imperative that we direct our attention to performances and sites of representation that are often extremely enigmatic. The dynamic of containment, response, and resistance within which performances manifest themselves, then, may itself be understood as power, which, as Foucault understands it, does not constitute an institution, a structure, or a strength with which one is endowed but rather is the name for "a complex strategical situation in a particular society" (*History* 93). The contradictions implicit in the structure of the prison writ large call into question the absolute function of power vis-à-vis black men. Black men know that they are being surveilled. Therefore, many act in orderly ways that may signal their willingness to see themselves as they are seen. In such cases, their behavior would seem to complete the cycle through which power is organized and containment is produced and reproduced in the prison writ large. An easy assumption would be that black men have no choice but to see themselves as they are seen. However, the extent to which black men can and do imagine themselves in ways other than they are seen qualifies the extent to which their apparent conformity to the behavior demanded of surveilled subjects renders them mere "objects of information" through disciplinary technologies (Foucault, *Discipline* 200). As John Edgar Wideman so brilliantly conveys in the fictional and nonfictional work to which I turn next, the performance of conformity is something quite different than genuine acquiescence to a subordinate position within a power arrangement.

Wideman, in his brilliant *Brothers and Keepers*, develops a theory of containment, response, and resistance that enables us to better understand both how this dynamic that Foucault calls power works and the role of representation within the prison writ large. Wideman's theory grows out of the way that he uses language and storytelling to examine the dichotomous constructions on which the criminalization of black males depends. His narratives take the form of what Karla F. C. Holloway refers to as recursive or translucent texts. Such texts blend figurative and symbolic processes to produce narratives that are "reflective (mirror-like)," while their "depth and resonance make them reflexive" (Holloway 55). The symbolic and figurative processes that characterize recursive texts tend to be both emblematic and interpretive of the culture that they describe (Holloway 55). The translucent qualities of Wideman's work are apparent in two ways. First, his writing is informed by African American vernacular traditions. Second, he uses vernacular forms to expose the hegemonic performances that require black men to live double lives. The translucent qualities of his writing, like the child who cries "The emperor has no clothes!" expose the hegemonic illusions and fictions that contain black men when such fictions become manifest in various forms of representation. The use of such forms to do just that is especially prevalent in rap and is in part what compels some of the most vehement opposition to the genre.

The translucent qualities of Wideman's narrative techniques are underwritten by W. E. B. Du Bois's concept of double consciousness, or the "sense of always looking at one's self through the eyes of others" (Du Bois 8). In his essay "The Language of Home," Wideman explains why the doubleness that underwrites many vernacular forms is so integral to his work: "EVERYONE lives a significant portion of life below the surface. Art records and elaborates this unseen dimension. A minority culture systematically prevented from outward expression of its dreams, wishes and aspirations must evolve ways for both individuals and the group to sustain its underground life. Afro-Americans have become experts at living in at least two places simultaneously, celebrating a sensitivity to the distance—comic, ironic, tragic—between our outer and inner lives." The notion that there are unseen dimensions, or lower frequencies, of African American lives refers to the myriad ways in which black people generally and black men specifically develop and perform what Zora Neale Hurston calls featherbed resistance. In *Brothers and Keepers,* Wideman's theory of containment, response, and resistance takes shape in narrative spaces out of which a double consciousness emerges and evolves. He employs this sensibility to develop and to make space for others to develop multiple angles of vision with respect to the organization of and black men's situation within the prison writ large. As Foucault tells us, although the effects of power within a disciplined society seem to be homogenous, they are not. Wideman's writing, like many of the representations with which I deal in this book, yields a constellation of perspectives that he situates in contest with one another as a means of exposing fictitious arrangements and representations that compel the subjection of black men in the prison writ large. In the process, he creates a narrative space in which black men may see how they are seen and where they may speak and be heard beyond malevolent systems of distortion.

Wideman's theory of containment, response, and resistance and his use of vernacular forms to construct it reflect one of his primary objectives as a writer and as a black man: to make his way to a place that he calls Home. In "The Language of Home," he offers a definition of *Home* through a discussion of his annual trip to Maine. He claims that when he is in Maine, he returns most easily "home again in fiction and nonfiction, to Homewood, the black neighborhood in Pittsburgh" where he grew up and in which he situates many of his stories. In Maine, he explains, it seems easier "to borrow, to internalize for a few quiet instants, the peace of the elements at play. Whatever mood or scene I'm attempting to capture, the first condition is inner calm, a simultaneous grasping and letting go that allows me to be a witness, a mirror." He notes, however, that

> [t]his state has gradually become more accessible to me only after fighting for
> years to believe again in my primal perceptions, my primal language, the words,
> gestures and feelings of my earliest memories. At some point I taught myself to
> stop translating from one language to another. I've learned I can say the things

I want to say using the words and telling the stories of Homewood people. The blackness of my writing inheres in its history, its bilingual, Creole, maroon, bastardized, miscegenated, cross-cultural acceptance of itself in the mirror only it can manufacture.

To Wideman, therefore, Home represents how he says what he knows, what he wants or needs to say, as well as the act of saying itself. Home is less a place than it is a process or strategy that guides him in his work. As we shall see shortly, Wideman's journey there has not been unfettered.

Toni Morrison also addresses the notion of Home and interprets double consciousness in a manner that complements Wideman's understanding of Home as a process. Morrison contends that double consciousness is most usefully understood as a strategy for liberation. To embrace double consciousness as a strategy for liberation is to embrace the exploration of "the inwardness of the outside, the interiority of the 'othered,' the personal that is always embedded in the public" ("Home" 12). But to see things differently and to articulate them in ways that compel others to do the same and act accordingly requires one's willingness to abandon an attachment to what are often very persuasive fictions. The extent to which Wideman's strategy is informed by double consciousness is apparent in his attention to how and why the lives of and relationships among many African Americans are influenced by what he calls "the impacted quality of utterance" (*Brothers* 76). This quality is apparent in the words and stories of Homewood people, which tend either to bury "a point too obscurely or insist . . . on a point so strongly that the listener wants the meat of the message repeated" (*Brothers* 76). As Wideman notes, "[P]eople in Homewood often ask: You said that to say what?" (*Brothers* 76). The doubleness that such a question recognizes has meaning for those who understand that what is unsaid invests words with special meaning and urgency (*Brothers* 76). Wideman claims to have lost what he calls his "Homewood Ear" when he left Homewood and became a star basketball player, a Rhodes scholar, and a university professor and to have struggled to relearn how to use it ("Language"). His recovery and mastery of his "Homewood Ear" is apparent in the characteristics that he identifies as the "blackness" of his writing ("Language"). Wideman's journeys Home have taught him that "words can be more than signs, that words have magic, the power to be things, to point to themselves and materialize" (*Brothers* 34–35). Armed with that knowledge, he turns the blackness of his writing into a theory that resonates with the urgency of his efforts to expose the fictions and images that contain black men as he restores clarity to their distorted images and voices.

In the author's note that prefaces *Brothers and Keepers*, Wideman locates his work within the African American vernacular tradition: "The style, the voices that speak this book, are an attempt to capture a process that began about four years ago: my brother and I talking about our lives" (ix). By way of this note, Wideman acknowledges the integral relationship that exists between style and subject matter in *Brothers and Keepers*. His elision of the preposition *in* after the verb *speak* signals to readers that he structures the narrative as a speakerly text. Henry Louis Gates Jr. defines a speakerly text as one in which free, indirect discourse is used as if it were a "dynamic character, with shifts in its level of diction drawn upon to reflect a certain development of self-consciousness in a hybrid character, a character who is neither the novel's protagonist nor the text's disembodied narrator, but a blend of both, an emergent and merging moment of consciousness. The direct discourse of the novel's black speech community and the initial standard English of the narrator come together to form a third term, a truly double-voiced narrative mode" ("Signifying" xxv–xxvi). Gates locates speakerly texts within the "signifyin(g)" tradition ("Signifying" xxv). Wideman's use of this vernacular form represents an integral part of the method by which he registers his participation in the strategic situation to which Foucault gives the name *power*. Wideman uses vernacular forms to integrate his writing into that strategic situation and to create a theory with which to mediate texts about black men's lives (Spillers 459) to "salvage [something] from the grief and waste" of "the tragic chain of circumstances that caused one young man to die and sent three others to prison for life" (*Brothers* Author's Note).

In particular, Wideman employs the metaphor of a two-sided mirror to theorize the ways that black men use different kinds of performances to respond to and resist representations of themselves as criminals. One of the most violent effects of incarceration within an actual prison is its imposition of "condition[s] of nonexistence" on prisoners, thereby providing those in the "free world" with absolution from "responsibility for the prisoner's fate" (*Brothers* 188). In *Brothers and Keepers*, Wideman relates how, as his brother Robby's appeals are rejected time and again, he feels as though the courts are intent on denying his "existence as being in any way meaningful or of having any worth at all" (170). Wideman draws an interesting comparison between Robby's feelings specifically, a convicted criminal's entry into prison generally, and the Orthodox Jewish practice of saying kaddish (187). Kaddish, he explains, may be said as a prayer of mourning or may represent "a declaration of death" by which a "child becomes . . . a nonperson, cut off absolutely from all contact, a shadow the father will not acknowledge, a ghost referred to in the past tense as one who once was" (187–88). The imposition of a state of nonexistence on prisoners is not unlike what the historian Orlando Patterson referred to as "social death" and identified as the effect of chattel slavery on Africans brought to the United States (Andrews 130). As William Andrews writes, summarizing Patterson's use of the term,

> [T]he system of chattel slavery was designed to prevent Africans and their descendants from building a new identity except in accordance with the dictates of their oppressors. Instead of an individual, slavery devised what Patterson calls "a social nonperson," a being that by legal definition could have no family, no personal honor, no community, no past, and no future. The intention of slavery was to create in the slave a sense of complete alienation from all human ties except those that bound him or her in absolute dependence to the master's will. (130)

Although the system that transforms the prisoner into a nonperson and that which subjected enslaved Africans to social death are very different, both systems wrought violent social and psychological effects.

As Wideman sees it, the illusion of a prisoner's nonexistence is created and sustained by a system of representation that functions like a "two-sided, unbreakable mirror" (189). One side of this mirror reflects images of order and justice, whereas the opposite side reflects prisoners as "deformed aberrations." Keepers of such systems of representation guard them against interference that might distort the images that make "the free world and the prison world" appear distinct (189). Wideman theorizes the performances through which black men make the two sides of the unbreakable mirror face each other, thus disrupting and undermining the containment wrought by dichotomous representations of black men as deformed aberrations and criminals on the one hand and an uncompromised system of order and justice on the other hand. Such performances distort the fictitious clarity of the racist system represented by the two-sided mirror by introducing a constellation of images that he intersperses throughout the fictitious arrangements that structure black men's containment. That is, Wideman's model features a two-sided, unbreakable mirror that represents a racialized system of binary representation. The two sides of the mirror reflect opposite images in opposite directions. The reflections structure a system of containment similar to that which operates through representation in the United States. The model is structured to prevent the images from confronting their inherent contradictions. Wideman appropriates the technology of the mirror model and incorporates it into his use of language and storytelling, thereby, in Morrison's words, forcing racial constructs "to reveal their struts and bolts, their technology and their carapace" and thus opening the doors and windows of the racial house and pointing the way toward freer spaces ("Home" 11).

In this way, Wideman's writing allows him to function as both witness and mirror in relation to the traditions and experiences of African American people. Through rhetorical practices that expose and sometimes disrupt the damaging effects of hegemonic representations of black men, his narratives function as would multiple mirrors if they were introduced into his two-mirror model. In a manner of speaking, that is, Wideman increases the number and alters the nature of the reflections or representations in such a system. He therefore transforms binary systems of representation into a system characterized by multiplicity and dissonance rather than by dichotomy and certainty. Such dissonance produces the tension between the models of containment, response, and resistance that Wideman theorizes. Moreover, it provides an alternative to representations of black men as seen through the lens of whiteness.

In *Brothers and Keepers*, Wideman accomplishes this transformation through analyses of his visits with his brother, Robby, who is serving a life sentence in Western Penitentiary. He examines issues of complicity and resistance as they pertain to the containment of black men in the prison writ large. His theory of containment and resistance and his understanding of the empowerment possible through performance grow out of his analyses. One of the most compelling aspects of this nonfictional narrative is Wideman's use of Robby's story to enable the author's story to emerge and to theorize his complicity in his own and his brother's containment. John Wideman draws on Robby's experiences in prison to identify and to expose the illusions and fictions that Wideman had allowed to structure his containment on the outside. As he puts it, he uses Robby's story as "a hiding place, a place to work out anxiety, to face threats too intimidating to handle in any other fashion" (*Brothers* 77). By connecting Robby's story to his, Wideman exposes the false dichotomy between actual prisons and the world beyond its walls.

Wideman was not always aware of the degree to which he was contained because he had fallen prey to the binary illusions about black people and black men that structure the United States as a prison writ large. Indeed, he initially viewed his trips to visit his brother in prison as no more than visits to a place with which he believed himself to be quite unfamiliar. Over time, as he came to better understand his brother's incarceration, he recognized his complicity in both his and his brother's containment, which stemmed from his long-term behavior and feelings about Homewood and his family's blackness and poverty. For example, he admits to having measured his success by the geographic, social, and economic distance that he put between himself and his family (*Brothers* 27). He likens his early decision to flee Homewood to Robby's postmurder flight to Wyoming, where

Wideman lived with his family and worked as a professor. Reflecting on how he felt about Robby's visit to his world at the time, Wideman writes,

> Robby was a fugitive. My little brother was wanted for murder. For three months Robby had been running and hiding from the police. Now he was in Laramie, on my doorstep. Robbery. Murder. Flight. I had pushed them out of my mind. I hadn't allowed myself to dwell on my brother's predicament. I had been angry, hurt and afraid, but I'd had plenty of practice cutting myself off from those sorts of feelings. Denying disruptive emotions was a survival mechanism I'd been forced to learn early in life. . . . Robby was my brother, but that was once upon a time, in another country. My life was relatively comfortable, pleasant, safe. I'd come west to escape the demons Robby personified. I didn't need outlaw brothers reminding me how much had been lost, how much compromised, how terribly the world still raged beyond the charmed circle of my life on the Laramie plains. (*Brothers* 11)

Whereas Robby was running from the law when he went to Laramie, Wideman "was running away from Pittsburgh, from poverty, from blackness" (26–27). Like Robby, who did not succeed in placing himself beyond the reach of the criminal justice system, such flights did not liberate Wideman in the ways that he had hoped: whenever he had "any hesitations or reconsiderations about the path [he'd] chosen," he relied on Homewood to remind himself how lucky he was (26). In other words, he used his Homewood relatives and their lives as the measuring sticks by which he gauged his success. Although he thought that he was running, he later realized that he was in fact "fashioning a cage" (32). Wideman realized that fundamental to his emancipation was his ability to "get over the shame of acknowledging" all that his community and family were and were not (17). As Wideman characterizes his relationship to his incarcerated brother, "I lived far away. Light-years away on a freezing planet, a planet empty except for the single solitary cell that I inhabited. Visiting was illusion, deceit" (*Brothers* 184).

Wideman's description of his relationship to Robby and to the prison functions ironically because it collapses the time and space that separates the brothers while emphasizing the solitary nature of their containment. The geographic and social distance that separates Wideman from Robby situates them in a relationship characterized by what Foucault calls "lateral invisibility," a relationship in which individuals do not come into contact with each other (*Discipline* 200). By melding Robby's story with his own, Wideman embarks on a mission to bring down those walls by disrupting the representations that structure binary relationships between inside and outside, guilt and innocence, good and evil, and—perhaps most importantly—brothers and keepers.

In *Brothers and Keepers*, Wideman is as much concerned with what the book eventually has to say as with the process that he, as a writer and as a black man, must master before he can say it. Whereas Wideman claims to have lived his story in ways that at times diminished those on its periphery, he writes his story to resolve the issues and dissolve the barriers separating him from the people in Homewood and his family, all of whom reside in cells that are in the end not so very distinct or distant from each other. His challenge, in other words, is to produce a narrative that functions as a mirror that reflects different ways for black men to see themselves, to conceptualize the nature and function of their containment, and to respond in the most emancipatory ways possible.

The emergence of such a narrative is complicated, however, by the limitations of the worldview to which Wideman once subscribed and which made him complicit in his own containment. As a young professional, he believed that there were "[j]ust two choices as far as I could tell: either/or rich or poor. White or black. Win or lose. . . . My mind was split by oppositions, by mutually exclusive categories." Driven by a worldview so divided, he believed that to "succeed in the man's world you must become like the man and the man sure didn't claim no bunch of nigger relatives in Pittsburgh." For Wideman, that meant functioning as though he were two people rather than risk exposing "in either world the awkward mix of school and home I'd become" (27–28). He illustrates the devastating effects of his double life in the "sawing dream" that he relates to Robby. In the dream, he explains, "I am a man, myself, but not myself." The dream is set in a "honeycomb of steel" where the dream man cannot see the stars, where he is surrounded by the smell of death, and where he is doomed to reside forever among fifteen hundred other men. He can hear but cannot see the other inmates. As the dream man tries to retreat into the "deathly sleep that's the closest thing to mercy prison ever grants," he becomes aware of a "monotonous sawing sound," which turns out to be the sound of the other men snoring. The sound "reminds him of the funny papers, the little cloud containing saw and log drawn above a character's head so you can see the sound of sleeping." As he closes his eyes and listens more closely to the sound, he envisions himself as the cartoon figure sawing off parts of his own body. The dream man imagines the cartoon figure methodically "lopping off his own flesh and blood" in a manner that seems "almost bored, almost asleep, ready to snore like the saw's snoring as it chews through his body" (193–94).

Wideman's description of this dream theorizes containment and resistance in ways that are extremely provocative. The image of a "honeycomb of steel" in which fifteen hundred men are caged invokes the compartmentalized structure of the prison writ large. Although the dream man who is contained therein cannot see beyond his cell, he can hear the "fitful stirrings, clattering bars, groaning, the sudden outcries of fear, rage, madness, and God knows what else" that signify the presence of other prisoners whose behavior disrupts the order of the system (193). The noise that they make undermines the effects of "lateral invisibility" by signifying the possibility that they might become "subject[s] in communication," even though they remain subject to the "axial visibility" that renders them "object[s] of information" (Foucault, *Discipline* 200). Wideman juxtaposes the disorderly sounds of one group of prisoners with the monotonous snoring of the sleeping prisoners. He then links the dream man's focus on the snoring emitted by docile, sleeping bodies to the similarly sleepy manner in which the cartoon figure violently dismembers himself. In Wideman's dream, the cartoon figure is twice removed from Wideman. Wideman re-members that cartoon man through the imagination of the dream man and through his retelling of the dream to Robby. In the process, he also re-members himself as a man who has learned that a mind "split by oppositions, by mutually exclusive categories," can only reproduce its own containment and self-destruction and can never so much as dream of freedom and wholeness (27).

Wideman theorizes the processes of compartmentalization and decompartmentalization as methods by which to evade the oppressive effects of containment wrought by binary worldviews and systems of representation. Compartmentalization is a process that involves chopping "your world into manageable segments" and "segregating yourself within safety zones white people have not littered with barricades and landmines." It "begins as a pragmatic reaction to race prejudice" but in time becomes an "instinctive response" that makes a "special way of seeing . . . second nature." That "special way of seeing" requires that one "ignore the visible landscape" because "it will never change" and instead "learn a kind of systematic skepticism, a stoicism, and, if you're lucky, ironic detachment" (*Brothers* 221). However, Wideman explains, compartmentalization is also an ironic process that "begins with your black skin, and your acknowledgment of racial identity, and becomes both a way of seeing and being seen. Blackness is a retreat to the security of primal night. Blackness connects me with my brother but also separates us absolutely, each one alert, trembling behind the vulnerable walls of our dark skins" (221–22). For compartmentalization to structure blackness as a retreat instead of a barrier that separates, it must occur in conjunction with the process of decompartmentalization. Decompartmentalization involves seeing, naming, and finding ways out of spaces that are not safety zones but rather sites of containment.

It involves reconstructing and sometimes demolishing such sites to counteract the oppressive effects of particular technologies of containment. It requires that one "always take second readings, decode appearances, pick out obstructions erected to keep you in your place. Then work around them" (*Brothers* 221). As with compartmentalization, decompartmentalization involves using what Wideman calls a "special way of seeing" (*Brothers* 221) to structure places in which to foster the signs and sounds of resistance and solidarity rather than docility and complicity.

For Wideman, *Brothers and Keepers* represents just such a space. Indeed, writing *Brothers and Keepers* was an integral part of Wideman's effort to teach himself to decompartmentalize. As he explains,

> This book is part of the unlearning of my first response to my brother's imprisonment. In spite of good intentions, I constantly backslide. In large matters . . . or small, neglecting to relay somebody's greeting to my brother or a hello from Robby to some friend on the outside, I'll revert to my old ways. My oversights embarrass me, shake me up, because I'm reminded that in crucial ways my brother still doesn't exist for me in the intervals between visits. The walls become higher, thicker, unbreachable when I allow myself to become part of the conspiracy. (222)[1]

During the early stages of writing the book, Wideman describes his imagination as a "curving mirror doubling the darkness." Lying latent in his imagination are the words through which Wideman eventually structures a zone of "sweet, solitary pleasure," a place that is "velvet-soft and black," a story of brothers and keepers in which he and Robby become enfolded and enclosed. Initially, however, his imagination fails to function as a "curving mirror" but rather reproduces a "trick of the [two-sided] glass" that renders the brother subordinate to the keeper and then proclaims to the latter, "You're the fairest of them all" (*Brothers* 87). The failure of Wideman's first draft is attributable to this "trick of the glass," which compels him "to impose a dramatic shape" on Robby's story even though, as a consequence of Robby's life sentence, it was unlikely that there would be any "dramatic, external changes in Robby's circumstances" (194). The failure of the first draft was inevitable as long as Wideman envisioned it as a "powerful engine being constructed to set [Robby] free" (195) and to enable his return from the state of nonexistence imposed on prisoners. In contrast, the final draft of the narrative becomes a safety zone wrought through processes of compartmentalization and decompartmentalization and by the "curving mirror" of Wideman's imagination only when he relates what about Robby enables "his slow, internal adjustment day by day to an unbearable situation" (*Brothers* 194–95).[2]

Wideman attunes himself to Robby's voice, which "issues through a crack" in the "curving mirror" of Wideman's imagination, insisting on its right to be heard (*Brothers* 88, 87). Although the writing of *Brothers and Keepers* does not free Robby from prison, it does free Wideman from his role in the conspiracy of black men's containment and as his brother's keeper. The collaborative writing process teaches Wideman to abandon his inclination to remain "two or three steps ahead of [Robby], making fiction out of his words" (88). Wideman learns to resist the urge to overwrite what Robby says and to clean up Robby's image by manufacturing "compelling before-and-after images" and making "the bad too bad and good too good" (195). To manufacture such dichotomous images is to fall victim to the tricks of the unbreakable two-sided mirror. Instead, Wideman is careful not to represent Robby as "a man whose qualities were self-evident cause for returning him to the world of free people" (195). As Wideman puts it, "The character traits that landed Robby in prison are the same ones that allowed him to survive with dignity, and pain and a sense of himself as infinitely better than the soulless drone prison demands he become. Robby knows his core is intact; his optimism, his intelligence, his capacity for love, his pride, his dream of making it big, becoming somebody special. And though these same qualities helped get him in trouble and could derail him again, I'm happy they are still there. I rejoice with him" (195).[3] Wideman's prison visits with Robby teach the author to see the world in ways that do not rely on dichotomies. Wideman acquires a way of seeing that makes it possible for him to represent his brother as a man whom prison had changed but not broken and whose behavior was informed by "a certain consistency . . . a basic impetuous honesty that made him see himself and his world with unflinching clarity. He never stopped asking questions. He never allowed answers to stop him" (195). And, as Wideman puts it, "therein lay the story" (195), for he succeeds in seeing and then representing Robby in ways incongruous with the fictions and dichotomies that structure hegemonic representations of black men.[4]

Through the shared process of writing *Brothers and Keepers*, Wideman realizes that his visits to the prison are less journeys to an unfamiliar place than descents into the deepest, most closely surveilled compartments that contain black men. An important aspect of Wideman's theory of containment, response, and resistance arises from his recognition and exploration of the "artificiality of *visiting*" actual prisons (*Brothers* 184). Since a person cannot visit a place where he or she already resides, a visit to a prison for black men—who are merely passing from one sector of the prison writ large to another—is an oxymoron.[5] Yet the rituals to which visitors must submit to enter the prison delineate a line between inside and outside, freedom and containment. Theoretically, visitation rituals facilitate the temporary passage of visitors from their lives as free people to places in which they become subordinate. This fictitious divide tricks the unsuspecting black male visitor into believing that he is entering a world that differs significantly from the one that he inhabits on the outside. To enter the prison as a visitor requires one's acquiescence to rituals that make it seem that one is giving up "one version of reality for another" (Wideman, *Brothers* 183). One of the most significant rituals involves passing through a series of physical barriers that includes a metal-detecting machine. In the case of the latter, Wideman notes that although the "reason for such a security measure is clear; the extreme sensitivity of the machine is less-easily explained." Given that women are required to remove wedding rings, underwire bras, and structured undergarments, he surmises that the point of the machine is to humiliate visitors (185). On one occasion, for example, as he passes through the metal detector, Wideman ponders what will happen when he brings his sons, who just had metal braces put on their teeth: "Whose responsibility will it be to inspect the kids' mouths for weapons? Will the boys feel like horses on sale? Have I taught Dan and Jake enough about their history so that they'll recall auction blocks and professional appraisers of human flesh?" (186). As a black man, Wideman feels particularly susceptible to the effects of such rituals, which require that one endure being treated like a criminal to secure passage from one section of the prison writ large to another. Although Wideman is permitted to pass through the barriers to the prison, the process reminds him of occasions outside the prison when his passage through similar technologies was impeded by his membership in a criminalized class. For example, he relates an incident "during the early seventies when paranoia about skyjacking was rampant and a lone black male, youngish, large, athletically built, casually dressed, 'fit' the profile of an air pirate" (186). On that occasion, Wideman was pulled aside and subjected to a special search. A similar incident occurred while he was traveling with his family at Christmastime: his "sons were forced to unload their new cowboy pistols from [their] carry-on bag and stow them in the baggage hold" (186). An off-duty white male cop, however, was permitted to board the aircraft with a .38 in his briefcase. The processes by which visiting rituals designate what appears to be a rigid division between the worlds inside and outside prison walls disguise the extent to which such a division is considerably less distinct and at times—particularly for black men—nonexistent.

Over time, Wideman realizes that passage into a prison leads to a sector of containment that is governed by far more than a "dramatic flip-flop of values." Such a simple reversal, he explains, "would be too easy. If black became white and good became bad and fast became slow, the players could learn the trick of reversing labels, and soon the upside-down world would seem natural." Accordingly, "prison rules are designed to keep you ignorant, keep you guessing, insure your vulnerability" (183). Such rules enable keepers to both define and control deviance and "deviants" such as Robby. Not only are keepers "empowered to say *You go to the right. You go to the left*," they are also empowered to define what is right and what is left (48). As Robby so aptly puts it, the rules make it seem as though black men are "just spozed to fuck up and keep on fucking up and that's why we in the mess we in the first place" (149).[6] Any prisoner who "insists on seeing other versions of himself, is in constant danger" (183). Further, "you were supremely eligible for a bullet if the guards couldn't press your button. If they hadn't learned how to manipulate you, if you couldn't be bought or sold . . . then you were a threat" (82–83). The prisoner or the black man on the outside who literally sees his way outside of mirrorlike systems of containment of the sort that Wideman theorizes is at risk of being violently (and permanently) resubjected whether through the barrel of a gun or other means (101, 75).

On the one hand, it would seem that there exists no real possibility for inmate agency or resistance as it puts Robby "in no less jeopardy than going along with the program. Because the program [itself is] contrived to kill you" (Wideman, *Brothers* 83). Robby understood that "he was sentenced to die. That all sentences were death sentences" (83). He could choose to see other versions of himself, in which case "the guards would do everything in their power to kill him" (83). Or he could accept the ways in which he was seen, thus succumbing to the pressure "to surrender dignity, self-respect, control over his own mind and body," in which case he would "become a beast, and what was good in him would die" (83). On the other hand, as Robby sees it, resistance begins with his acceptance that prison "was the white man's world and wasn't no way around it or over it or under it" and with his knowledge that his survival depends on his willingness to "get down and dance to the tune the man be playing" (114). In Robby's case, this dance involves engaging in performances that worry the line between complicity and resistance and enable Robby to "maintain sanity" while minimizing opportunities for the keepers to destroy him (83).

Wideman relates a compelling example of a performance that involves dancing to the "tune the man be playing" in his short story, "All Stories Are True" (1992). In this story, Robby's fictional counterpart, Tommy, explains the nature and function of a performance through which he and other black inmates play on guards' fears of black men as a way of exerting some control over the conditions of their containment:

> I think I'm finally beginning to understand why they so evil to us. They're scared of the Blackman. Really scared. More scared than I ever knew. More scared than

they know themselves. When I first come in the joint I knew something about the fear. Knew we had something on them. Wild as we was we didn't give them no chance to run game on us. We had learned the hard way coming up running the streets what they thought of us. Crazy Killers. Animals. Dope fiends. Niggers you got to lock up or kill before they kill you. That was the deal. So we played the hand dealed us. We was stone outlaws. Fuck wit us you better be prepared to take us down cause if you don't we coming down on you. . . . We saw fear in their eyes. We fucked with them to keep it there. . . . Wasn't really me in the first place. I was just playing the outlaw role I thought I needed to play to survive the joint. I changed but they stayed scared of me. (13–14)

In one sense, the black inmates, through their performances as outlaws, become complicit in the reproduction of images of black men as a criminal class. However, their performances are underwritten by their knowledge that people can exploit such images to gain leverage within the system that contains them. That is, they can manipulate such images in ways that are resistant because they offset the effects of absolute control. How does this work exactly? First, as I argue later in relation to the return of the black brute figure in rap, performances of the figure haunt white America's racial house. Such images perpetuate the guards' fears of black men. Inmates then reinforce that fear by behaving in ways that cause the guards to modulate how they deal with the black inmates to avoid provoking their "wild" and "crazy" impulses and becoming their victim. From the inmates' points of view, the material and psychic benefits of their performances outweigh the costs that their apparent complicity exacts. The inmates, like many rappers, step out of "scenes" of violence in which they have been cast as silent subjects and into roles as players in a game of power (Baker, "Scene" 39). Double consciousness underscores the performance, which requires knowledge of where the role begins and ends, what is the man and what is the mask, what is real and what is counterfeit.

To put it in other terms, the inmates can see beyond the guards' performances of power to identify the ideologies that drive them (whiteness, racism). The inmates' refusal to acknowledge as accurate images of black men as "Crazy Killers. Animals. Dope fiends" empowers the inmates to deflect the counterfeit images with which they are confronted if not the full effects of the containment that such images produce. The inmates "run game" on the keepers by using the latter's methods of control and containment against them, thereby transforming perpetual systems of containment into systems in which these and other kinds of performances can destabilize hegemonic operations.

It is possible, then, to view the inmates' performances through the lens of blackface minstrelsy. As I will discuss further in chapter 2, blackface performances by whites were "a means of exercising white control over explosive cultural forms as much as [they were] an avenue of derision" (Lott 115). Eric Lott introduces the notion of the counterfeit to refer to such performances. He also introduces the notion of the "seeming counterfeit" as a figure for blackface performances by blacks. If we posit a loose relationship between the guards who are designated keepers of black male bodies and white blackface performers and black black-face performers such as Master Juba and the black inmates who perform in "All Stories Are True," it is possible to see both the counterfeit and the seeming coun-terfeit at work. In Wideman's story, the inmates recuperate some control over their own images through performances as outlaws. In the context of the prison, such performances by black inmates cause the counterfeit to break down and the constructed image to become frighteningly real. The breakdown of the counter-feit forces the guards to negotiate the tension caused by these "acts of unsettling authenticity" (Lott 113). The resultant tension signifies that a dynamic of contain-ment, response, and resistance is at work in which the control of black men is at stake.

Whatever else Wideman's visits to Robby become, they begin "as compromise, an acceptance of defeat."[7] As Wideman explains, visitors and prisoners have just two choices about how to respond to the humiliating rituals of passage: they can either resist overtly on the grounds that "dying with your hands on an enemy's throat is better than living under his boot," or they can agree to go along with the rules one more time, knowing that "the other way, the alternative is always there" (*Brothers* 190, 191). Out of concern for his brother's safety, Wideman endures the visiting rituals because he knows that the guard remains in power after the visit is over. As he puts it, when the visit ends, the guard is "free to take out on [Robby] whatever revenge he couldn't exact from me and my smart mouth" (*Brothers* 192). Accordingly, in instances where it seems that he and Robby are subjected to unrea-sonable restrictions and the inconsistent enforcement of constantly changing rules during their visits, Wideman's strategy is to "take low. Shake my head but stroll away (just enough nigger in my walk to tell the guard I know what he thinks of me but that I think infinitely less of him)" (*Brothers* 190–92).

Still, as Tommy explains in "All Stories Are True," Wideman's visits to the prison teach him that a kind of freedom can be had through finding ways to name the "tune the man be playing" while one is dancing to it (*Brothers* 114). In Wideman's case, he uses language and storytelling, the modes of performance most readily available to him, just as the inmates use their performances as outlaws. An example of such a performance is Wideman's description of a guard with whom Robby has had trouble on more than one occasion:

> The guard's chest protrudes like there's compressed air instead of flesh inside the gray blouse of his uniform. A square head. Pale skin except on his cheeks, which are bluish and raw from razor burn. His mustache and short curly hair are meticulously groomed, too perfect to be real. The stylized hair of comic-book superheroes. A patch of blue darkness etched with symmetrical accent lines. His eyes avoid mine. He had spoken in a clipped, mechanical tone of voice. Not one man talking to another but a peremptory recital of rules droned at some abstraction in the middle distance where the guard's eyes focus while his lips move. (*Brothers* 192)

Wideman's description interrupts the constancy and consistency of hegemonic technologies that contain black men. It does so in a number of ways. First, the description dehumanizes the guard by depicting him not as a figure of absolute power or even a man but as an air-filled doll with features that resemble those of a comic-book superhero. Second, it exposes the markers of the guard's authority—his uniform, his clean-shaven appearance, and his articulation of rules—as a costume that disguises the contrived nature of the authority that the guard performs. Third, it undercuts the authority and accuracy of the guard's gaze, which seems only vaguely to register the evasively abstract prisoner whose subjection he oversees. Finally, it denies the import of the guard's speech by reducing it to the unspecific sound of a drone. As Wideman puts it, "Nazi Gestapo Frankenstein robot motherfucker. . . . He's what he is and there's no way to get around that or for the moment get around him because he's entrenched in this no-man's land and he is what he is and that's worse than any names I can call him" (*Brothers* 192). By way of this description, then, Wideman passes the guard and all that the role of the keeper represents through a fun-house mirror.

Wideman's visits with Robby ultimately leave the author unprepared either "to step through the looking glass" (*Brothers* 182) that separates him from his brother or to acknowledge the terms of its reflections. He theorizes his conundrum through a story about a time when he went to visit Robby by way of a new route. Although he reaches the prison in record time, Wideman is not yet ready to pass through the gates. He is unprepared because the trip to the prison is as much a psychic journey as it is "a matter of miles and minutes" (182). Both journeys require that he traverse a "vast, uncharted space, a no-man's land" (182) that marks a divide between prison and Homewood, prisoner and man, brother and keeper.

To visit the "alien world inside 'The Walls'" (182) of the prison, a visitor must cross from one side of the two-sided mirror to the other, knowing that on the other side "the rules change. Visitors must take leave of the certainties underpinning their everyday lives" (182). The visitor does so knowing that "the setting has been contrived not so much to allay your grief, your sense of loss but to profit from them, mock them, and mock the one you need to see" (185).

Wideman's desire to confirm that Robby is still alive, still inside, as well as the author's inability to alter the visitation processes in literal terms compel him to reimagine the rituals in the form of a personal narrative of ascent.

> I focused on the ritual, the succession of things to be done in order to enter the prison. In my mind I passed through the iron gates of the official parking lot, I glanced at the stone walls, the river as I crossed the crowded lot to the visitors' annex. I climbed the steep concrete stairs. I faced the guard in his cage outside the waiting room, presented my identification, stated my brother's name and number, my relationship to him, wrote all that down on a sheet of mimeo paper, then found a seat in the dingy room, avoiding the blank faces of other visitors, frustration and anger building as I wait, wait, wait for the magic call that allows me down the steps, across a courtyard, up more steps, through steel doors and iron-barred doors into the lounge where my brother waits. (*Brothers* 184)

The processes that enable Wideman's physical ascent to a space where he is reunited with his brother—passing, crossing, climbing, facing, writing—signify structural or systemic transgressions of one type or another. Such transgressions also characterize the processes that Wideman undergoes in his psychic journey that leads to his reunion with Robby and reconnection to his Homewood roots. Unlike the shortcut to the prison, this journey prepares Wideman to take up arms with his brother(s), to refuse to remain a "conspirator" in the process of making the prison walls for black men "higher, thicker, unbreachable," and to move beyond compartmentalization to commence his journey toward Home (*Brothers* 224).

So deeply entrenched are the ideological foundations and institutional frameworks of the U.S. prison writ large that at times it seems futile to think that black men might one day function freely outside its parameters. In "Home," Toni Morrison celebrates the potential to sidestep such futility through racial projects that envision "a-world-in-which-race-does-*not*-matter" and represent it as "something other than a . . . failed and always-failing dream" (3). As a writer, Morrison considers her challenge to be that of moving "the job of unmattering race away from pathetic yearning and futile desire . . . to a manageable, doable, modern human activity" (3–4). She employs the notion of Home as a model for racial projects that are underscored by visions similar to hers. She uses *Home* as a metaphor for such projects for two reasons. First, a home is a place where people can live safely and comfortably. Thus, Home represents both a race-specific and a nonracist space (5). Home is a place where safety exists without walls and where difference is prized but not privileged (12). It is a space characterized by "the concrete thrill of borderlessness—a kind of out of doors safety" (10). Second, Home signifies the transformation that has to happen if writers, scholars, artists, prisoners, and all of the people whom we cannot locate within such handy categories are to "domesticate" the various racial projects in which they are wittingly or unwittingly engaged. As this and subsequent chapters suggest, the U.S. prison writ large makes it impossible to see the nation as a Home. It is possible, however, to view the United States as a racial "house." A racial house, Morrison explains, is a space that we all inhabit. It is governed by "the master's voice and its assumptions of the all-knowing law of the white father" ("Home" 4). Morrison is careful to emphasize that Home cannot be constructed by simply redesigning a racial house and decorating it with names such as *multiculturalism* and *diversity* (8). However, it is possible to make a racial house habitable by transforming it from a windowless prison "from which no cry could be heard" into "an open house, grounded, yet generous in its supply of windows and doors" (4).[8] Racial projects that undertake to do the latter involve finding ways to "carve away accretions of deceit, blindness, ignorance, paralysis, and sheer malevolence embedded in raced language so that other kinds of perception" are not only available, but inevitable (Morrison, "Home" 7). As the emphasis throughout this book shifts from lockstep toward dance, we will see how black men are carving away these obstacles.

Morrison's designation of the United States as a racial house and her cautiously optimistic description of it as a prison with windows and doors accord with the notion of the United States as a prison writ large for black men. The prison writ large compartmentalizes black men in ways that encourage them to become complicit not only in their own containment but also in that of their brothers. Power must be distinguished from the performances that produce the subjection of black men. Rather, power is more usefully understood as the tensions among containment, response, and resistance that grows out of performances taking place at all levels within the prison writ large. The performances in which black men engage while incarcerated, on the job, at play, and through story and song help to prevent the prison writ large from becoming a windowless prison in which only their silence and subjection prevails. Although a Home of the sort that Morrison envisions has yet to be realized through the racial projects in which people of all races are engaged, black men engage in representational practices through which different visions of the world may be seen and through which roars of battle may be heard. Contemporary representations of black men, however, have not taken shape in a vacuum. Rather, they bear the signs of their ancestors, which included the blackface minstrel tradition and the images, practices, and rituals associated with lynchings of black men during the Jim Crow era. Chapter 2 focuses on these histories and their legacy.

THE LEGACY OF TYPE
Minstrelsy, Lynching, and White Lore Cycles

Phillip Brian Harper, in *Are We Not Men?: Masculine Anxiety and the Problem of African-American Identity* (1998), states that it is not novel for a cultural studies critic to focus on the relationship between representation and reality. However, Harper rightly argues, "we cannot hope . . . to construct an effective critique of the racial politics of popular culture until this rather elementary proposition is more fully elaborated to account for some of the specific *ways* that such conditioning occurs" (154). *Lockstep and Dance* undertakes such an accounting as it traces the genealogies of contemporary representations of black men in popular culture that play a significant role in preserving the social order and the prison writ large in the United States. My investigation of the racial politics of popular culture helps to unravel what David Marriott refers to as the "legacy of type." To examine the legacy of type with respect to representations of black men is to consider what it means for black men "to be, or be seen to be, a 'type,'" to identify the various for(u)ms of representation in which the politics of type are embedded, and to consider how black men respond to hegemonic notions of black masculinity trafficked in the forms of images, icons, and idols (Marriott 43–44). To that end, I locate contemporary representations of black males within constantly turning cycles of white cultural lore. Such representations are produced and reproduced through the mechanisms of whiteness that shape such lore. Subsequent chapters explore the ways in which black men respond to and create various forms of cultural production that circulate within realms of representation that have been shaped by white lore. Chapters 3–5 consider the nature and function of some of the contradictions that attend black men's participation in certain representational practices and the resultant cultural products. This chapter, however, establishes the peculiar genealogy of the legacy of type that infiltrates popular culture and reinforces the nature and function of the prison writ large in myriad ways. Such a genealogy is apparent in the seemingly disparate representational practices and performances associated with lynching, blackface minstrelsy, and print and television advertisements. Taken together, the connections among the three areas constitute revealing indices of representations. These indices provide insight into how white America has managed and continues to manage its fear of and fascination with black men.

Advertising not only shows consumers what products are available for use but also shapes how white America sees such products as well as the people who endorse them. Advertisements influence consumers' perceptions of the contexts in which the products are presented. They shape consumers' perceptions of what is desirable and what is not. They instruct consumers about the use value of products. At the same time, advertisements sculpt images of a desirable social order through narratives and images that reflect racial, class, and gender hierarchies; the use value or roles of particular groups of people within such strata; and the behavior that can be expected of individuals within such groups.

Until relatively recently, black men's appearances in advertisements were minimal in frequency and scope. Today, more and more companies employ black men to endorse products and companies. Such changes notwithstanding, many, if not most, print and television advertisements depict black men in ways that reveal the representational limitations wrought by white lore about black men and the cycle through which it is produced and reproduced. That is, the images of black men that circulate in many advertisements today reflect legacies of violence, of exploitation and, to borrow Eric Lott's term, of love and theft (40). The application of a telescoped gaze to the ways in which lynching and minstrelsy inform contemporary white lore about black men provides a lens through which to view the manifestations of such lore in advertisements and with which to consider how such representations lock black men into what Joseph Boskin calls "imagic straitjacket[s]" (121). As we shall see, the realms of sport, film, and rap reveal similar genealogies in areas in which black men participate quite audibly and visibly. These areas reveal not only the form and function of imagic straitjackets but also black men's efforts to mediate the production of these bindings.

An important relationship exists among whiteness, economies of representation, and white lore cycles. W. T. Lhamon Jr.'s concept of a lore cycle enables us to trace patterns of continuity and change as they pertain to historical and contemporary representations of black men. The lore cycle functions as a paradigm in which to locate and link lynching rituals and blackface minstrel performances, particularly the ritual of castration and the minstrel man's association with the black penis. White America's ways of seeing, representing, and disciplining black men today can be traced to the historical images and disciplinary methods that characterized both traditions. The apparent drive to figuratively castrate the black male figure remains evident in realms that invite black men's participation if they perform the role of the hypersexual criminal, the clown, or a "depoliticized, racially denuded, conscienceless" figure (Dyson, *Open Mike* 253). The evolution and persistence of the Sambo figure in print and television advertisements provides evidence of such a pattern. This pattern represents the paradoxical dialectic of controlling images of black men at work in American popular culture. As the close analyses of advertisements in the latter part of this chapter reveal, variations of the Sambo figure market both threatening and entertaining images of black masculinity along with various products. Indeed, the legacy of the Sambo figure is prominent enough that a wide range of advertisements and advertising patterns may be characterized as examples of what Anne McClintock calls "commodity racism" (207).

Michael Eric Dyson, in *Open Mike: Reflections of Philosophy, Race, Sex, Culture, and Religion* (2003), uses three categories of analysis to conceptualize whiteness and thereby enhance our understanding of how and why such images circulate. Whiteness, Dyson argues, manifests itself as identity, as ideology, and as institution. Although each of these categories of analysis is as impure as it is complex, all are useful tools with which to discuss the mechanisms of whiteness. For my purposes, Dyson's notions of whiteness as identity and ideology seem especially useful. As identity, whiteness comprises the "self-understanding, social practices, and group beliefs that articulate whiteness in relationship to American race, especially in this case, to blackness" (*Open Mike* 99). Further, white identity depends on the recognition and negation of blackness as a competing racial identity. White identities are produced within structures of domination, and the preservation of white identity is largely contingent on the mechanisms through which it is reproduced. The minstrel show, the practice of lynching, the circulation of images of black men associated with it, and contemporary advertisements constitute examples of mechanisms that reproduce white identity. Such mechanisms complement the work of other structures of domination—for example, institutions, codified policies, and entrenched practices—that enable the United States to function as a prison writ large for black men. Ideologies of whiteness reproduce the support necessary to sustain the structures of domination that uphold the hegemony of white identity, which is contingent on the precept of black inferiority. As ideology, whiteness systematically reproduces the legitimacy of its own dominance and thus sustains one of the most powerful and long-standing myths within American culture. Ideologies that construct white identities and white superiority as both normative and natural are codified in myriad structures of domination. Such structures help to ensure the longevity of the precept of black inferiority that underscored the enslavement of African Americans and their subsequent subjugation through "debt peonage, sharecropping, Jim Crow law, the assault on the welfare state" (Dyson, *Open Mike* 101), and the criminal justice system. As ideology, whiteness protects the precept of black inferiority because it shifts attention away from the racist operations of the structures of domination that contain black men. Whiteness accomplishes this via techniques that reinforce views of black men as one of the most significant threats to the protection and security of mainly middle-class whites, creating the illusion that they do not deserve such protection and security unless they conform to certain prescribed roles. Whiteness also protects the precept of black inferiority via techniques that reinforce ideas about when and for whom black men are useful commodities as well as ideas about appropriate and profitable ways to exploit them as such (Dyson, *Open Mike* 99–101).

Ideologies of whiteness are rearticulated within economies of representation that rely on a precept of black inferiority, reinforce stereotypical views of black men, and make it possible for whites to justify particular kinds of violence and abuse inflicted on black men in different eras. Accordingly, as Mark A. Reid notes, we must understand the formation of identity as an ongoing process that occurs within fields of representation. This is because ideologies create fertile frameworks—lore cycles, as Lhamon calls them—within which the meanings attached to representations change (Reid, *Postnegritude* 8). In turn, historical representations of black men and those that circulate in contemporary popular culture reveal the extent to which the production of white identity is a relational process, growing out of efforts to distinguish itself as that which it is not. Both past and present cultural performances by whites and representations that situate black male figures at the center of such performances provide "a relational model in contrast to which masses of Americans could [and still do] establish a positive and superior sense of identity . . . established by an infinitely manipulable negation comparing whites with a construct of a socially defenceless group" (Harris 116–17). The rituals common to lynchings of black men, the images used to justify lynchings, the images common to minstrel shows, and the images that circulate in contemporary print and television advertisements played and continue to play significant roles in shaping such fields of representation, in which images of black men are made to accord with the negative half of that black/white binary. Although remarkably different in form, minstrel performances, lynching rituals, and advertisements are quite similar in function. All three inscribe inferiority and/or criminality onto the image and body of the black male and allow whites to claim a superior identity.

Lynching, minstrelsy, and advertising have important and related places within economies of representation that have contributed and contribute to black and white identity formation. Such traditions and texts reinforce the notion that white identities and images are ideal and normative, doing so, more often than not, at the expense of black men's images. In particular, all three sets of images circulate within economies of representation that negate and misrepresent black male identities and images by demonizing, devaluing, eroticizing, and criminalizing them. Such representational processes reassure whites that the imagined threat of black men is controlled, while often (and sometimes at the same time) exploiting images of black men as threatening for purposes of white pleasure and consumption. In this way, contemporary economies of representation provide the rhetorical and philosophical underpinning for the social and cultural practices that sustain the nature and function of whiteness (Dyson, *Open Mike* 107–8).

Lhamon's notion of a lore cycle conceptualizes complex systems and processes of representation that function in culture as do stereotypes in discourse (70). Cultural lore precedes and parallels ideology while working in much the same way (90). Cultural lore creates, expresses, and is structured by the values and beliefs of a group. It functions as a system of documentation through representations saturated with history and meaning, widely recognized and understood, and highly adaptable to changes in current belief systems and contexts. This system of documentation shapes the texts and contexts, the stories and the images, through which people understand, construct, reconstruct, negotiate, change, and represent themselves and others in relation to the cultural contexts in which they live. These functions work collectively to shape a lore cycle in which representations must be understood in relation to their genealogy. On the one hand, lore seems to produce tautologies in which beliefs prompt, license, and modulate actions, which in turn appear to authenticate the group's beliefs. In fact, what appears to be a pattern of repetition and sameness is actually a process of recursion and difference. That is, lore cycles are more cyclical than circular, more dynamic than static, and more inclusive than exclusive in the most dangerous senses of the words. As such, lore is both determinative (because it culls and enforces the beliefs on which a group predicates its actions) and adaptive (because of the ease with which it mutates across time and space in accordance with changes in social, cultural, political, and economic environments) (Lhamon 69–73).

Lore includes but is not limited to all manner of expressive behavior. Various gestures become fetishized and over time signify to insiders as well as to outsiders one's affiliation with a particular group. The gestures that take on this significance or have this significance attached to them are chosen selectively—that is, not all of a group's gestures or characteristics will become part of the lore cycles in which they circulate with the help of another group. To study a lore cycle, then, is to study both the gestures, styles, and attributes that have been deemed representative of a group (whether accurate or not) and the nature and function of the economies of representation within which insiders and outsiders have employed these phenomena. The process that is the lore cycle or the process of lore maintenance enables us to see how whiteness and white identity have been and continue to be formed, practiced, and reproduced at the expense of the black male image (Lhamon 69).

When outsiders employ what they see as the defining qualities of a group's behavior, lore often circulates and becomes available for consumption. The processes of consumption afford lore meanings that change across time and space. Even in instances where the lore about a group has its origins in the culture of the group that is being represented, once separated from the group that produced it and the context within which it was produced, a space opens between the original and the reproduction, and violent distortion often occurs. It is possible to excavate white America's ideas about itself and black men from the performances and rituals on which white lore cycles turn(ed) and which were and are used to justify acts of racial violence and murder. Extinguished species are rare when we are talking about cultural lore and its circulation within various realms of representation. In other words, white America's injurious ways of seeing black men have not disappeared but have adapted to the historical, social, and political contexts through which such images circulate (Lhamon 65). Moreover, the actions that result from these ways of seeing have undergone similar adaptations.

Ralph Ellison's "Change the Joke and Slip the Yoke" provides further insight into how we might understand the process by which white lore is articulated through representation and how it informs white America's ways of seeing black men. Ellison contends that the "physical hardships and indignities of slavery were benign compared with [the] continuing debasement" of the image of black people. Indeed, he claims, this debasement has occurred with such frequency and in so many contexts that "it is almost impossible for many whites to consider questions of sex, women, economic opportunity, the national identity, historic change, social justice—even the 'criminality' implicit in the broadening of freedom itself—without summoning malignant images of black men into consciousness" ("Change" 48). The irony is that human beings act as agents of interpretation, translating what we see and have been taught to see as archetypal into representations that take shape within particular historical and social contexts. Such contexts inform the nature and form of the texts that represent such interpretations (Ellison, "Change" 46). Thus, white fantasies and narratives about black men circulate within economies of representation that make it seem as though black men really are as whites imagine them to be. Marriott sums up the fabricated image of the black male, a product of the white imagination, as "an imitative perversion of human kind, a being incapable of inhibition, morals or ideas; a being whose supernatural indulgence of pleasure and continued satisfaction cannot deal with the contrary of denial or pain; a being whose violent, sexual criminality is incapable of any lasting, or real relationships, only counterfeit, or trickery; a being who remains a perpetual child, rather than a father" (x). Blackface minstrelsy, lynching, and contemporary advertisements played and play significant roles in shaping such representations. The cultural texts associated with each represent(ed), deploy(ed), and destroy(ed) black male bodies in ways that confirm(ed) and reconfirm(ed) whites' views of black men as inferior and thus the latter's subordinate position in the prevailing social order of the United States. Representations of black men that circulate in popular culture thus function as a slate on which whites inscribe their angst about black men's equality and agency. Blackface minstrelsy, lynching, and advertisements capture the relational nature of white identity and of the heterogeneous methods that sustain the lore upholding notions of white supremacy and authority.

Blackface minstrelsy in part constituted an outgrowth of one of the primary contradictions that underlay a capitalist (slave) economy in which humans represented both capital and labor: within such a system, human labor must reproduce both itself and surplus value (Lott 117). Lott reads the adoption of the black mask by white men during the nineteenth century as a method by which the latter negotiated the tension between their fears of "degraded and threatening" black men and the desire to control those fears through the corporeal mastery of the figures themselves (25). To fully recognize the body of the slave as human and the body of the male slave as a man within a slave economy was to acknowledge the exploitative nature of the slave economy and the latent masculine authority of the laborers. The lore through which whites mediated these contradictions manifested itself in blackface performances, which reduced the black male body to sexuality, dismembered it through medical discourse, and dehumanized it through discourses of racial biology (Lott 117–18). The blackface minstrel show functioned as a site of representation in which white men performed their obsession with the parts, functions, and attributes to which they reduced black male bodies. The frequency with which minstrel shows included the suggestion of miscegenation bespoke a somewhat obsessive fascination on the part of white men with black males and black culture. Interestingly, Lott reads the minstrel show's preoccupation with miscegenation as shorthand for "a relatively transparent white male attraction to and repulsion from the black penis." The assumption that white women's bodies needed to be protected from what white men perceived as black men's superior sexual potency informed the nature and function of the experimental race mixing that was the blackface performance (57). Blackface performers inscribed their acts with references to and plays on miscegenation, homosexuality, and transvestism, to the extent that the shows came to be defined by "white men's investment in the black penis" (Lott 121). Indeed, in a move that may be somewhat reductive but is compelling nonetheless, Lott argues that "in a real sense the minstrel man *was* the penis" (121) because of the recursive manner in which it appeared in different contexts. The lore of the black penis was played out in minstrel performances in ways that produced a titillating tension arising from the pleasure that the predominantly white male audiences "derived from their investment in 'blackness'" as well as the ever-present threat of castration that was "obsessively reversed in white lynching rituals" (9).

For this reason, blackface performance may be considered "one of the very first constitutive discourses of the body in American culture" (Lott 117). Minstrelsy enabled the commercialization of black bodies, a significant impetus for white men's perception of black men as both threatening and fascinating. The minstrel stage enabled the white performer and the spectator to experience both the creation and amelioration of the perceived threat of the black male. The end result was the simultaneous production and disintegration of the body through its representation (Lott 117–19). The need both to produce and to destroy through the counterfeiting of black male identity speaks to white men's doubt about the authenticity of their image (Ellison, "Change" 53). This peculiar dynamic of fascination and fear structured the minstrel show as a site of contradiction that invoked as it derided the power of blackness "in an effort of cultural control, through the very convention that produced its power—the greasepaint and burnt cork of blackface" (Lott 25–26). This trend continues today. As Greg Tate argues, "Though the cork-grease appliqué has faded away, the sight of white performers attempting to replicate black features still generates among African American spectators a host of responses—from joy to horror to sarcasm to indifference" ("Introduction" 8).

On the one hand, minstrel performances (and contemporary versions thereof) functioned as safe spaces in which white men imagined and experimented with the notion of their fraternity with black men. Minstrel performances allowed white men to appropriate—or at least to try on for size—what they perceived as a competing masculine identity. The "narratives of love and theft" that constituted the allure and lore of the minstrel show were the means through which white men both revealed and negotiated their anxiety about how they measured up against their own constructions of the black masculine figure and the imagined threat it posed (Lott 57). As Lott notes, to "put on the cultural forms of 'blackness' was to engage in a complex affair of manly mimicry. . . . To wear or even enjoy blackface was literally, for a time, to become black, to inherit the cool, virility, humility, abandon, or gaité de coeur that were the prime components of white ideologies of black manhood" (52). By inhabiting the black body, in other words, whites simultaneously articulated a desire to be on the one hand (like) blacks and on the other hand to overwrite the black presence with white representations of it. The forum of representation that was the minstrel show allowed whites to displace real black people with whites' images of them (Gubar 56). For white people, burnt cork provided a place from which to represent what they perceived as the essence of black behavior and black people. The minstrel show, like so many other sites of representation, became a space wherein whites could express feelings unexpressed elsewhere. Most significantly, the minstrel show displayed and helped to perpetuate a dangerous disregard for black people that was ultimately embodied in the structures and practices of domination, which reflected "formalized distortions of thought" (P. Williams 73). Such distorted ways of seeing and thinking blinded whites to the fact that "generally, statistically, and corporeally, blacks as a group are poor, powerless, and a minority"; therefore, only in white imaginations do blacks "become large, threatening, powerful, uncontrollable, ubiquitous, and supernatural" (72). The cultural productions that create such images not only violate a human responsibility to protect and foster the dignity of individuals and groups over whose images whites have some control but also seem to blind whites to or function as alibis for the horrors that blacks have suffered at the hands of whites (P. Williams 72–74). Such blindness shields whites from having to recognize the many forms that violence and containment takes, such as those wrought by representational practices. Cultural blindness enables whites to ignore or to deny the relationship between the historical and ongoing debasement of the images of black people generally and black men specifically and the ways in which African Americans have been tortured and terrorized. In this regard, a consideration of the practice of lynching provides a window into another form of theater in which rituals constituted literal performances of whites' sexual paranoia. Such paranoia fueled the ideologies on which whites drew to justify the ritualistic lynchings of thousands of black men at the end of the nineteenth and well into the twentieth century (Gubar 77).

During Reconstruction, African Americans experienced many political and economic gains. The Compromise of 1877, however, led to the withdrawal of northern troops from the South and, more importantly, of northern support for the advancement of African Americans in the South. The southern states took steps to undo African Americans' gains in terms of participation in politics and the economy. Southern regimes disenfranchised African Americans, passed the Jim

Crow laws that formally segregated public facilities, and mobilized the practice of lynching, of which African American men were the primary target (O'Malley). Lynching introduced an especially barbaric kind of racial violence to the South, making the years between approximately 1880 and 1968 distinctive in the history of the United States (Litwack 12). During this period, records document at least 4,742 incidents in which African Americans were killed by lynch mobs or, as was commonly reported despite literally thousands of witnesses to the murders, "at the hands of people unknown." Moreover, at least as many blacks were victims of what Leon Litwack calls "legal lynchings" in the form of quick trials and even quicker executions, private acts of violence by whites, or "nigger hunts" that led to blacks being killed in myriad ways and their bodies being discarded in isolated rural areas. As one black southerner recalled, whites "had to have license to kill anything but a nigger. We was always in season" (Litwack 12).

Prior to 1880, lynching had been employed in the West and Midwest as a means of extralegal justice. In the West, however, most (though not all) of the people who were lynched were white. Two things changed during the post-Reconstruction era. First, lynching was used not only to punish but also to terrorize and to control the black population, whose deference and subordination whites believed it was necessary to reinforce through both legal and extralegal means. Second, an unprecedented degree of sadism and exhibitionism characterized the murders. As Litwack explains, the "ordinary modes of execution and punishment no longer satisfied the emotional appetite of the crowd; the execution became public theater, a participatory ritual of torture and death, a voyeuristic spectacle prolonged as long as possible (once for seven hours) for the benefit of the crowd." Indeed, lynchings were often announced in advance, excursion trains were arranged, and parents packed picnic lunches and took children out of school so that they could attend. As many as fifteen thousand people at a time would gather to watch as victims were tortured—dismembered, frequently castrated, and burned alive in addition to being hung. Witnesses took home the victims' body parts—fingers, toes, bits of bones, and penises, which were especially coveted—to keep as souvenirs. In one case, a man's knuckles were displayed in the window of a grocery store. Photographs were taken, turned into postcards, and distributed around the United States (Litwack 11–16). As Christopher Booker puts it, black men and women "hanging from ancient southern trees" were "'the strange fruit' of a democracy" (140). Such images, many of which were captured on film and which I will subsequently discuss in more detail, provide "an apt symbol of how elusive freedom and equality were for African Americans" in the decades following Reconstruction (Booker 140).

Whites' fascination with and fear of black male sexuality and especially black penises inform what Robyn Wiegman refers to as the "anatomy of lynching." Wiegman locates lynching within a sexual economy in which the practice functioned as a disciplinary practice of racial control. The specificities of the lynching rituals—most notably, the severing of black men's penises—represented brutal and ritualized literal responses to the theoretical effect of emancipation, which was the definition of black men as socially the same as white males. A rereading of black men's relationships to patriarchal privilege clearly is in order, because all men were not and are not afforded the same masculine rights and privileges and power relationships were not and are not "uniformly based on sexual difference (men as oppressor, women as oppressed)" (Wiegman 83). The ironic motives for and implications of the ritual severing of the penis are of particular relevance here, for severing a black man's penis signified the mob's denial of both the physical sign of the masculine and the symbolic marker of patriarchal authority (82–87). The irony of the ritual lies in the fact that lynch mobs frequently justified lynchings by constructing their black male victims as threatening embodiments of violent masculinity, of which whites' fear was so great that they deemed it necessary to align even dead black male bodies with those of women, whom the theoretical effect of emancipation left untouched. As W. Fitzhugh Brundage argues, "The dramatic spectacle of each lynching taught all southerners, male and female, black and white, precisely where in the social hierarchy they stood. For black men and women, lynchings graphically demonstrated their vulnerability and debasement; for white women, the violence reaffirmed their dependence upon white men; and for white men, lynching was a ritual that manifested their intention to occupy the loftiest position in the racial and gender hierarchy of the South" (11). The construction of taboo lines, especially those forbidding sexual relationships between black men and white women, direct us to the relationship between the lore of the black penis in minstrel performances and its reappearance in lynching rituals, both of which delineated blacks' and whites' places in the various U.S. hierarchies.

The spectacular methods by which lynching rituals were carried out indicate that lynching came to represent and to be employed as a means to a desired end. As Wiegman explains, "Operating according to a logic of borders—racial, sexual, national, psychological, and biological as well as gendered—lynching figures its victims as the culturally abject—monstrosities of excess whose limp and hanging bodies function as the specular assurance that the racial threat has not simply been averted, but rendered incapable of return" (81). Speaking in 1907, U.S. Senator Ben Tillman of South Carolina conveyed the vehement conviction with which whites rationalized lynching as the most appropriate way of dealing with black men who had been accused of committing sex crimes against white women: "So far as I am concerned he has put himself outside the pale of the law, human and divine. . . . Civilization peels off us . . . and we revert to the . . . impulses . . . to 'kill! kill! kill!'" Tillman subsequently both denied that he hated blacks and expressed his nostalgia for "the negroes of the old slave days . . . the negroes who knew they were inferior and who never presumed to assert equality" (Wiegman 97). As Wiegman puts it, "[W]hile the slavery period often envisioned the Uncle Tom figure as the signification of the 'positive good' of a system that protected and cared for its black 'children,' once emancipated, these children became virile men who wanted for themselves the ultimate symbol of white civilization: the white woman" (96). The literal violence of the lynching rituals thereby extended the violence wrought by the cultural constructions and representations of black males as hypersexualized rapists that emerged in response to the officially sanctioned theoretical inclusion of black males within the newly integrated category of masculinity (96–97).

Lynching also reinforced a sense of community and commonality among whites. As the agents of and witnesses to acts of terror and territorializing, whites claimed their perceived entitlement to control of the black body. Whereas blackface performances distorted and assassinated the character of blackness and the image of black men, white lynchers set out to literally annihilate the black male body (Gubar 56–57). It is not altogether surprising to discover, as Orlando Patterson points out in *Rituals of Blood: Consequences of Slavery in Two American Centuries* (1998), that such annihilations bore all the characteristics of "classic human sacrifice[s]" (173). The function of a human sacrifice is to perform and symbolically re-create a social order that has been disrupted or threatened. The act of sacrifice constitutes an attempt to resolve the resultant crisis of transition through bloodshed. In this regard, human sacrifices function as rites of passage for entire communities. It is not surprising, Patterson concludes, that the practice of human sacrifice has been common in slaveholding societies. The ritualistic practice of whites' lynchings of blacks and the sociohistorical contexts in which they occurred accord with virtually all of the components of human sacrifice. For example, sacrifices are always ritualistic; they always involve some degree of drama or celebration, a pattern of continuity, and a climax that is marked by the killing of the victim; they usually occur in a designated or sacred place and involve fire; the victim is usually tied to a stake; there usually exists a particular set of beliefs or ideas about the victim; and the victim's remains are often literally or symbolically eaten or kept as mementos of the sacrificial act (Patterson 182–83). Sacrifices have been most common at historical moments when communities are undergoing extraordinary changes in their ways of life. As a community attempts to make sense of and reconcile itself to the change and its effects, human sacrifices have served as a method of doing so. The postemancipation period in the United States certainly was characterized by such conditions. The Old South dealt with the "period of acute liminal transition" that it faced when Reconstruction failed by initiating what was possibly one of the worst periods in African American history, when blacks "paid the expiatory and propitiatory price of the South's transition" as victims of "increasingly savage rituals of human sacrifice" (Patterson 185).

Given whites' horror regarding supposed cannibalistic practices in Africa, Patterson's claim that the burning of black bodies during lynching rituals amounted to literal acts of consumption by lynchers is not only ironic but compelling. During rituals of human sacrifice, cannibalism and other forms of blood sacrifice are often enacted in conjunction with one another. Patterson makes this argument by drawing on scientific evidence concerning the nature and function of the sense of smell. The correlation between the senses of smell and taste is so strong that many scientists consider the two senses to be conjoined because the brain does not differentiate between them. Thus, to smell the victim's body as it burned was akin to eating it. Lynchers' tendency to liken the burning of black bodies to the barbecuing of meat, to carry away mementos in the form of pieces of burning flesh, to hold celebratory picnics after the lynchings, and to refer to the odor of burning flesh in subsequent accounts of the events provide a supportive context for Patterson's claim that southern lynchers were, for all intents and purposes, eating the black victim while they inhaled and smelled the fumes created by the burning body. Whereas whites often commented on what they perceived as the distasteful smell of blacks, the ritualistic act of burning that accompanies human sacrifice seems to have altered whites' attitude toward the smell. Perhaps the change in attitude can be attributed to the lynchers' perception that the incinerated black body had been sufficiently tamed and culturally altered into a form that could be safely consumed (Patterson 198–200). On the one hand, white men and women sacrificed black male bodies to affirm their white identity and to distance themselves from blackness. On the other hand, ironically, they did so by taking the tortured black body into themselves through smell, touch, and even the gaze, directed as it was at the spectacle of the Other being tortured and sacrificed. The act of taking the black male body into themselves, of forcing the black male body into both male and female white bodies, seems at once to cohere and to be at odds with whites' frequently articulated fear of the black male rapist, whose perceived superior masculine potency constituted a threat to white masculine authority and white women's virtue. The torture, annihilation, consumption, and ultimate expulsion of black male bodies allowed whites to exorcise their fear of and desire to partake of the potent black male body by theatricalizing the act of rape through the rituals of human sacrifice. As I discuss in chapter 5, the return of the black brute with a voice in rap constitutes a haunting legacy of this history.

James Baldwin's disturbing short story "Going to Meet the Man" (1965) addresses precisely the sorts of masculine contests theatricalized in lynching rituals and demonstrates how castration rituals in lynchings marked an especially violent turn in the white lore cycle. In "Going to Meet the Man," Baldwin tells the story of Jesse, a white sheriff who finds it difficult to adapt to the ways in which social and political changes require him to alter his methods of exercising authority over the black people who reside in his jurisdiction. The story begins with a scene in which Jesse is unable to have sex with his wife because of an episode of impotence. Jesse's unwillingness to ask his wife to "do just a little thing for him, just to help him out ... the way he could ask a nigger girl to do it" leads him to revive his impaired virility by reimagining, as he lies with "one hand between his legs," the day's events in relation to a day long ago when he accompanied his parents to a lynching (229).

On that earlier day, Jesse witnessed a black man being burned alive and dismembered for allegedly knocking down an elderly, white woman. As Baldwin writes,

[The victim] wanted death to come quickly. They wanted to make death wait: and it was they who held death, now, on a leash which they lengthened little by little. *What did he do?* Jesse wondered. *What did the man do? What did he do?*—but he could not ask his father. He was seated on his father's shoulders, but his father was far away. There were two older men, friends of his father's, raising and lowering the chain; everyone, indiscriminately, seemed to be responsible for the fire. There was no hair left on the nigger's privates, and the eyes, now, were wide open, as white as the eyes of a clown or a doll. The smoke now carried a terrible odor across the clearing, the odor of something burning which was both sweet and rotten. (246–47)

Baldwin's description of the event captures the rhythm of the lynch mob's response to its own pleasure. The image of Jesse masturbating as he remembers the lynching to revive his impaired sense of masculine virility is reproduced in Baldwin's description of the two white men who enhance the mob's pleasure by flaunting their complete control over the timing and method of the black man's torturous death. Baldwin's description of the white men using their hands to manipulate the seemingly enormous body of the black victim between them draws its power from Jesse's recollections of the relative size of the victim—"he was a big man, a bigger man than his father, and black as an African jungle Cat, and naked" (246)—and yields an astonishingly subversive caricature of white, masculine power vis-à-vis black masculinity. The image of the older men raising and lowering the chain on which the black male victim is suspended links the white men's nurturing of their own desire (and Jesse's masturbation) to their corresponding dependence on, obsession with, and fear of the black male body and its literal and figurative markers of masculinity and authority. Although the black man's head bears a cranial marker of masculine sameness in the form of a widow's peak that resembles one borne by both Jesse and his father, such markers of sameness are interrupted by corporeal differences between the bodies of the white male spectators and participants and that of the black male victim. Jesse's memory of the older white men lifting and lowering the large, black male body between them emphasizes their enormous power over the man whose life is literally in their hands. At the same time, Baldwin's description undermines the image of the white men's power over the black male body, which, engorged as it is by historically and culturally constructed images of black masculinity, seems almost to control them. As I discuss in chapter 5, more subtle enactments of white men's fear of the black masculine signifier are apparent in uncritical opposition to rap and responses to athletes who test the parameters of their celebrity status.

In the final, climactic moments of the story and of the lynching itself, one of the white men cradles the victim's "privates in his hand . . . as though he were weighing them." Baldwin writes, "In the cradle of the one white hand, the nigger's privates seemed as remote as meat being weighed in the scales; but seemed heavier, too, much heavier, . . . and huge, huge, much bigger than his father's, flaccid, hairless, the largest thing he had ever seen till then, and the blackest." As the white man severs the penis, "cutting the dreadful thing away, and the blood came roaring down," Jesse experiences a surge of love for his father as he realizes that his father "had revealed to him a great secret which would be the key to his life forever" (247–48). Jesse is reassured by his memory of "what had been a wound between what had been [the victim's] legs" that he still knows the secret and, therefore, still has the key his father had given him years earlier. His memory of the wound left by the severing of the black man's penis reassures Jesse that the threat to his adult, white, male body has been averted, temporarily at least, and that for the moment, it bears no marker of such lack. As Marriott explains, "Jesse knows that what he had witnessed was a gift from his father. That gift, the desire and power to castrate—to take and so to take in—the sexuality of black men, brings them together and forges their futures as white men. Disconcertingly, what sustains Jesse (and his wife) 'as he laboured and she moaned' are the correspondence between that gift and the terrible, gaping wound" (Marriott 18–19). Interestingly, Marriott adds, "There is much more here than simply coming. Jesse's blackface imitation of those two *scenes*—the lynching, his parents' sex which precedes it—may be sadistic, but his performance also thrives on imitating derogatory images of black men as either dangerously oversexed and/or emasculated or dead. One thing he knows for sure is this: blackness is a vicarious, disfiguring, joyful pleasure, passionately enabling as well as substitutively dead" (19). As the story concludes, Jesse turns to his wife and assures her that he is now able to "do [her] like a nigger" (249). Jesse's memory of the lynching and his use of that memory as a fantasy to stimulate himself illustrates in sexually graphic detail the literal effects of white males' mythic conceptions of black sexuality (Wiegman 97).[1]

Although the primary function of lynching was to destroy the black body, the transformation of the annihilated black body into a permanent representation was as, if not more, important in terms of the ritual's residual cultural import. The practices of taking and circulating photographs were consistent with the primary function of lynching, which was to instill terror in black communities and thus discourage both black and white resistance to the injustices wrought by Jim Crow generally and lynching specifically. Moreover, the circulation of photographs of dead black men was critical to the process of white identity formation. The invention of the Kodak camera and roll film system in the mid-1880s coincided with the rapid increase of racialized lynchings in the South (Wood 96). Thanks to the invention of the inexpensive Brownie camera, amateur photography became a "social practice" that provided an efficient and cheap method of recording both the actual murders and "the carnival-like atmosphere" and the eager—indeed, festive—mood of the crowd (Wood 196; Litwack 11). This new technology enabled pictures of lynchings and burnings to be turned into postcards, which were kept and circulated as souvenirs of the events. The circulation of the photographs allowed the message of terror to be carried a long way. For example, on one occasion, a "Unitarian minister in New York, John H. Holmes, opened his mail one day to find a postcard depicting a crowd in Alabama posing for a photographer next to the body of a black man dangling by a rope. Responding to the minister's recent condemnation of lynching, the person who sent the card wrote, '*This is the way we do them down here. The last lynching has not been put on card yet. Will put you on our regular mailing list. Expect one a month on average*'" (Litwack 11). Furthermore, the popularity of amateur photography generated the practice of taking photographs at social or familial gatherings. Just as such photographs became records of the "social harmony and unity" of a family or group of friends, so too lynching photographs became records of a community's sense of solidarity and supremacy. Consequently, many lynching photographs seem to focus more on the white people, mostly men, surrounding the victim than on the victim (Wood 201). As Joseph F. Jordan, the curator of the Without Sanctuary exhibition of lynching photographs, notes, "You will see in the exhibit a good number of images with onlookers and large crowds attending the murder of the victims. Many of those onlookers gaze directly into the camera lens, posing as if they were honorably gathered, and would be remembered over the passing years in honorable terms" (Jordan). Most photographs were taken by the lynchers themselves; efforts by out-siders, such as journalists, to take pictures were usually thwarted. In this way, the lynchers both retained control over which images would be recorded on film and integrated picture taking into the lynching ritual. Furthermore, as Wood argues, the rituals of mutilation and dismemberment rendered the "lynching victim . . . a 'representation.' . . . To take a photograph of the victim in this state of debase-ment . . . froze the moment of representation in time. The visual representation of the violence was thus inextricable from the violence itself, becoming a sort of visual discourse that substantiated white supremacy and legitimized the supposed social need for lynching" (196). In this way, the lynching photographs "enhanced the cultural work of lynching by making the social and racial meanings enacted through the violence [both] visible" and recursive because of the degree to which they circulated at the time (Wood 195–97).

Taking and circulating photographs were practices consistent in other ways with the spectacle and ritual that characterized the actual murders. The produc-tion and circulation of lynching photographs extended the possibility not only of seeing the sacrificial act but also of partaking in the consumption that frequently accompanied it. Marriott reads the act of looking at a photograph as akin to the act of incorporation (25). Citing German psychoanalyst Otto Fenichel, Marriott argues that the camera both consumes that which its lens sees and subsequently projects outward what it has taken in. Thus, Marriott argues in relation to the black male body, "[T]o look at the penis and to castrate, and destroy it, can amount to the same thing" (27).

The meanings attached to the photographs vary according to the perspective from which one views them. On the one hand, they reveal the degree to which the lynchings were staged galas for the white lynchers (Marriott 5). Describing one such image, Marriott writes, "The assembly of (largely) white men and boys look out at the photographer/spectator—as if they have sated their appetites for look-ing at the black corpse hanging above them (only one or two still look up). What they want to see now is themselves looking at the camera: judges and execution-ers in the lives, and deaths, of black men. Above all, they are vigilant. An image of white identity emerges from a spectacle of annihilation: the lynchers posing, grimly, alongside their black 'trophies' " (6). On the other hand, such photographs are likely to evoke different reactions—at times visceral—in black males by suggesting inevitability. Elizabeth Alexander calls attention to the differences that attend whites' and blacks' ways of seeing violent images in which the victims are black. She contends that an important difference exists between looking at and witnessing the kind of violence that the photographs represent. In her essay " 'Can You Be BLACK and Look at This?': Reading the Rodney King Video(s)," Alexander argues that African Americans share a collective memory. Such a memory has been wrought through images of black bodies in pain that have been available for public consumption in American spectacle for centuries (92). Viewing images of black bodies in pain traumatizes African American people by teaching them a "sorry lesson of their continual, physical vulnerability in the United States, a lesson that helps shape how [African Americans] understand [them]selves as a 'we' even when that 'we' is differentiated" by class, sexuality, or gender (95). Accordingly, the images captured in lynching photographs and those that circulated following incidents such as the Rodney King beating and the subsequent trials and insurrections suggest that "there is such a thing as 'bottom line blackness' with regard to violence, which erases differentiations and highlights race" (95). Though cognizant that her claim might be labeled essentialist, Alexander argues that this "bottom line blackness" grows out of a "traumatized collective historical memory" (93, 94) that is developed and preserved through storytelling practices and individual experiences and is recalled at contemporary scenes of violence. In these ways, "both individually experienced bodily trauma as well as collective cultural trauma—comes to reside in the flesh as forms of memory reactivated and articulated at moments of collective spectatorship" (93–94). As the title of Alexander's essay suggests, then, perhaps one cannot be black and just look at images of black bodies in pain; instead, if one is black, one is compelled by this bottom line blackness to witness the violation, which may provoke an immediate, inevitable, and painful identification.

Hinton Als's description of his initial reaction to the lynching photographs seems to support Alexander's argument. In his contribution to the book *Without Sanctuary*, Als writes about the anger and trauma that he experienced when asked to write about his reaction to the photographs: "I looked at these pictures, and what I saw in them, in addition to the obvious, was the way in which I'm regarded, by any number of people: as a nigger. And it is as one that I felt my neck snap and my heart break, while looking at these pictures" (38). The photographs cause Als pain, and he resents them "for making [him] feel anything at all" (40). Tired of being asked to articulate his suffering to make "the coon situation 'clear' to a white audience" (39), he resents that his point of view becomes just another thing for whites to look at. At some level he is considered a more reliable witness to the images of atrocity that some whites seek to understand. But by agreeing to view and then write about the photographs, Als "paradoxically had to witness [his] own murder and defilement in order to survive and then to pass along the epic tale of violation" (E. Alexander 106). To look, in other words, requires only one's ocular investment. To witness demands that one register the meaning of what one sees at a far more visceral level. If Alexander is correct, viewing lynching photographs seems to risk invoking the trauma of that collective historical memory for black men, who may read the images in relation to their own histories and collective memories of racial violence. One can but imagine, then, the effect of such photographs on black men during the lynching era. Yet the legacy of the violence that the photographs capture is apparent, albeit in considerably more subtle ways, in representations of black men today.

Many realms of representation featuring black men provide evidence of the extent to which and the ways in which the white lore cycle continues to turn in the twenty-first century. For example, many if not most print and television advertisements that depict black men reflect the legacies of cultural exploitation and unspeakable acts of violence associated with the blackface minstrelsy tradition and lynching. In particular, images of black men as both comic clowns and criminals are incorporated into advertising texts in ways that are rarely if ever acknowledged by anyone other than cultural critics. The last part of this chapter begins the process of tracing the legacy of type through contemporary manifestations of the Sambo figure in advertising. The complexities of the Sambo stereotype, which remains a persuasive presence in American culture, and the representations of black men in which it is reproduced suggest that white America has yet to fully reconcile itself to the idea of black men as free U.S. citizens who are equally entitled to the nation's bounty.

Sambo is a childlike black male figure characterized by a constant grin; the ability and the desire to work for, to entertain, and to serve whites; and the absence of anything resembling wisdom or political potency (Boskin 12, 73). He has long been represented in different forms, such as a worker and an athlete, and his image has appeared in just about every imaginable cultural venue. Sambo was a concept long before the figure connoted a specific identity. Over time, the concept came to be personified as a figure that was ultimately institutionalized in popular culture. To understand the significance of Sambo within popular culture, the figure must be considered in relation to the nature and function of stereotypes. Joseph Boskin argues that Sambo may well represent the "perfect stereotype," which "precedes reason," functions "as a form of perception[, and] imposes a certain character on the data of our senses" (4). Boskin attributes Sambo's longevity in American culture to his endurance as a comic image. The Sambo figure is extraordinarily complex and has undergone many changes over time depending on the context in which it is mobilized. At all times, however, in one way or another, the figure has always been "a comic performer *par excellence*" (4). Sambo inhabited images of plantation darkies and the performances of minstrel men and appeared in Negro jokes, on postcards, and in film. In some respects, Sambo bears a relationship to the figure of the fool in medieval Europe. Like the medieval fool, Sambo is seen to be naturally funny, and his humor is seen as obliquely related to the world on which it provided commentary. However, whereas the medieval fool was ascribed qualities of wisdom and perspective and assumed to be able to direct his humor toward sophisticated ends, Sambo is rarely accorded such qualities. Instead, Sambo is considered both the instigator and the butt of his comic antics. Sambo's ubiquitous presence in American culture often functions as shorthand for the racialized views and assumptions that structure various hierarchies within American society. The longevity of the figure, although its appearances in popular culture are arguably subtler than they once were, confirms on an ongoing basis the perceived use value of blacks as entertainers. As Walter Lippmann claims of stereotypes generally, those personified in the Sambo figure have been "consistently and authoritatively transmitted in each generation from parent to child" to the extent that today many whites take them as biological facts (qtd. in Boskin 12). For these reasons, the constantly grinning figure still functions as a powerful means of social control. Even so, very little attention has been directed to his continued presence in American popular culture and the relationship between the Sambo figure and the persistence of stereotypes of black men in popular culture (Boskin 4–15).

The controlling images that white America constructed of black men resulted in perpetual contests of representation in which opposing images of blacks as savages, criminals, and clowns were often entwined and circulated throughout postbellum culture. Out of this culture arose two competing ideas about blacks: first, that the fundamental characteristic of black men was bestial savagery; and second, that the more positive characteristics embodied in the Sambo could be attributed to enslavement. According to George M. Fredrickson, "A concept of the duality or instability of Negro character was in fact one of the most important contributions made by Southern proslavery propagandists to the racist imagery that outlasted slavery" (53). There existed a notion among whites that "slavery 'civilized' black men and that they would otherwise be limited by innate racial traits and doomed to an existence in 'a more or less tenuous state of semi-civilization,' a conception which provided an unequivocal justification of permanent servitude" (53). Black men were thus viewed as savage brutes who were civilized and domesticated under the institution of slavery. Accordingly, proponents of slavery believed that if freed, the supposedly civilized savage would revert to unchecked barbarity and thus pose a significant threat to whites—in particular, to white women. Together, these competing ideas provided the raw materials for systems of representation that justified the oppression of blacks, suggested ways of preventing the supposedly innate savagery from emerging, and "legitimiz[ed] a conditional 'affection' for the Negro. As a slave he was lovable, but as a freedman he would be a monster" (Fredrickson 55).

It is not surprising, given such systems of representation, that with a few rare exceptions, Sambo is represented almost exclusively as a black male. This is likely so, Boskin explains, because "[m]en posed a far more complex and trying challenge. To effect power over males was to control their women and children." Moreover, Sambo was "an illustration of humor as a device of oppression, and one of the most potent in American culture. The ultimate objective for whites was to effect mastery: to render the black male powerless as a potential warrior, as a sexual competitor, as an economic adversary" (14). A most interesting and relevant characteristic of the Sambo figure is the extent to which it is an emasculated version of the black male criminal. Historical narratives that featured Sambo as a character depicted him as someone with a penchant for stealing chickens and watermelons. In its current manifestations, the character retains elements of what many whites still believe to be the black male's innate criminality. At the same time, Sambo's comic elements continue to appear in representations of black men to ameliorate whites' fears and resentment of black men's resistance, agency, and authority. As Boskin explains in relation to the combined function of Sambo's comic and criminal traits, "To make the black male into an object of laughter, and, conversely, to force him to devise laughter, was to strip him of masculinity, dignity, and self-possession" and thus of the markers of citizenship (14).

This burial of criminality within the comic figure and/or the context of comedy directs the analyses of advertisements in the remainder of this chapter and throughout subsequent chapters. Such images not only appear in advertisements today but also inform other realms of cultural production as well as policies and practices that routinely subject the black male image to what might be likened to a ritualized stripping of the signs of masculine identity and citizenship. Boskin claims that Sambo has all but disappeared from American culture (224). However, Sambo-like images of black men not only are far from gone but also appear frequently enough to reveal the extent to which white America continues to deal with its anxieties about black men via the aforementioned dialectic. Together, the recurrence of the entwined figures of the clown and the criminal in advertisements featuring black men make legible the ways that whites have managed the fear of and desire for black men that white lore about them has generated.

As Anne McClintock discusses in *Imperial Leather: Race, Gender, and Sexuality in the Colonial Context* (1995), advertisements for products, which are often quite benign outside of the realm of representation, reproduce hegemonic ideologies pertaining to race, class, and gender by manipulating both "the semiotic space around the commodity" and "the unconscious as a public space" (213). That is, advertising thrives—indeed, relies—on the production of textual characteristics that fall outside of the parameters of industrial rationality, such as ambivalence, sensuality, chance, unpredictable causality, and multiple time. By manipulating these characteristics, advertising influences consumers' spending habits through narratives and images. On the one hand, such narratives and images may appear to be both coherent and rational. On the other hand, they may allow consumers to venture into a "repository of the forbidden" through subtle allusions to "subterranean flows of desire and taboo" (McClintock 213). As a case in point, McClintock offers a compelling analysis of the ways in which early-nineteenth-century advertisements for soap fostered the development of middle-class values and helped to disseminate imperialist ideologies. In its move from an invisible object with its place in the hidden realm of domesticity to commodity, soap circulated as an item of exchange within the capitalist system in ways that created a dominant form of racialized representation (208). That form of representation was produced and mobilized through advertisements that marketed soap using texts and images. Such texts and images constituted extremely effective means of reinventing hegemonic notions of racial difference, particularly ideas concerning blackness and whiteness. The soap advertisements enabled hegemonic ideas of class, gender, and race identity to circulate through images that made legible all that "black" and "white" connoted in the colonial empire. Soap advertisements not only advocated the use of a product but also marketed the promise of moral and economic salvation for Britain's nonwhite populace and thus "the spiritual ingredient of the imperial mission itself" (211). As McClintock explains, "Soap offered the promise of spiritual salvation and regeneration through commodity consumption, a regime of domestic hygiene that could restore the threatened potency of the imperial body politic and the race" (211). Soap advertisements reproduced images and attitudes that evolved into what McClintock characterizes as a system of commodity racism, reproducing itself through the marketing of commodity spectacles that circulate both images and attitudes (208–11).

McClintock's notion of panoptical time enriches our understanding of the legacy of type as it pertains to advertisements and their place in the structure of the prison writ large. McClintock defines panoptical time as "progress consumed as a spectacle from a point of privileged invisibility" (214). The concept of panoptical time helps elucidate the ways in which commodities represented and marketed through narratives and images reveal the meaning of progress and the form and function of cultural domination within a society. As does the arrangement of power within the prison writ large, economies of representation shape a body of expectations about how individuals and groups are expected to think and behave while they compel—without direct force, in many cases—conformity to those expectations. Both commodities and the advertisements that represent them take on lives of their own as they circulate within economies of representation. However, many consumers too easily forget that commodities are tethered to other structures of domination.

Grace Hale calls attention to such connections in her discussion of the relationships among minstrel performances, spectacle lynchings, and the marketing of stereotyped images of blackness through various forms of mass entertainment and advertisements in the late nineteenth and early twentieth centuries. For example, the minstrel show offered counterfeited black identities to white audiences for their consumption even during the period when black bodies were themselves considered commodities (153–54). In addition, spectacle lynchings functioned for southern whites as forms of amusement that reinforced the social order regulated by segregation laws. Both blacks and whites could consume goods that they purchased, providing that they did so in the spaces designated "for colored" or "for whites." Hale argues that a certain "commonality" defined "this spatially divided experience of consumption" (205). Spectacle lynchings, however, disrupted this commonality because only whites could witness the brutal murders of blacks and only blacks could be "extralegally and publicly tortured and killed" under the prevailing social codes. This "grisly dialectic" furthered the construction of "consumption as a white privilege" and reinforced the "structure of segregation where consumption could take place without threatening white supremacy" (205–6). Finally, the invention of photography enabled whites to represent blackness using technology rather than white bodies, as minstrel performers did. Photographs taken by whites of black individuals and circulated within various realms of consumption and later movies such as D. W. Griffith's *Birth of a Nation* further objectified black subjects whose identities were overwritten by the figurations that were the products of whites' fascination and disdain (Hale 154). These seemingly disparate modes of consumption had a shared function: transforming a commodity into a desirable product, which human agents of interpretation then marketed through advertisements that upheld hegemonic ideas about race, class, and gender.

Today, the privileged point of invisibility that operates within economies of representation in the contemporary United States remains a surveilling white gaze that sets and enforces many of the terms and conditions of black men's participation in society generally and popular culture specifically. The gaze produces and reproduces the parameters of their participation in the form of a spectacle—contemporary advertisements. Such spectacles and the historic narratives that they recall function as yet another type of theater or theater of type in which racial boundaries are occasionally negotiated, tested, and pushed but are most often reinscribed (McClintock 216). More often than not, advertisements featuring black men reflect white anxieties. Such ads also frequently reflect the contradictory desire to utilize black men to further projects of capital accumulation and the pursuit of pleasure. These advertisements reinforce long-standing ideas about what can be expected of black men and the realms in which the expected behavior will take place. In this regard, like the soap in the advertisements that McClintock analyzes and the many examples of advertisements that Hale discusses, ads featuring black men can be seen as allegories of the body politic, and the representations of black men can be said to mark places of contradiction in social value (McClintock 214). The representation of black men in advertising reveals the contradictions that inform their reception as well as the absence of a complete resolution to their contradictions, the only resolution that whites can imagine at any given moment, and/or those resolutions that have been explored as possibilities in other theaters of type and at other historical moments. Contemporary advertisements thus constitute another realm of the prison writ large because they support invisible structures of racism that masquerade as neutral or benevolent institutions and texts.

In a 1949 article, "Advertising Jim Crow," Walter Christmas recounts a postwar visit to Belgium. After viewing several copies of the *Saturday Evening Post*, his hosts asked why no blacks were depicted "enjoying the pleasures and gadgets of life in America." The only advertisements in which blacks appeared were a soap ad that depicted a black woman hanging a load of whites on the line and another in which "a distinguished-looking, gray-haired man . . . carried a tray with a Hiram Walker whiskey and soda set-up" (54). Christmas explained that the U.S. advertising industry molds the ways in which people both see and think about the world and conditions them to believe in a "strange world" wherein the material effects of social, economic, racial, and gender divisions are neither apparent nor important. In reality, Christmas explained, the images and narratives through which advertisements construct this strange world are distorted representations of race relations in the nation. The ads' depictions of happy black people performing menial tasks impress "upon the mind the menial, second-class 'place' of the Negro" (55). Ultimately, Christmas determines, recalling the conclusions reached by a group of advertising experts at a conference addressing the Negro in the Arts, "advertising's greatest offense is its denial of the Negro's proportionate existence in our society" (55).

Referring to the advertisements that the group of experts studied before reaching this conclusion, Christmas notes that in not a single ad was a black person represented (55). The 23 April 1949 *Saturday Evening Post* contains 187 advertisements, only one of which depicts a black person. That ad for International Trucks is a photograph of an African safari and shows "natives" "loading one of the trucks while others peer with disbelief under the hood of another truck. Here the medial angle is combined with the simple-minded-black-men stereotype clear to the hearts of all imperialists" (57). Ads in the 2 May 1949 *Newsweek* and 30 April 1949 *Saturday Evening Post* feature the familiar smiling white-jacketed figure of the Negro Pullman porter. The 23 April 1949 *New Yorker* contains 199 ads, only one of which shows a black person—the persona of "the familiar, white-coated Negro bearing the luggage to the room" (57). Such elisions were no oversight, according to Christmas. Indeed, it was not uncommon for commercial artists to be asked to paint blacks out of crowd scenes. The elisions of blacks appear to have been calculated and deliberate. The operative pattern seems to have been one of absence or carefully contained presences.

As one 1950 news article reported, Jim Crow policy was reinforced through advertising practices that sanctioned the depiction of blacks only in menial roles. Far from being represented as a significant component of the American population and thus the American market, "Negroes may never be depicted in national ads in any but standard stereotypes. They can be used as 'Uncle Toms' or 'Aunt Jemimas,' or as wild savages, comic buffoons or grinning redcaps. . . . According to these ads, Negroes are simply not part of the American public, except in the stereotypes commonly accepted" ("Reveal Jim Crow Policy"). A similar pattern persists within the realm of advertising today: blacks continue to be represented as either absences or contained presences. A close analysis of popular contemporary advertisements provides a representative reading of the terms and conditions that apply to black men's participation in commodity culture today and thus offers something of a measure of the terms and conditions that apply to their participation as full citizens in American culture generally.

Contemporary advertisements endorse hegemonic notions about and expectations of black men by depicting them through images and narratives that are often as limited as those to which Christmas referred more than half a century ago. This recurrence indicates the extent to which the preservation of the strange world that Christmas described to his Belgian hosts continues to rely on age-old stereotypes. Indeed, there remains an ongoing tendency to depict black men in ways that continue the pattern of absence/presence established during the Jim Crow era, when the advertising industry was, as it is now, but one institution that upheld the places of whites and blacks in the social order. Whereas lynching functioned as a violent means of reinforcing ideas about black men and controlling the black community as a whole, advertisements, like blackface minstrelsy, preserve stereotypic images of black men as figures whose impulses, when mediated by whites, are entertaining and worthy of fostering and therefore beneficial to whites. However, because certain traits and behaviors are not perceived as desirable when they are not contained within the frame of the commodity spectacle, the spectacle text must always remind audiences that the agency and/or the perceived threat of the black male figure has been appropriately contained and that they are safe to enjoy what it has to offer in the way of entertainment.

Today, continuing disparities in income, education, and other kinds of opportunities notwithstanding, the black middle class is expanding, and African Americans are now gainfully employed in a range of fields far more expansive than ever before. Advertisements in magazines such as *Essence* and *Ebony*, which target an African American audience, reflect these changes. In contrast to publications targeting a primarily white audience, which rarely depict black men outside the parameters of long-standing stereotypes, however subtly inscribed on the texts they may be, the advertisements in magazines geared toward an African American market depict black men as competent, capable, and successful members of businesses and families who have attained some degree of material wealth. Far from representing black men as unthinking laborers, dumb jocks, or barflies with dog-eyed lust for white women, advertisements in magazines geared toward an African American demographic represent black men as responsible sons, fathers, and husbands. For example, an *Essence* ad for *Little Bill* products features a black man in his thirties playing with his young son. In another *Essence* ad, Nationwide Insurance and Financial Services proclaims, "Houses appreciate in value. Families do, too," and shows a young black couple admiring their new baby while standing outside a lovely middle-class home. An *Ebony* advertisement sponsored by Miller Brewing Company advocates educating children about drinking and features a black man holding his daughter on his lap over the caption, "You teach her to look both ways. You teach her not to talk to strangers. It's all about making responsible choices." A Merck pharmaceuticals ad in *Ebony* shows a black man helping his daughter build a sand castle under the words, "What's it like to look forward to the first few steps of the day?" An ad for Chevy trucks shows a father roughhousing with his son and is captioned, "Year after year, it's good to have someone you can depend on." Ads for General Electric, Chevy Malibu, and AC Delco foster similar images of black men as dependable, reliable, and successful citizens. Images of black men wearing aggressive facial expressions and gold chains while running through or from scenes of chaos and so on are all but absent from the pages of such publications. This is most certainly not the case in magazines and television advertisements that are geared toward a broader (that is, white) demographic, where such ads constitute the rule rather than the exception.

Advertisements not geared specifically toward an African American audience feature myriad manifestations of the Sambo figure. Black men, with rare exceptions, are represented as workers, athletes, laborers, entertainers, criminals, or some combination thereof. In advertisements that feature both white and black men, the black man is likely to be depicted in a subordinate posture or position relative to his white counterpart. The captions and the images tend to emphasize the supposed innate athleticism and brute strength of the African American male, his less-than-superior intellect and decision-making skills, and his aggression and hostility—usually safely contained by the literal or latent narrative of the advertisement.

For example, a GM Certified Used Vehicles ad in *Sports Illustrated* depicts the back of a black man's head atop a very thick neck. Across the back of the head are two Polaroid pictures. One shows a sign that says "GM Certified Used Vehicles" and is captioned "Good decision"; the other shows a black man poised, broom in hand, beneath a large wasp nest, presumably ready to knock it down, and is captioned "Bad decision." The ad's message is clear. It is stupid to get rid of a wasp's nest in the manner suggested, and it is smart to buy a GM Certified Used Vehicle. On the one hand, it is difficult to argue with that logic. On the other hand, GM's use of a black male to depict the dumb behavior that the ad contrasts with the decision to purchase a used vehicle from GM is an extension of a historical tendency to employ the black male as a representative example of foolishness, carelessness, and downright stupidity.

Other advertisements reinforce the notion that black men are most suited to work as laborers and blue-collar workers rather than as employees with the desire and opportunities to think and to make decisions that impact the world around them. For example, an ad for Best Buy depicts a young black man sporting dreadlocks, wearing only a pair of long shorts and sneakers, and waving a shovel and laughing exuberantly while sitting atop a huge pile of compact discs. The caption for this ad reads, "Thousands of Possibilities. Get Yours." Evidently, if a person goes to Best Buy, s/he can buy a lot of things. However, this advertisement implies that, thousands of possibilities notwithstanding, those available and/or desirable to a young black man are a pile of thousands of CDs and a job as a ditch digger. What other than a job as a laborer and access to lots of music, the ad seems to ask, could a black man possibly wish for? Along the same lines, an ad for the Toyota Tundra depicts a black man wearing overalls and leaning against a truck, over which a crane is lifting what appears to be a steel bar. The caption reads, "There's a difference between lifting things and raising the bar." The fact that the black man is standing beneath the bar makes it clear that he is not the one raising it, though perhaps he has lifted it at one point or another. Rather, the bar is being raised by an unseen figure guiding the operation from the crane. Black men lift things. Invisible agents of power set and raise the standards by which quality and value are measured. Such ads do not depart significantly from a 1957 Payloader ad that appeared in *U.S. News and World Report*. That ad featured a black man driving a bulldozer beneath the caption, "Dig more, carry more, deliver more." The piece of equipment being advertised, one is led to believe, increases the worker's ability to exceed his current output. The advertisement reinforces in the minds of the audience the idea that black men are the ones who do the digging, the carrying, and the delivering. Whereas in 1957 black men were most likely to be employed in blue-collar jobs, such are most certainly not the only kinds of jobs performed by black men today. Yet most print advertisements in magazines marketed to white audiences do not convey the impression of such diversity and thus, through elision and repetition, perpetuate an impression of black men as blue-collar workers who are not well suited to the important, thinking jobs that reap greater material benefits.

Other advertisements perpetuate the stereotype of black men as lazy individuals who would rather listen to music and dance than take on the responsibilities of a real job. Puma, for example, ran an ad in *FHM* in May 2002 that overtly made this suggestion. That ad depicted a group of black and Hispanic young men wearing headphones and dancing under the caption "The problem with 'real jobs,' as Angel saw it, was the lack of opportunities to dance." In addition to perpetuating stereotypes of black men as lazy and interested only in dancing, the Puma ad calls attention to the large numbers of unemployed or underemployed black males and subtly unloads the responsibility for their lack of employment onto their shoulders. A recent Office Max television ad featuring a character called the Rubberband Man suggests a solution to such a dilemma for black men. The Office Max ad depicts a black male who "starts to jam," as the song goes, while delivering the mail to his office coworkers. In contrast to Angel and the other black and Hispanic men in the Puma advertisement, the Rubberband Man is evidently able to withstand the demands of a "real job" as long as he can dance while performing his duties, entertaining his coworkers in the process. Likewise, the Office Max commercial reinscribes the place of the black male in the lower echelons of employment hierarchies. The commercial valorizes the Rubberband Man not for his ability to use Office Max supplies in ways that increase the efficiency with which he carries out his regular duties but rather for his ability to entertain his coworkers (and the television audience) by dancing as he completes his tasks. The elasticity of his body makes him as functional within the office environment in which his performances break up the monotony of the daily routine as the inert office supply item to which his name invites comparison.

Similarly, a pair of V8 Juice television commercials that aired in 2003–4 speaks to the ways in which black men's performances bring relief into the monotonous lives of hardworking whites. In the first of the two commercials, Savion Glover is depicted frantically tap dancing his way around a Laundromat. As the commercial draws to a close, the dancer starts to sit down and is transformed into a white woman who is leaning back as she enjoys a refreshing swig of V8 Juice. In the second commercial, Glover tap-dances around a high school science classroom. At the end of the commercial, Glover is transformed into a white male teacher, whom we see settling into his chair and drinking deeply from a bottle of V8. In each case, the black male dancer seems a figment of the white imagination, conjured to relieve the monotony of tedious routine and structured work. The black male's disappearance into the bodies of a white female and a white male also references a tradition of whites' aversion to and fascination with the black male body generally and miscegenation specifically in a subtle yet titillating fashion. The suggestion is reminiscent of the ways in which blackface minstrel performances and lynching rituals danced around the complex dynamics of fear and fascination, desire and repulsion, for which whites evidently continue to seek catharsis. Both commercials capture the place of the black male in the white imagination and offer insight into the relationships among black male performance, the imagined threat posed by black men, and white fantasies.

A common trend in print advertisements is to depict black men as aggressive figures or fleeing criminals. For example, an ad for Degree antiperspirant depicts an angry black man who looks as though he is on his way to kill someone. He is running while holding up a bottle of Degree as though it were a shield. The man's visage is in the center of a mirage of smaller versions of his angry face. The first of two captions reads, "A new breakthrough, now with high-response protection made for men." The second reads, "Degree kicks in in the clutch." Degree apparently will protect men from sweat and body odor, which, in the strange world of advertising, are made to seem as scary as the black man being used to sell the product.

The advertisement invokes the angry face of a black man to assure male consumers that when men are threatened, they will be protected. Since the only threatening image in the advertisement is the black man's face, it stands to reason that it is being used as shorthand for the threat rather than the source of the protection that the ad promises. Along the same lines, an ad for the Nike Pro Vent top depicts football player Terrell Owens dashing through a city street and leaving chaos in his wake. Street vendors' carts have been toppled, products have been spilled all over the street, and people are fleeing in every direction. Owens, however, appears to be making a clean getaway despite the efforts of a street vendor in hot pursuit. The caption reads, "Through. Around. Over. Whatever. The unstoppable Terrell Owens wears the Nike Pro Vent top." (Nike, "Pro Vent Top"). Were he not Terrell Owens, the man in the scene would be just another black male, a figure to be feared and apprehended. However, Owens's popularity and superior athletic skill (along with the shirt he wears, of course) allows Nike to use the familiar image of the fleeing black male criminal who has wrought havoc within the community while containing the fear the scene generates within a commercial script that banks on its audience's familiarity with Owens and its confidence in the corporate giant that pays Owens heartily to play on the end of the tether to which he is attached.

Among the most illustrative examples of the legacy of type are Nike's Fun Police commercials, which aired during the 1997–98 basketball season. The series of eight television commercials featured NBA stars such as Gary Payton, Stephon Marbury, and Kevin Garnett and purportedly represented an effort to highlight the fun aspects of the game and alter Nike's image, which some observers had criticized as too serious. The methodology that Nike employed to reassociate its corporate image and basketball more closely with fun was driven by subtle references to and inversions of black/white power dynamics with powerful referents in both the antebellum and postbellum eras. The commercials promoted the fun aspects of the game at the expense of images of both black males generally and the athletes whom the ads featured specifically. In one of the commercials, for example, the Fun Police—in this case, three players, two black and one white—are hotly pursuing a white referee who allegedly calls too many ticky-tack fouls during games. The implied purpose of the search is to hold the referee accountable for using his authority to undermine the flow of the game and inhibit the style of play that provides so much of the game's entertainment value. The locale and the methods employed in the search, including the use of bloodhounds, allude to historical images of searches in which plantation patrollers, vigilantes, and police sought fugitive slaves, prospective lynching victims, and escaped prisoners (Nike, "Fun Police: Find the Ref").

The commercial alludes directly to such historical referents when one of the Fun Police discovers a white fugitive prisoner cowering beneath a pile of leaves. The officer releases him after quickly identifying that he is not the referee that they are seeking. The search is interrupted again when the most vigilant of the three Fun Police discovers his two colleagues pausing to enjoy a marshmallow roast. "It's fun," the white officer explains. His black comrade appears to support the explanation for the unauthorized break by way of a minstrel-like grin enhanced by the marshmallow-stuffed black cheeks that lend it form. The search and thus the commercial conclude when the hounds locate the referee, who has been treed, not insignificantly, like a coon. The referee's whiteness signifies a racial reversal that at best negates and at worst mocks the often horrific outcomes of historical searches in which black fugitives were sought. Not only does the commercial gloss over the frequently violent nature of the sorts of searches the Fun Police reenact, but the naming of the Fun Police; the fact that they are dressed in bright yellow raincoats, like children; the stereotypic depiction of and the denial of a voice to the marshmallow-eating character; and the release of a white fugitive prisoner imply a clear distinction between the authority afforded real police and that which the Fun Police are permitted to enact in off-court settings. The commercials play on as they effectively sever links between black males and officially sanctioned authority to carry out their purported agendas while reassuring white audiences that the actors pose no threat either on or off court.

Another of the Fun Police series of commercials employs an even more overtly racialized structure. The commercial features NBA players Jason Kidd and Damon Stoudamire barging unexpectedly into the middle-class home of a white family. Their entrance frightens the white female resident, who cowers on a sofa as she pleads with her young son to concede to the demands of the black men who have invaded their home. A white male adult hovers fearfully and silently in the background. The Fun Police, however, are not there to steal from the family or rape the woman but wish only to confront the boy, who has been hogging the ball during basketball games. The Fun Police search the house and discover a closet full of balls, which provide evidence that the boy is guilty as charged (Nike, "Fun Police: Kid"). Although on one level the commercial advocates a congenial message that condones good sportsmanship, it relies on the easily recognizable image of black males as criminals to do so. The commercial assumes that viewers will recognize the black crime narrative that cultivates viewers' pleasure produced by feelings of fear and relief. The popularity of the Fun Police commercials suggests that Nike was correct in its assumption that there exists a common discourse among viewers as to what can be expected of black men when they are not otherwise occupied on athletic courts.² Indeed, Nike banked on its belief that viewers would grasp the subtexts that the commercial campaign employed to replicate the experience of the spectator in an off-court setting. The company employed those subtexts to produce the undercurrent of excitement and fear that make the experience of viewing the commercial similar to that of watching the basketball games that it aims to promote. Nike's use of such racialized discourses to alter its image and that of the game of basketball leads me to suggest that the real policing of the "game" is carried out by the various media campaigns that construct and control the images and behavior of professional black athletes. Indeed, like the commercial featuring a fugitive referee, this one reassures viewers that big, black, athletic men pose no threat in off-court settings as long as they are kept running down balls that white boys wish to claim as their own.

Taken on their own, many people would dismiss out of hand the notion that the advertisements and commercials that I have invoked as representative examples of the legacy of type portray black men in limited and limiting ways and that they have undertones characteristic of the subtle manner in which racist beliefs and attitudes are expressed and circulated today. Many would find it easier yet to dismiss the claim that such images impact the day-to-day lives of black men in the United States. However, these images constitute but a few of thousands that circulate each day in various realms of popular culture. As such, unless one is determined to ignore the recursive nature and the historical traditions that underscore such images—as many whites and some African Americans are—it is difficult to deny the nature and function of the stereotypes that such texts reproduce. Those who would deny the relationship between such advertisements and commercials, the legacy of type, and the white lore cycle within which it circulates fail to question the differences between the kinds of texts that companies use to market products to black audiences and those that are deemed likely to appeal to largely white audiences. The marked differences between the kinds of advertisements directed to each market surely indicate a rather basic recognition that African Americans are not likely to respond favorably to negative images of themselves, whereas white audiences are quite likely literally to buy into representations of black men that accord with stereotypes about them.

Perhaps the greatest irony of the white lore cycle is that, however violent its effects, at times and sometimes at the same time, it can and has both enabled and regulated collective agency on the part of black men and whites (Lhamon 72). Contemporary popular culture reveals the extent to which black men remain shackled to the negative side of white America's binary ways of seeing, interpreting, and representing the world and the place that it imagines for itself and others in it. It would be wrongheaded—downright silly, in fact—to think that black men are unaware or unresponsive to the ways in which whites see and represent them. Black men have always dared to dream of themselves and to act in ways that do not accord with how they have been typecast. The possibilities inherent in such daring and dreaming are not to be underestimated. As Marriott argues, whatever the limitations of dreaming, for the world and one's place in it to be different, it must first be imagined as such (vii). The manner in which popular culture today represents black men suggests that white America remains unable or unwilling to imagine black men's place in the United States other than as it is and has been. And while the onus ought to be on whites to reimagine the place of black men, they are not holding their breath and waiting. Instead, many black men are determined to participate in a twenty-first-century version of reconstruction because their images and lives remain threatened. Thus, as Marriott puts it, "Daring to dream is thus a double commitment to pursue the wished-for risk and revolutionary hope that by dreaming the unthinkable—namely, wanting, rather than hating, one another— we can contest the dreamwork of racist culture in its verisimilitude, address and imagine another kind of *experience*, another kind of living present and future" (vii). This is not to say that black men have consistently reimagined themselves in accordance with the revolutionary possibilities inherent in the acts of dreaming or seeing the world as it might be. On the contrary, black men's behavior and cultural productions frequently reveal an understandable anger at being constantly reduced to type and/or their complicity in wittingly or unwittingly reproducing stereotypic images of black men (Marriott viii). It is not, I think, too great a stretch to posit that the absence or presence of a collective historical memory may inform the ways in which and the extent to which whites and blacks recognize, perceive, and react to manifestations of that legacy. It ought not to come as a surprise that the black male psyche has been conditioned to be in conflict with itself through racial dramas and traumas in the United States. But neither should we be surprised by the myriad ingenious ways in which many black men dance within the parameters of the cultural lockstep created and imposed on them by white fears and fantasies (Marriott x). In this regard, it would be a mistake to assume that the segments of a lore cycle that indicate desire for black gestures on the one hand and disdain for them on the other function independently of one another. Just as the symbols that were part of blackface performances were at various times and sometimes at the same time disdained, fetishized, buried, enhanced, and elaborated, so too desire and disdain become intertwined in contemporary representations of black men that circulate, often covertly, within fields of representation to which both blacks and whites contribute (Lhamon 76–77).

The complex array of stereotypes embodied in the Sambo figure, in the black-face minstrel tradition, in lynching rituals, and in the lore of the black male as criminal remain operative and visible in the realms of advertising, basketball, film, and rap. Today, such lore informs the racialized, masculine games (both literal and figural) played out in television and print advertisements, sports arenas, movie houses, and the recording industry. The form and manner of the "games" through which whites managed the tension between their fear of and desire for black men in the past are contiguous with the methods of protecting and recuperating white masculine authority deployed in and around such realms today. I turn now to a discussion of these realms.

COURT GESTURES
Cultural Gerrymandering and the Games
That Black Men Play

The white lore cycle centered on the hybrid figure of the black male as brute/comic continued to turn throughout the twentieth century and into the twenty-first. The figure circulates within contexts that are inscribed with both the subtleties of the minstrel show and the violence of lynching rituals. In particular, white lore about black men remains operative and visible through representations within and around the realm of professional basketball. It informs the racialized, masculine games (both literal and figural) that continue to be played out on the professional basketball court and through media representations of black male athletes. Clyde Taylor contends that black men in the United States are players, though not by choice, in a high-stakes game in which the prize "is the soul, spirit, and creative energy of black men themselves" (167). The notion of the game did not originate with Taylor, of course. Todd Boyd addresses the broad usage of the term in the preface to his coedited volume of essays, *Basketball Jones: America above the Rim* (2000): "The Game. This is the metaphor used by so many Brothas that it ain't even funny. Michael Jordan talks about raising his game to a higher level; Ice Cube incites us to be true to the game; and down in the dirty south, Silk the Shocker encourages us to charge it to the game. The metaphor has a historical precedent as well. Back in the day, Iceberg Slim pontificated on the game, and Richard Pryor's memorable character from *The Mack* (1973) told us the game was strong. In the present, Snoop Dogg tells us that the game is to be sold, not to be told" (ix). Although there is no single definition of the game, Boyd offers a starting point:

> Life in America, for far too many Brothas, has been about playing a concerted game of chance, with the odds definitely stacked against them. These Brothas have attempted to turn a game of chance into a game of skill, and because of this, life itself becomes an ongoing game. This influence pervades black culture, and because sports has been one of the arenas where there has been a consistent black presence, even dominance, the notion of the game is that much

more a part of everyday life. The three most commonly referenced games in contemporary black popular culture are basketball, the rap game, and the dope game. (ix)

The game, then, as referenced by Taylor, is ironic because the souls of black men are what is at stake, but "the contest is carried out on the body of the Black male" (C. Taylor 167). Furthermore, the game is oblique because "many Black men, players all, don't even know the object of the contest, have no clue of the rules, the stakes, or even that they are both in the game and the quarry" (167). Taylor's thesis that there exists a game within which black men become forced participants provides the framework for my consideration of the ways that historical stereotypes of black men inform the construction of professional basketball as a racialized site of containment and contemporary representations of black male basketball players. The methods by which white America manages its fearful and voyeuristic responses to black male athletes are representative of how whites generally manage relationships to black men. Thus, applying a telescoped gaze to basketball and representations of professional black basketball players enables a better understanding of the cycle of white lore within which historical images of black men circulate.

The contributions of black athletes to basketball led to the gradual structuring of the sport as a racialized site within the United States. The nature of this restructuring reveals the ways in which the historical images and disciplinary methods that I discussed in chapter 2 inform white America's ways of seeing, representing, and disciplining black men today. Specifically, the dynamic of fear and desire enacted in literal ways in minstrel performances and lynching rituals relates to the more subtle ways that the same dynamic informs contemporary responses to and representations of black male athletes. The infamous coach-choking incident involving Latrell Sprewell and the images and representations of now-retired players Dennis Rodman and Michael Jordan are cases in point. Both Sprewell's anger and (arguably) resistance to his coach's derogatory coaching methods and Rodman's blatant disregard for the rules and regulations governing the behavior of black males generally and black male athletes specifically made visible and pushed the boundaries within which white America is most comfortable identifying black males. In contrast, Jordan's aestheticized body and gentrified image offered no categorical challenges to the social control and discipline that define the prison writ large (Fiske, "Understanding" 99). In sum, I link the game of basketball to the broader games in which black men are implicated and of which so many are masters when it comes to finding ways to incorporate the pleasure of undisciplined sites into the closely curtailed and regimented structure of the prison writ large.

A look at the important and paradoxical place that basketball occupies in African American culture and communities helps us to see its location both in black culture and in cycles of white lore about black men. Basketball courts in black neighborhoods represent sites where verbal and athletic skills are honed, reputations are acquired or lost, and the tensions of everyday life are released and temporarily overshadowed by the game's pleasure and intensity. As Nathan McCall recalls in his autobiography, *Makes Me Wanna Holler: A Young Black Man in America* (1994), in the neighborhood where he grew up, "[e]verybody was tradition-bound to learn to shoot hoops. Those who could hawk ball were respected almost as much as those who could dress well, rap, and fight" (56). John Edgar Wideman offers us two very different perspectives on basketball games played by black men on neighborhood courts. These points of view meld together in a reference to the racialized games that take place off court, in which black men are implicated and which function as paradoxical sites of containment wrought by white lore concerning black masculinity. In his novel, *The Lynchers* (1973), Wideman describes the dynamics of a Sunday-morning pickup game, empha-sizing the unique relationship between players and spectators by describing how "reputations were made and dismantled as the bystanders with the words and noises participated in the game. There were no passive spectators" (107). In keep-ing with this relationship, Wideman makes a compelling link when he compares the flow and rhythm of the game, which resembles "the sound of the ocean as sudden pauses in the game would be marked by a crescendo of angry voices, deep, male voices disputing a foul or an out of bounds," to a performance of "gut bucket jazz" (107). This comparison is provocative when considered in relation to the gradual and much-resisted shift toward the so-called schoolyard style of play.

It is possible to compare the characteristics of the schoolyard style of play to those of a jazz performance. As Boyd notes in *Am I Black Enough for You?: Popular Culture from the 'Hood and Beyond* (1997), although "there is no exclusive way of defining 'Blackness,' . . . a certain criteria must be in place. The heart of these criteria is the sustained articulation of an oral culture, which is most often pre-sented in the form of improvisation. Thus jazz is an obvious signifier of African American culture" (113). Further, he argues, the best basketball players play the best of classroom ball while adding nuance to the formal performance through their "reliance on tenets of Black oral culture as they relate to the game" (111). Finally, prior to the popularization of the schoolyard style, the performance of the team as a whole was considered more important than that of any individual. The incor-poration of showy moves such as the slam dunk has had the effect of highlighting individual performances. The changes in the style of play may be likened to one of the primary differences between blues and jazz performances. Whereas blues performances traditionally feature a single performer, jazz performances take the form of a complex pattern of interaction in which the performances of individual musicians and those of the entire band are highlighted at different points in time. Similarly, basketball has evolved into a game in which individual players and their unique skills become more or less visible at various points throughout the game yet always remain important to the team's performance as a whole.

To those not privy to the meanings of the calls and responses that flow across the boundaries of the court, the patterns of action and interaction in a neighborhood hoops game signify only misdirected, unintelligible chaos and confusion. As Wideman puts it, to "a stranger the anger would seem violently out of proportion" (*Lynchers* 107). However, to those whose senses are attuned to the "lower frequencies" of the Sunday-morning games won or lost depending on players' skills, the performances represent nothing less than brilliantly crafted narratives of survival.[1] In these games, the black men, who on the other six days of the week were "classed as dishwashers and janitors or men who carried mail, men who scuffled to make ends meet for themselves and their families," exit those roles to "play . . . the game the way it should be played" (109). The game, as it is played on Sundays at least, takes the men "as far away from this earth as the sanctified people in the storefront churches just down the block, singing and shaking their way to glory," offering the men both an escape and the wherewithal to "slip into the nonentity, the innocuousness demanded of them as they encountered the white world" on Monday morning (109, 108). That is, in important ways, their participation in the Sunday games reassures the players that their workaday worlds have not extinguished the "fluid inevitability" that, "no matter how high the others jumped, no matter what impossible refinements their skills brought into the game," enables them to return to the playground courts each Sunday. On the court, strength and pride "bloom again and again" in "these men so real, so richly full of life" (109). Like Tupac Shakur's thug life and EXODUS 1811 tattoos, which I analyze in chapter 5, Wideman's description of the Sunday-morning basketball games reflects a similar disregard for a boundary between the sacred and the secular. Just as the churchgoers attend weekly services, so too the players return to the courts each week to again have the "emotional experience of being filled with the power of the spiritual" that will sustain them in the week to come (Smitherman 91–92).

In *Hiding Place* (1988), however, Wideman suggests that limits exist to the freedom that black men find on playground basketball courts. *Hiding Place* tells the story of Tommy, a young black man who is trying to elude capture by the police. In this text, Wideman describes a basketball game from Tommy's perspective.

The players appear to be engaged as enthusiastically as those whom Wideman describes in *The Lynchers*: "Ball players half-naked out there under that hot sun, working harder than niggers ever did picking cotton. They shine. They glide and leap and fly at each other like their dark bodies are at the ends of invisible strings. This time of day the court is hot as fire. Burn through your shoes. Maybe that's why the niggers play like they do, running and jumping so much because the ground's too hot to stand on" (61). The players seem less like free agents and more like marionettes whose performances are underscored by complex dynamics of pleasure and pain, desire and fear. The playground court, which takes the form of "a big concrete hole . . . where people piss and throw bottles like you got two points for shooting them in" and which is marked by "[w]hat's left of a backstop dropping like a rusty spiderweb from tall metal poles" and "the flaking mesh" of a screen, seems in both form and function less like a sanctified church and more like a prison cell (62).[2] In significant ways, the contradictions and paradoxes of the neighborhood game are reproduced in the professional arena, where racial power plays are highly visible and regularly enacted.

Arguments that locate professional basketball as a place where racism remains operative are frequently met with doubt couched in references to the salaries of NBA players and the fact that for many black males the sport offers an alternative to a life assumed otherwise to be destined for places considerably less desirable. For example, McCall recalls watching professional ball games and admiring the black players, who seem more self-assured on the basketball court than anywhere else: "I concluded that brothers shone so well shooting hoops because the basketball court was the one place white Americans let them know they believed in them" (373). Similarly, Boyd, in "The Game Is to Be Sold, Not to Be Told," admires black men whose superior basketball skills enable them to take advantage of the myriad opportunities that go hand in hand with playing in the NBA, not the least of which is getting paid for displaying those skills (xi). Perceptions notwithstanding, studies conducted during the 1990s revealed certain troubling racial inequalities in terms of wages and job security in the NBA. One such study revealed a wage gap between white and black players, with whites receiving salaries between 11 and 25 percent higher than those of black players. A 1999 study took note of exit discrimination in the NBA, finding not only that white players are 36 percent less likely to be cut but also that their careers tend to last on average two seasons longer than those of black players of like caliber (Shropshire 78–79). John Hoberman addresses the issue of resistance to the notion that racist worldviews and agendas manifest themselves in sport, contending that resistance to the argument that race relations inflect the world of sports in the United States "is rooted in an uncritical faith in the model of equal opportunity, which envisions a linear expansion of minority participation and power over time" (32). Such uncritical faith may not seem startling when one considers that basketball constitutes a form of entertainment. Indeed, some would argue that its status as a sport and a form of entertainment renders basketball unworthy of critical investigation and political interrogation. Yet Boyd and Kenneth L. Shropshire, in their introduction to *Basketball Jones: America above the Rim* (2000), assert that basketball bears a far greater influence on American popular culture and national identity than any other sport, including baseball and football.

Whereas baseball continues to occupy an important place in U.S. sports nostalgia and tradition, basketball functions "perfectly as a symbol of contemporary America" (Boyd and Shropshire 5, 3). In contrast, Boyd and Shropshire contend that baseball and football are primarily American sports and thus relatively insignificant globally. They note that the U.S. global prowess is especially visible during the Olympic Games and was especially so during the 1992 Olympics in Barcelona, where it became apparent that both Michael Jordan and basketball had achieved unprecedented global significance in ways that other sports and their participants have not (1). Given basketball's importance on the American scene, it seems more accurate to characterize uncritical faith in notions of equality and opportunity as critical blindness. That is, in a way that no other sport (with the exception of boxing) has, professional basketball reflects histories of racist practices and racialized representations of black men in the United States. The history of professional basketball and the images of black players represent compelling subjects because of the ways that they shape and are shaped by white lore of the black male as a criminal and a black brute/comic. Critical blindness with respect to the significance of basketball within the racial organization of the United States is particularly dangerous because it fosters the continuous turning of lore cycles that structure a broader system of containment in the form of a prison writ large. As Boyd puts it in "Mo' Money, Mo' Problems," "[I]n basketball, race, directly or indirectly, *is* the conversation at all times" (60).[3] Accordingly, I read basketball as a site in which subtle forms of racism directed toward black players replicate those that structure the United States as a prison writ large. Basketball in the United States is rife with examples of what John Fiske calls the "two main strategies by which the dominant attempt . . . to control the leisure and pleasures of the subordinate." Those strategies include both the construction and enforcement of repressive legislation and the taming of uncontrolled leisure pursuits into "respectable" and disciplined forms (*Understanding* 70). As Fiske explains,

> Anything out of control is always a potential threat, and always calls up moral, legal, and aesthetic powers to discipline it. The signs of the subordinate out of control terrify the forces of order (whether moral, legal, or aesthetic), they

constitute a constant reminder of both how fragile social control is and how it is resented; they demonstrate how escaping social control, even momentarily, produces a sense of freedom. That this freedom is often expressed in excessive, "irresponsible" (i.e., disruptive or disorderly–the adjectives are significant) behavior is evidence both of the vitality of these disruptive popular forces and the extent of their repression in everyday life. (*Understanding* 69)

The evidence of such strategies for control of the leisure, pleasure, and work of black male athletes and some players' resistance to such control is evident at all levels of the professional game. The nature and function of the containment to which black athletes are subject in the NBA becomes apparent when we look more closely at the social, political, and literal positions of the players vis-à-vis management and spectators; the athletes' attire; the dimensions and layout of the court; and the style and rules of play. These arrangements and characteristics function collectively to tease the boundaries between (black) players and (white) audiences by both encouraging and controlling activities and interactions between black men and whites that are interpreted and responded to quite differently in less controlled settings.

For example, at its most rudimentary level, basketball represents yet another site in which black men do the work and provide entertainment for mostly white audiences while whites run the show. As Julianne Malveaux notes in "Gladiators, Gazelles, and Groupies: Basketball Love and Loathing," the "rules and profit of the game reinforce the rules, profit, and history of American life. . . . Black men who entertain serve as stalkers for white men who measure profits. Neutered black men can join their white colleagues in cha-chinging cash registers but can never unlock the golden handcuffs and the platinum muzzles that limit their ability to generate independent opinions" (56). As documentaries such as *Hoop Dreams* (1994) suggest and as Todd Boyd notes in his preface to *Out of Bounds: Sports, Media, and the Politics of Identity* (1997), something indeed seems innately criminal about a system that offers young, often disadvantaged black men opportunities for upward mobility only to subject them to alternative forms of bondage within the NBA (ix). Lindon Barrett, in "Black Men in the Mix: Badboys, Heroes, Sequins, and Dennis Rodman," makes a similar point when he notes that the desire to derive uninhibited pleasure from the exploitation of African American young men is manipulated for profit in post-civil-rights U.S. culture (108).

But giving massive amounts of money to a tiny percentage of black men does not ease white America's burden of guilt. The money and adoration bestowed on black athletes is not sufficient reparation for the abuse and indignities suffered by blacks for centuries past (Shields 120). White America at once worships and resents the success enjoyed by black athletes in the NBA (Shields 120). It comes as no surprise, then, that there exists no evidence of a trickle-down effect in terms of white America's tolerance toward black men generally. It is one thing for white America to celebrate the achievements of a few black athletes, but too many white Americans assume that such reverence indicates significantly improved perceptions of blacks more generally. Just because a white person is a fan of a black male athlete who scores a lot of points for the team does not mean that such appreciation extends to matters of interracial dating, workplace authority, or class mobility (George 138). Hence, a figure such as Michael Jordan is appealing both because of his prowess on the court and because he demonstrated it without reminding fans "of the conditions that helped nurture it" (George 234).

Public receptiveness both to basketball and basketball players grows out of or is, in part, the product of the intimacy of the game itself and the identification between fans and individual players (or at least the images of those players) that such intimacy fosters. Basketball may have greater intimacy than other popular sports in which black athletes predominate in part because it is easier to see the players' faces and therefore easier to exploit their images in advertising campaigns (Boyd and Shropshire 3). Boyd and Shropshire call this phenomenon the "cult of personality" and claim that it grows out of such intimacy, which can be likened to that between Hollywood celebrities and their fans (5). David Halberstam also highlights the intimacy of basketball relative to baseball and football when he links improvements in various types of technology, including satellites, cameras, and televisions, to fans' increased perceptions of closeness between themselves and basketball players. In addition, basketball players' minimal uniforms, along with their acrobatic movements and their ability to play both offense and defense, enable players to project a degree of physical and emotional intimacy that is not apparent in football. As Halberstam puts it, a "superstar in basketball, one truly surpassing player with only four other men on the court with him, playing both offense and defense, could dominate the play and fire the imagination of the public as one baseball player among nine or more or one football player among twenty-two never could" (131). Further, in contrast to football and baseball uniforms, basketball uniforms neither protect or conceal the athletes' bodies nor hide their expressions of emotion during play. A basketball fan observed, "In football, they've got all these pads and they've got this helmet on; they don't even look like human beings anymore. In basketball, they're very clearly real men: you can see their faces, you can see their bodies, they're not distorted in any sense, and they're sweating. You can see their muscles, and they're up against each other. . . .

[I]t's just, you know, bodies on bodies and it's totally erotic" (Shields 59). The same fan attributes the NBA's imposition of rules that make it illegal for players to touch each other on the back, to hand check, or to taunt each other to the homoerotic nature of the game. Whereas the NBA explained its imposition of such rules as efforts to control the increasing level of violence in basketball games, the fan reads the rule changes as an effort to limit audiences' exposure to images of emotional black men touching each other. The fan concludes that in "American culture the most dangerous symbol, the most frightening symbol, for white people, is black men in love. The moment black men love each other, the United States is done for" (Shields 59–60). This fan is right, given that the image of an emotional, loving community of black males does not accord with hegemonic images of aggressive black males whose sole purposes in life are to destroy self and community. In ways absent from other sports, then, the blackness, sexuality, and physical and emotional vulnerability of the majority of the players are stamped on the face of the game of basketball.

Whereas basketball has changed considerably since the professional game was integrated in 1951, one trait that has remained constant at all its levels since its inception is the aggressive manner in which the game is played. Today, basketball is not a sport that one immediately associates with aggressive play in comparison to, say, prizefighting. If one stops and thinks, however, the basketball court and the game itself bear a striking resemblance to the battle royals that were popular throughout Reconstruction and into the twentieth century (George 14).[4] In the early years of the twentieth century, basketball was renowned for its overt, physical violence. In 1908, Harvard President Charles Eliot called for a ban on basketball on the grounds that the game had become more brutal than football. As Thomas G. Bryant, a player for the University of Kentucky Wildcats from 1905 to 1907, remarked, "We didn't play for championships but for bloody noses" (qtd. in George 7). One response to the violence of the game was the installation of mesh and wire screens around basketball courts, a practice that continued until the 1940s. The screens were intended to protect fans from players, players from fans, and the referees from both players and fans (George 7).[5] The removal of the protective screens just prior to the integration of the game created a heightened sense of intrigue and risk that the presence of black players would only increase. This is not to say that the removal of the protective screens was a conscious attempt to play on white spectators' racialized fears. Actions that feed whites' fears of and desire for black men have rarely been so overt. Rather, the timing of the screens' removal, which coincided with the addition of black players to professional leagues, may have affected the ways that whites perceived and experienced their increased exposure to black male athletes in the particularly provocative context of a basketball game. Nowadays, the perimeter of the court is defined only by chairs that are occupied by athletes; formally attired members of the mostly white, mostly male, management conglomerate; and members of the press and celebrities. This human barrier serves two paradoxical functions in relation to the court. On the one hand, like the cage, it reminds players of the boundaries within which they are expected to perform in ways that are innovative, aggressive, and entertaining without violating the rules of the game. On the other hand, the human boundary denies spectators the security of a more solid physical barrier between themselves and the ten very large, mostly black, very aggressive male athletes who control the tenuously contained and relatively small space of the court. The physical layout of a basketball court and the figures who assume roles on and around it thus create a framework that mobilizes a peculiar combination of desire and fear wrought almost entirely on the backs of black male athletes.

The size of the court and the "black" or schoolyard style of play that has come to characterize professional basketball games also contribute to the sensation of fear and desire that the absence of a stable boundary between spectators and players produces. The court itself is small compared to a football field or an ice surface and seems even smaller when ten large players take the floor. Jeff Greenfield notes in "The Black and White Truth about Basketball,"

> It takes a conscious effort to realize how constricted the space is on a basketball court. Place a regulation court (ninety-four by fifty feet) on a football field, and it will reach from the back of the end zone to the twenty-one-yard line; its width will cover less than a third of the field. On a baseball diamond, a basketball court will reach from home plate to just beyond first base. Compared to its principal indoor rival, ice hockey, basketball covers about one-fourth the playing area. And during the normal flow of the game, most of the action takes place on about the third of the court nearest the basket. It is in this dollhouse space that ten men, each of them half a foot taller than the average man, come together to battle each other. (374)

The dimensions of the court did not change when the professional game was integrated. However, the stylistic changes that black players brought to the integrated game could not but alter the ways in which both spectators and players perceived and situated themselves in relation to that contained space. One of the changes that preceded the integration of the game but became more pronounced in the years that followed was a shift away from the ritualized, orderly style of play known as classroom ball toward a more stylistic, improvisational "schoolyard" style. Many critics have argued that this style reflects the influences of a black aesthetic. For example, Gena Dagel Caponi, citing Michael Novak, identifies basketball as a medium that enables "the mythic world of the black experience" to enter American life while undergoing minimal change. According to Novak, the "game is corporate like black life; improvisatory like black life; formal and yet casual; swift and defiant; held back, contained, and then exploding; full of leaps and breakaway fluid sprints" (Caponi 2). Similarly, the influence of a black aesthetic is apparent in the definite distinctions between "black" and "white" styles of play. Both styles of play bear the mark of different ways of responding to the contained space of the court. Whereas white players tend to gain mastery on the court by sheer intensity, black players more often employ their athletic skills to work the compressed space to their advantage. The black style of play is better suited to the restraints of the size of the court, which demand that players master "the subtlest of skills: the head fake, the shoulder fake, shift of body weight to the right and the sudden cut to the left," to defeat an opponent through clever acts of deception. Thus, Greenfield concludes, in basketball, as in many a black man's life, "[d]eception is crucial to success; and to young men who have learned early and painfully that life is a battle for survival, basketball is one of the few games in which the weapon of deception is a legitimate rule and not the source of trouble" (374).

As has frequently been the case in other areas of performance, the styles of play that characterize professional basketball—the slam dunk in particular—are indicative of the ways in which black men incorporate the vernacular into a formal structure (Boyd, "Game" x). The slam dunk is a move where players jump and with either one or two hands and with great force stuff the ball through the basket. The ability to execute a dunk had eluded most players, and coaches had discouraged the move from the game's inception in 1891 until the 1950s, when black high school players began to use the slam dunk as a means of intimidating other teams. During the 1970s, the "Black ability to dunk 'with authority' became, in the wide-open American Basketball Association . . . an integral part of professional basketball's tapestry" (George xvi–xvii). The inclusion of the slam dunk shifted play from a horizontal to a vertical plane, thereby literally elevating the game and transforming the court into a three-dimensional playing field. Further, the slam dunk is attended by a culture of violence signified by the sheer force with which players slam. Indeed, bruises on athletes' hands, wrists, and forearms frequently reflect the force of the dunk. The emphasis produced by the aggression of the gesture suggests that the move is as much about violence as it is about artistry, grace, and athleticism. Moreover, the best dunks are those considered directed at an opposing player, rendering the move arguably the "ultimate 'weapon' on the basketball court, an expression in the literal sense of the word ... accompanied by the vernacular of violence" (Houck 153–56). The combination of an increasingly disorderly, improvisational, and unpredictable style of play and the almost entirely black makeup of professional basketball teams creates the illusion of a smaller, more aggressive, and less secure court from the spectator's point of view.[6] Proximity to and the openness of the athletes and the action on the court creates the unease that derives from the structure of fear and desire so important to spectators' pleasure.

Today, the style of the game has become such that basketball spectators expect to see players—most of them black males—engaging aggressively with one another. Although the structure of the court denies spectators—most of them white—a protective distance from the objects of their voyeuristic gazes, the style of the game reinforces the pervasive image of black males as dangerous figures. This image is in keeping with one of the most overt methods of containment to which black athletes are subject and which arises from the dominant image of black masculinity in the United States. That image arises from what Hoberman identifies as "the merger of the athlete, the gangster rapper, and the criminal into a single black male persona that the sports industry, the music industry, and the advertising industry have made ... predominant" (xviii). This merger leads to the dangerous twinning of the violent black male with the spectacular black athlete. White America's eagerness to conflate the black athlete, the rap artist, and the criminal into a single image of black masculinity leads to the construction of all black males as dangerous, frightening, and offensive figures (Hoberman xviii–xix). White America remains comfortable with—indeed, derives enormous pleasure from—the physical and cultural space that professional basketball occupies as long as black men's displays of aggression are confined to the court itself. However, white America becomes far less comfortable when it encounters black males behaving aggressively in off-court settings. An even closer look at the off-court game(s) in which black male athletes are implicated provides strong evidence that white America manages its discomfort by mobilizing in peculiar and often ironic ways images of black males both as childlike creatures and as innately violent and hypersexualized men.

Take, for example, the incident involving Latrell Sprewell while he was a member of the Golden State Warriors. On 1 December 1997, Sprewell allegedly choked and threatened to kill Warriors coach P. J. Carlesimo.[7] The incident, according to Shropshire, "had varying undertones of the dominant form of racism that permeates American society: aversive or unconscious racism" (76). The extent to which the media represented the incident in ways that vilified Sprewell through the use of derogatory images of black men and as though it occurred outside of any explanatory context and without provocation suggests that Shropshire is correct in his assertion. According to Sprewell, he was provoked by verbal abuse from Carlesimo, who is renowned for his aggressive, insulting, and confrontational coaching style. Sprewell's explanation seems quite plausible in view of the suggestion that his violent behavior may well have been a reaction to the tendency of many coaches, including Carlesimo, to use racial expletives to "motivate" their players (Malveaux 53). San Francisco Mayor Willie Brown would seem to concur with such a position given his response to a request for his take on the incident: "His boss may have needed choking.... I'm not justifying what Sprewell did as right. But nobody is asking why he did it or what might have prompted him" (Shropshire 86). During an arbitration hearing that upheld most of the league-imposed penalty against Sprewell, NBA Commissioner David Stern stated that "the severity of [Sprewell's] punishment was based on the 'clearly premeditated nature' of the attack" (Barkin B11). The degree to which the attack was premeditated remains open to question. The NBA Players Association claimed that there "was no premeditated attack" because Sprewell never became calm enough to "premeditate anything" (Shropshire, "Deconstructing 86). Rather, the association maintained that the "incident was an instantaneous reaction resulting from a month of tension and confrontations between" Sprewell and Carlesimo (Shropshire 81–82). Finally, Shropshire and many other critics locate Sprewell's action within a larger framework of resistance by reading it in the same light as the players' positions in the NBA lockout that followed closely on the heels of the incident as "a stand against power" (77). As a result of the attack on his coach, Sprewell received a sixty-eight-game, seven-month suspension that ultimately cost him $6.4 million (Branch 5C). Sprewell's punishment was significantly harsher than that of white NFL player Kevin Greene, who just over one year later "attacked one of his coaches on the sidelines, in full view of a stadium full of fans and a network television audience" and received only a single-game suspension (Brunt A32). One journalist questioned such disparities when he observed that "these things certainly upset the country a lot more when it is a Black player going after a white coach.... Why aren't they as outraged about a stringy-haired Hollywood Hogan wannabe as they were with a rich African American basketball player, his hair arranged in neat cornrows?" (J. K. Miller 39).

Although some observers would argue that Carlesimo's reputation as a coach was tarnished by the incident, his ethnicity was not used to contextualize his behavior, as race was in Sprewell's case. In fact, in contrast to Carlesimo, whose role in the incident received little, if any, serious attention, Sprewell was sharply criticized by the NBA, the media, and basketball fans. As Sprewell claims,

"I've been looked on as a negative person. . . . I've been vilified. Every time I look at a clip it's always a picture of me looking mad and being aggressive" (Gloster D4). Considerable evidence suggests that Sprewell's claim is not far-fetched. Indeed, in one article about the incident, Carlesimo's infamous coaching style is characterized merely as behavior that "often annoys players" (Feschuk, "Sprewell's" B12). In contrast, the same article employs considerably more inflammatory language when it characterizes Sprewell's response to Carlesimo's "annoying" behavior as an "ugly incident [that] was the culmination of Sprewell's long-simmering dislike of Carlesimo" (Feschuk, "Sprewell's" B12). Upon Sprewell's return to Oakland as a New York Knick, an article labeled him a "corn-rowed anti-hero" and characterized his response to the crowd's "predictably rude reception" as "akin to that of a garbage-picking raccoon" (Feschuk, "Sprewell's" B12). Other examples of the ways in which the media vilified Sprewell include an article titled "The Game Within" that claims that "[n]o matter what Sprewell does with the rest of his life, he will forever be known as the Bench-Boss Strangler" (B12). In addition to depicting Sprewell and his action as one and the same, the same article misrepresents the language characteristic of competitive sport, which, ironically, spectators consider to be desirable and motivating in other circumstances to the extent that many appropriate it for their own use in the stands: "Sprewell . . . is still thinking violent thoughts about the Warriors. 'I just want to go in there and crush them,' he says. 'I'd just love it if we just killed them. . . . Bitterness, hatred, whatever you want to call it, it's there'" ("Game Within" B12).

Another example of Sprewell's vilification is an episode of the syndicated cartoon "In the Bleachers" that aligns Sprewell with tamed lions (subordinated jungle beasts) who have been made into circus performers. The cartoon depicts three lions being directed by a trainer holding both a whip and a pistol. One lion is performing his tricks as directed. The other two are not. One of the resistant lions says to the other, "I can't take it anymore. If he gets in my face again, I'm gonna go Sprewell on the guy" (Moore D4). This cartoon draws on stereotypical associations of blacks with the jungle and wild animals as well as the tools that slave masters and overseers and more recently the police have employed to punish blacks, representing Sprewell as synonymous with violent acts of resistance and insubordination. Such representations of the incident highlight the media's racialized language and imagery and its resultant racist implications that the incident was the consequence of Sprewell's inability to control himself or his emotional responses. The Sprewell incident brought to the forefront of white America's racial consciousness images of uncontained black male aggression, thus positioning him in opposition to black male athletes such as Michael Jordan, to whom acceptance is offered on the condition that he perform the role of a raceless, colorless, and apolitical subject (Shropshire 83).

Just as the Sprewell incident made visible white America's readiness to criminalize the images of black male athletes who display aggression outside of controlled settings, so too the 1998–99 NBA lockout made visible the extent to which the blackness of most of the players increased the league's determination to maintain control over the bargaining process. Jesse Barkin linked the lockout to the Sprewell incident when he claimed that "the Sprewell affair left the entire league with a black eye. . . . Sprewell became the poster child for all that is wrong with professional sports. Oddly, Sprewell can no longer be considered the worst blight to hit the NBA since drug scandals rocked the league two decades before. That dubious honor belongs to those responsible for a labor impasse that has forced the cancellation of the first two months of games and threatens to wipe out the entire season" (B11). During the lockout, however, it became apparent that the "black eye" with which Barkin claims Sprewell left the league assumed more than one form and represented more than one perspective. Indeed, the perspectives offered from the black eyes of the players and the white eyes of the management and media revealed a good deal about the degree to which race informs hierarchies in the NBA. For example, the union leaders and all but two players on the negotiating committee were black, whereas all of the owners and the league's top two officials were white ("National Basketball Association" B11). One journalist suggested that the players had a significant advantage over management in NBA labor negotiations because of their relative size (C. Jones B10). Although one NBA spokesperson denied the suggestion, he revealed an underlying fear that it might be true when he noted in the same breath that Stern is "not a particularly small man" (C. Jones B10).[8] Karen Bentham, an instructor at the University of Toronto's Center for Industrial Relations, articulated the fear of physical attack that underlies the effort to connect physical stature with negotiating power when she commented, "I'm not sure size is that important. . . . You're separated by a table, you have a whole army of supporters on your side, and the likelihood of a physical attack is remote" (C. Jones B10). The notion that a boundary such as a table might lessen the likelihood of a physical attack recalls the seemingly perilous court arrangement that resulted from the removal of protective screens shortly before the integration of the professional game. In the case of the lockout, however, too much was at stake to savor the titillating nature of such tenuous divides. As Bentham succinctly noted, "More important than your physical size is your economic strength. . . . And the owners are much bigger in that sense" (C. Jones B10).

According to some of the players, however, the NBA management's confidence in the justness and the strength of its position stemmed from far more than its sense of its fiscal health. As Alonzo Mourning of the Miami Heat noted during the strike, "I think there is a perception from the owners to even some fans that we're blacks who should be happy with what we've got—fair or not. . . . There's a lack of respect given us in large part because we're athletes. I'm not saying it's all about race because it's not—but it plays a factor" ("National Basketball Association" B11). Similarly, Sam Cassell, who at the time played for the New Jersey Nets, commented, "I think the owners look at us as black ghetto guys with tons of money that we don't deserve" (Brunt A32). Shropshire concurs with Cassell, arguing that such assertions epitomized the dominant (white) public's reaction to the lockout, which was that the players "should be grateful for what [they] have" (83). In contrast, Stern, using language that recalls Hoberman's notion of uncritical faith in equality, denied assertions that race had a role in the stalemate and argued instead that "the league has successfully promoted a sport whose player population is nearly 90% black" (Brunt A32). One black executive dismissed the idea that race was a mitigating factor by suggesting, in equally troubling language, that from the "time they're 12 years old, [the players are] catered to by AAU coaches, sneaker companies, college recruiters, coaches, agents. We're left dealing with the end result, and no one knows what to do. What the players perceive as racism is . . . a lack of sensitivity based on ignorance" (Voisin B11). Such dismissals of the players' perspectives entirely overlook their experiences and knowledge of what it means to be black males in the United States. As Stephen Brunt astutely puts it, the players are not "just talking about what's going on now. They're talking about their experiences as black men in America, about history, about culture, about what they've come to understand to be true" (A32).

The media's reaction to the Sprewell incident and the efforts to suppress issues of race during the lockout make visible the degree to which audiences construct and rely on less threatening off-court images to counterbalance those of the powerful, aggressive, and assertive black males who populate NBA courts. As the strange invocation of the players' size relative to management in the bargaining process during the lockout suggests, white audiences' fear and desire in relation to aggressive black male athletes becomes genuine fear when they encounter such aggression—or even its possibility—in off-court settings where power instead of points is at stake. The consequence of such fear is the construction of off-court images that gentrify and domesticate on-court images of black athletes to "defuse the 'undertone of violence'" that represents such an important component of the pleasure that spectators experience as witnesses to a game (Hoberman xxi).

Although no one could claim that his image was ever gentrified, Dennis Rodman, the flamboyant, talented, and controversial former player for the Detroit

Pistons (1986–92), San Antonio Spurs (1993–95), Chicago Bulls (1995–98), Los Angeles Lakers (1999), and Dallas Mavericks (2000), is a compelling figure because of the extent to which images drawn from white lore about black men seem to cluster around him. For example, Dan Bickley, author of an unauthorized biography of Rodman, refers to him as a "prisoner to impulsive behavior" (xiii). Bickley also claims that Rodman is driven by a "nocturnal rage" that gives rise to an "uncontrollable temper . . . that surfaces in tremors, always leading to the inevitable quake that tears down the walls" and exposes the "sandbox of hedonism" in which he thrives (xi, xii). The images and stereotypes that Bickley uses to characterize his subject invoke the familiar stereotype of the black male as a beast driven to commit acts of destruction by uncontrollable corporeal impulses. Representations of Rodman gerrymander within the lore cycle that scripts narratives of containment for black men. Rodman's appearances on the covers of *Sports Illustrated* (1995) and *GQ* (1997) are underwritten by discourses of miscegenation, rape, and black male sexual excess and exemplify the ways that his eccentricities make him a useful focal point in discussions about the processes through which normative configurations of black masculinity are represented, recuperated, and sometimes rejected. As a figure of "cultural gerrymandering," Rodman causes the lines of racial taboo to be drawn and redrawn within white lore cycles in ways that perpetuate the nervous condition that characterizes white America's relationship to African American men (Lhamon 79).[9]

Whatever else one can say about Rodman, he unquestionably possesses a unique ability to make people squirm. He addressed that ability between segments of the made-for-television movie *Bad as I Wanna Be: The Story of Dennis Rodman*, which ABC aired on 8 February 1998, when he asked the audience, "Do I make you nervous?" The answer, of course, is yes. During the heyday of his NBA career, Rodman made a lot of folks nervous. He forced into public view an image of a black man who in many—though certainly not all—respects did not conform to the images of the disciplined athlete, of a criminal, or of a gentrified, domesticated, and politically neutered black man. He was notorious for refusing to adhere to rules both on and off the court. In on-court settings, he was frequently disciplined for missing or showing up late for practices and was criticized for avoiding team huddles and for removing his shoes during games (Boyd, *Am I* 122). His refusal to obey even the most basic rules for NBA team members, combined with his occasionally angry outbursts toward people in and around the court during games, fanned the flames of public fears about the sorts of rules for which he might harbor similar disregard in off-court settings. Ironically, the off-court rules he most frequently violated had no relationship to actual acts of violence or criminality of any kind. Rather, in off-court settings, the social rules with which his image became so imbricated were those that circumscribe the black masculine subject through white lore.

In "Black Men in the Mix: Badboys, Heroes, Sequins, and Dennis Rodman," Barrett questions the extent to which the notion of the individual is valuable as a lens through which to assess and to understand the "potent conjunction of racial, commercial, gendered, and moral economies" that are so compellingly and conveniently located in Rodman's figure (106). Rather, Rodman's transgressions, eccentricities, and inconsistencies are more usefully examined not as unique to Rodman as an individual but as characteristic of the fractures, contradictions, and historical continuities that characterize post-civil-rights U.S. culture. Barrett claims that these "peculiarities" of U.S. culture wreak havoc on the coherence of Rodman's representations of himself and on others' representations of Rodman, which are more productively examined in the context of a broader cultural narrative (106). With this in mind, I locate representations of Rodman in the context of the white lore cycle, which configures and reconfigures white America's methods of preserving and negotiating changes in the shorthand forms through which it articulates its mythologies, fascination, and fear concerning black masculinity.

Representations of Rodman were more often than not situated contentiously in relation to more disciplined images and cultural roles of other black male athletes. Rodman's multicolored hair, tattoos, nose rings, painted fingernails, and passion for cross-dressing were strikingly at odds with the carefully tailored image of Michael Jordan, for example, who epitomizes the image of a black man with which white America is most comfortable identifying. Rodman's chameleon-like construction (or destruction) of his black athletic body disrupts the celebration of beautiful bodies in sport and recontexualizes it as something other than "an active hegemonic agent" created by sport's "ideological celebration of physical labor in capitalism" (Fiske, *Understanding* 97–98). Rodman, in *Bad as I Wanna Be* (1996), takes pride in what he claims is his refusal to conform to the demands of the NBA: "The NBA didn't make me. They're in the business of taking these young guys who come into the league and marketing the hell out of them until they become stars. . . . They choose the players they think show the NBA in the most positive light. . . . *They create the image, then they control the image. But they didn't create me, and they can't control me.* I didn't need the league's help to get where I am. I made it in spite of them" (94). As an example of his resistance to the aesthetically demure, apolitical image of the ideal player as configured by the NBA, Rodman calls attention to his 1995 appearance on the cover of *Sports Illustrated*. The cover depicted Rodman seated in a chair upholstered with fabric resembling the skin of a wild cat, wearing leather shorts and a tank top and holding a parrot on his arm in front of him. The parrot is turned so that it is facing Rodman. Rodman boasts that, with the exception of the swimsuit edition, the edition of *Sports Illustrated* with his image on the cover sold better than any other that year. He reads the volume of magazine sales as a direct affront to the league's efforts to discourage public receptiveness to his image and as evidence of his successful marketing of an image that he believes to be marked by a liberating form of difference (Rodman and Keown 94).

Rodman fails, however, to recognize the ironies and contradictions to which the success of the cover points as well as the degree to which the cover plays directly into the same discourses of black masculinity that compel the NBA's marketing of nonthreatening images of the young, mostly black men in its ranks. Whereas the NBA image celebrates the "sporting [black] male body" that "offers no categorical challenges to social control" (Fiske, "Understanding" 98, 99), Rodman's image, through its references to an untamable wildness, provides the titillating component of excess that is the necessary partner to the NBA's normative image of the black male athlete. The parrot seated on Rodman's arm in the picture adds a particularly ironic touch to the picture. Although Rodman reads the parrot as a sign of "exotic" difference written into the photograph's statement of nonconformity, the parrot, a species of bird recognized for its ability to mimic the sounds and words of its keepers, signals the ease with which acts perceived by their agent as resistant can be recuperated in ways that reproduce hegemonic discourses. Rodman's image thus provides the essential second term in the dyad of desire and fear that remains integral to white America's pleasure in the "game." The *Sports Illustrated* cover therefore allows Rodman to test the elasticity of his tether—in his words, to "color . . . outside the lines" (Rodman and Keown 97)—while inscribing a narrative of recuperation and repetition into his departure from the normative structures built into the moral imaginary of U.S. mass culture.[10]

The off-court images of athletes who pose no threat whatsoever to the color line also are not exempt from such narrative policing of black masculinity. Consider the Hanes underwear commercial featuring Michael Jordan who, prior to his retirement from professional basketball and in contrast to Rodman, made only his opponents on the court nervous. The Jordan commercial features two white women sitting on a park bench, speculating about whether passersby are wearing boxers or briefs. An impeccably dressed Jordan approaches. The camera, assuming the gaze of the white women, targets his crotch briefly but shifts quickly upward to his face. The women and television viewers immediately recognize Jordan, who has figured out what the women are trying to discern. He strolls by and comments with an endearing smile, "They're Hanes—let's just leave it at that." The commercial implies that close scrutiny of a male's groin may reveal some evidence as to the style of undergarment that he is wearing and perhaps its contents. The Hanes commercial denies the white women and television viewers the opportunity to scrutinize Jordan so closely. Rather, the camera focuses only briefly on Jordan's lower half, clad in not-very-revealing pleated slacks, effectively denying Jordan's off-court audience the opportunity to gaze at his crotch for an indiscreet length of time. The camera's strategic shift, together with Jordan's comment, imposes a safe distance between Jordan, whom the camera paradoxically sexualizes as it castrates, and the white women whom he encounters beyond the disciplined boundaries of the basketball arena. The commercial's tentative gesture toward the myth of the black male rapist is ironic because it briefly releases Jordan from the confines of the sanitized image that inscribes his powerful, masculine, black body with lack. Although Hanes sells undergarments by capitalizing on Jordan's athletic black body, attractive features, and popular image, the company does so in ways that domesticate and gentrify his far more aggressive on-court image.

Rodman's images on the cover and inside the February 1997 edition of *GQ* situate him more daringly beyond white America's normative structures through overt references to taboo crossings of racialized sexual lines. The cover features Rebecca Romijn (a blond, white model) and Rodman. Clad in a white string bikini, Romijn poses in front of Rodman, who wears a bikini-style swimsuit made of black satin with white trim. Romijn assumes an ambiguous position with respect to Rodman. She appears to be fully in control of the black man who stands behind her—she rests one hand on Rodman's right thigh while her other hand reaches up and back as if to grab his ear.[11] However, the photo exploits the potential danger that Rodman—big, strong, nearly naked, tantalizingly close, and most importantly black—signifies to the model specifically and to white women generally.[12] Rodman stands behind the model; one arm is out of sight, the other hangs passively beside him. Except for the slight jut of his hip, there is nothing overtly sexual about Rodman's stance. In fact, his bikini-clad groin, but for the slightest hint of a wrinkle or a bulge, is almost entirely hidden behind the model. Although Rodman's penis may be out of sight, the pose ensures that it remains front and center in the audience's mind.

Whereas Jordan's Hanes commercial is very conservative in its allusions to and uses of the narrative of the black male rapist and the black penis, the *GQ* cover draws the cultural function of white lore about black men into much clearer focus. *GQ* imposes no safe distance between the black male and the white female who grace its cover, thus capitalizing on the racialized discourses of white women's desire for black men and the resultant construction of black men as threats to white women. However, when it comes to the issues and images featured between the covers, so to speak, GQ imposes considerably more distance between Rodman and Romijn. Inside the magazine, Rodman does not appear in any photographs with Romijn in which she models swimsuits. Rather, Romijn, who appears topless in many of the shots, poses in full, frontal contact with only white male models in the spread "Romijn Dressing." The imposition of distance between Rodman and Romijn "rescues" the white woman from Rodman by returning the cover's suggestion of miscegenation to the realm of the white imagination, leaving intact a normative order of racial and sexual relations.[13] However, GQ does not entirely evacuate the threat of black masculinity from the scene. Indeed, the photos that accompany the article about Rodman depict him alone, wearing a very small, hot pink swimsuit around which he swirls a leopard-spotted robe, teasing the camera by alternately revealing and concealing the evidence that his participation in this and previous off-court projects has most certainly not gentrified, domesticated, or castrated him (Raab). Much like the Sports Illustrated cover, the GQ cover demonstrates how white lore about black men and black men's sexuality continues cycling through stages of meaning that mark a continuous process of cultural struggle, negotiated in and around representations of black men as figures of criminality and sexual excess.

Contemporary representations of black male athletes occupy a stage in the constantly turning cycles of white lore concerning black men. There are connections between the highly structured "game" in which black athletes participate today and its earlier forms. The consequences for black men who have lost the game have, at times, been unspeakably dire. Others, such as the athletes discussed in this chapter, have been able to transform game forums into profitable venues in which many performances have proven translucent enough to be entertaining for both sides and opaque enough to protect and sustain the spirits and lives of the black players. Others, such as Rodman and Sprewell, have found themselves ostracized within the forums in which they perform or exiled to other forums by those with a vested interest in protecting the game in both letter and spirit. It is fortunate for their sake that black men have played the game for so long and so well that the skills they acquire on and in various courts and arenas transfer fairly easily to the many settings in which they find themselves forced to play. Black-focused film represents another setting in which black male filmmakers enter the "game" in compelling, sometimes complicit, and often resistant ways.

THE LAST BLACKFACE?
Forays into Film's Empty Space of Representation

Charles Johnson and John McCuskery, in their introduction to *Black Men Speaking* (1997), caution us not to get so caught up in studying criminological and sociological statistics about black men that we forget that the numbers are actually real people with stories that need to be told and heard. To discover such stories, they propose that we concern ourselves with the ways that black men develop and sustain a sense of self in relation to the black community generally, other black men specifically, and white America. The discovery and in some cases recovery of such narratives are complicated by the fact that the perspectives and activities that produce them often circulate and take place in invisible spaces, thus decreasing the likelihood that they will be recorded or expressed (xvii). The African American narrative tradition constitutes an important site within which have emerged black men's tales of survival and resistance, of success and failure, of grief and joy, of anger and empathy, and of love and hate. In film, however, what Ed Guerrero calls an empty space in representation still waits to be filled with cinematic texts of equal breadth and value. The empty space in representation is an untapped yet fecund space in which the potential to represent black men as other than what Ralph Ellison called "Prefabricated Negroes" has yet to be fully realized ("World" 123). If taken advantage of, the empty space of representation is a site from which to counter the damaging tradition in film of superimposing stereotypical images on black men and furthering their containment within the prison writ large. If tapped, this empty space of representation can be filled with complex renderings of black men's experiences and worldviews. That is, just as African American writers have exposed and challenged both the one-dimensional image of the black male wrought by white-looking practices and the various methodologies that sustain that image, so too the empty space of representation in film can offset the containment wrought by reductive and stereotypical representational practices.

Ironically, given its womanist emphases, Alice Walker's well-known essay "In Search of Our Mothers' Gardens" offers useful insight into both the possibilities inherent in the empty space of representation and the multiple ways in which filmmakers are making headway into it. Walker eloquently situates past events and lives already lived in relation to contemporary black women's writing. She expresses regret that images of black women as "mule[s] of the world" (232) have overshadowed the lingering signs of their resilience. She disputes suggestions that the harshness of African American women's lives extinguished the spirituality that compelled their artistry. Although Walker admits that few black women were able to express their spirituality in the forms with which we tend to associate artistic expression today, she is convinced that black women found ways to foster their creativity across time and space. The key to discovering evidence of such creativity lies in believing that although "contrary instincts"—those produced by the many methods of discipline, control, and abuse—may have muffled the voices of poets and suppressed other forms of artistic expression, those instincts did not negate "the living creativity *some* of our grandmothers were not allowed to know" (237). According to Walker, others "knew, even without 'knowing' it, the reality of their spirituality, even if they didn't recognize it beyond what happened in the singing in church—and they never had any intention of giving it up" (237–38). Accordingly, Walker embarks on a search of black women's writing for "the secret of what has fed that muzzled and often mutilated, but vibrant, creative spirit that the black woman has inherited, and that pops out in wild and unlikely places to this day" (239). She encourages others to undertake critical searches for evidence of the creativity to which we have not heretofore had access. Such evidence is to be found not only in physical bodies but also in other kinds of narratives that connect present lives to those past, traversing space and time via forms that free ancestral voices to speak. Such voices are free to speak today because they have received forums as characters in fictional narratives and are beginning to be offered such forums in film. Although I use it here to direct critical focus to places that she did not, Walker's insightful argument provides a useful lens through which to examine films that complicate notions of racial identity and bring the visions of black filmmakers and the experiences and voices of black men into the light.[1]

Black filmmakers increasingly are attempting to articulate concerns about the policies, practices, and environments that structure a prison writ large for black men today. Ironically, the need to articulate such grievances and concerns is heightened by greater class heterogeneity among African Americans. Although class mobility among African Americans is greater than ever before, an unfortunate effect of what is otherwise a positive sign has been the increasing denial of the problems facing black residents of inner-city U.S. communities. Such denial and representational practices in popular culture that perpetuate antiblack attitudes and practices have compelled filmmakers to respond in ways that constitute forays into the empty space of representation. The relative abundance of black films made in the 1990s can be attributed in part to a climate in which African Americans' anger and frustration concerning the ongoing erosion of political and economic conditions in urban centers have been dismissed and ignored. In keeping with the ways in which African Americans have historically dealt with the weight of racial terror and its material consequences, the by-products of the deteriorating urban centers—rage, frustration, and the threat of being rendered politically and socially mute—fuel contemporary black film and manifest themselves in artistic critiques of whiteness and racism (Guerrero, *Framing* 159–60).

Films that are favorably received by mainstream audiences tend to entertain white audiences while reassuring them that the threat of blackness, which is embossed in the white imagination as the image of a black male, has been contained. More often than not, the perceived threat is contained by a comedic frame and/or a narrative in which criminality is severed from structural and systemic inequities and violence. Such reductive portrayals take shape within a vacuum wrought at best by naïveté and ignorance and at worst by racist worldviews. The characters are contained within a system of representation that demands black political quietism in exchange for tokenism and accommodation. Thus, we see films that condemn the criminality of the ghetto dweller while disregarding the systemic violence that yields an environment in which poverty and disenfranchisement are the rule rather than the exception (Guerrero, *Framing* 163). The paradox that informs how society manufactures and consumes the black male image on television and in film grows out of the general and reductive tendency to represent black men in two ways. Images of well-to-do black men who have succeeded as athletes and entertainers are situated in opposition to representations of black men as criminals whose self-destructive tendencies become linked in the national imagination as the cause of "the real-time devastation, slaughter, and body count of a steady stream of faceless black males on the 6 and 11 o'clock news" ("Black Man" 183). The former are regarded as proof that if one works hard enough, one can rise above anything. The news images, Guerrero argues, are "coordinated with a wave of neo-blaxpoitative, violently toxic, ghetto-action flicks, which too often package and sell the extermination of black men as entertainment, while profiteering filmmakers offer up shallow alibis about only depicting 'what is real'" (183). These binary representations create a comfort zone for white America that fosters what is often a naive or disingenuous faith in its openness with respect to matters of race; it is a misguided belief that racial equality has been achieved in the United States, and it is underscored by the conviction that white America's attitudes and practices constitute proof of such equality. "Look how liberal we are. We enjoy movies with black people in them." "Some of my favorite movies have black people in them." "Denzel? He's hot!" The irony, of course, is that when the daughters of many black-film-loving white folks date someone who resembles Denzel in complexion, the tune and rhythm of their song and dance quickly changes. When the evening news attaches black male faces to virtually all things criminal, the facade of comfort and acceptance becomes the scaffolding for a platform from which black males are judged as inferior, innately flawed, and inherently criminal. Films that ameliorate white anxieties about black men by turning them into comics or criminals to be laughed at and/or condemned further the state of racial denial that plagues the United States. Films that adhere to such patterns of representation appeal to white America's desire to gaze at without engaging with black men. They ease white America's discomfort and make it easy to sidestep its responsibility to acknowledge and to address persistent racial inequalities and conflicts (Guerrero, *Framing* 163).

Reductive, binary images do little to foster a more sophisticated understanding of the complexities of African American culture and of black men's identities, experiences, and struggles. Rather, such images reproduce one-dimensional, inaccurate, and degrading images of black men. The consequence of polarized representations is the absence of more complicated and thus more accurate depictions of black men, their experiences, and their perspectives. Those who receive space on screen often are caught in either the positive image trap or the negative image trap. Since neither represents black men in ways that capture their heterogeneity, the empty space of representation functions within the industry as a realm of invisibility. This realm is defined by latent possibilities concerning ways to fill it with films from all genres that feature black men in roles that do not reduce them to comedians or criminals (Guerrero, "Black Man" 185). If African Americans were represented on screen as they have been in the African American literary tradition, then we might really begin to witness approximations of the real complicated and brilliant black men whose stories populate the rich texts of that tradition. Yet it is difficult not to be sympathetic to the conundrum that black filmmakers face when commercial success depends largely on a film's appeal to a white audience. On the one hand, they are expected to produce texts that bring to life the black experience and the struggles and joys that attend it without minimizing its complexity or compromising the honesty its portrayal demands and deserves. On the other hand, filmmakers who aspire to attain mainstream status for their work must find ways to do so without compromising the revenue-earning potential of appealing to a white audience by confronting the audience with images and narratives that white America refuses to see, let alone acknowledge, as legitimate or accurate representations of black life (Guerrero, *Framing* 168). How does one create and market a product to an audience willing to pay only to see counterfeit representations of African Americans?

The three films I explore in this chapter offer a glimpse of the different ways that filmmakers at all levels of involvement in the industry and at all stages of their careers have ventured into the empty space of representation. Aaron Blandon, Spike Lee, and Ice Cube navigate this empty space in ways that encourage more skeptical approaches to questions of racial identity. Their forays, in different ways and to varying degrees, constitute attempts to counter the effects of uncomplicated renderings of racial identities and representations that reduce black men to criminals and clowns. Each film that I address speaks to both the difficulties and the possibilities that attend efforts to do so. Their films both reflect and critique reductive representational practices that mobilize the white lore cycle discussed in chapter 2. As was the case with blackface minstrelsy and lynching and as is the case with contemporary representations, these films provide a window into how white America sees black men and understands its relationship and responsibilities to them.

Blandon's *The Last Blackface* (2002), Lee's *Bamboozled* (2000), and Ice Cube's *Barbershop* (2002) can be situated on the stage of the "theater of social and political struggle" (Watkins 137) where filmmakers grapple with tough questions and issues.[2] Their work explores and makes visible the legacies of type that contribute to the conundrum of the black filmmaker generally and the criminalization of black men in contemporary popular culture specifically. As such, these films represent compelling case studies. In distinct ways, each film comments—directly in the cases of Blandon and Lee and obliquely in Ice Cube's case—on the recursive and ubiquitous nature of blackface minstrelsy; its violent, ideological underpinnings in the United States; and its effects on the psyches and lives of black men. Each film promotes critical awareness of the nature and function of the containment in question. They make apparent the legacy of type in a self-conscious manner. This triad of filmmakers makes visible the complexities of black men's involvement in the production of cultural products that both comment on and/or reproduce white anxieties about black men. Each provides engaging and succinct reflections (or at least partial reflections) of and on the legacy of type.

The paradoxes that attend the peculiarities of white audience receptiveness to black-focused films today parallel those that Eric Lott associates with blackface acts. As I discussed in chapter 2, blackface acts represented whites' propensity to ridicule while gazing with wonder at black people and what were thought to be representations of aspects of black culture. Whereas minstrel shows provided a stage on which to bring blackness into the public eye, white audiences often were not receptive to the representation unless it was offered to them by a white dancer in blackface (Lott 111–13). White audiences desired the distance signified by the blackened faces. The blackface mask afforded whites a tantalizing albeit imaginary distance from the objects of their ridicule and wonder. The resultant illusory closeness to blackness created through blackface minstrelsy performances protected whites from the real difference that at once compelled and repelled them. This symbolic distance enabled whites to fulfill their desire both to be taken in by and to consume counterfeit constructions of blackness. That is, blackface minstrelsy drew whites into a world wherein distorted counterfeit figurations of blackness enabled viewers safely to indulge their imaginations by gazing on the fetishized representations with ridicule and wonder.

The Last Blackface, an independent film by Aaron Blandon, manipulates the irony of white America's desire for such distance. It draws attention to the unreliability of the mask in ways that create or re-create an unnerving sense of disorientation in the viewer. If an audience is receptive to the representation of blackness offered by a white dancer in blackface, the film suggests, perhaps it also will be receptive to a critique of whiteness and racism offered by black actors in whiteface. By imaginatively manipulating the desire/distance contradiction, *The Last Blackface* identifies itself as a subversive version of a blackface performance and in the process signifies on the tradition of blackface minstrelsy and the obsession with blackness that compelled whites' theft, misrepresentation, distortion, and destruction of black culture, black bodies, and black identities. The title of Blandon's film gestures toward the ironic relationship between the lynching, which is the focus of the film, and the nature and function of blackface performances. In the cases of both blackface performances and ritualized lynchings, a white audience's obsession with and desire for distance from the blackface figure structure the context in which they find their entertainment. However, just as the film's representation of a lynching conjoins the white individual with the ideology of whiteness and its violent material effects, it also distinguishes them from one another. In so doing, the film suggests the possibility if not the likelihood of emancipation for whites and logically, therefore, for blacks from the containment that whiteness as ideology structures.

The Last Blackface revolves around a typical series of events that preceded a lynching. The approximately nine-minute film opens with a scene in which a mother lays out a picnic lunch for herself and her children, with all of these characters played by black actors in whiteface. We learn via the dialogue between the mother and the children that the picnic lunch will be well received because the family has been waiting for more than seven hours. We also learn that they are waiting for a lynch mob to return with its chosen victim. The carefully prepared meal suggests that the event and the picnic that precedes it have been planned and are eagerly anticipated. Indeed, we learn people have come from Atlanta, which we assume is far away from the site of this particular lynching, given the excitement with which the information is conveyed, to witness the event. While the mother lays out the picnic lunch, one of the children awaits his father's return from the search and expresses his desire to join the men when they come back with the victim. The child's mother reprimands him on the grounds that his desire to participate is not appropriate for a Christian. It is difficult to miss the irony here. Seemingly unfazed by the thought of her children witnessing an unspeakable act of violence, the woman merely threatens that if the child reiterates such a request, she will not bring him "next time." The picnics, searches, tortures, and murders appear to be frequent family affairs from which a child would feel his or her exclusion to be a punishment.

The Last Blackface is compelling because of the reversals and language that Blandon employs to structure the narrative. The film defamiliarizes the lynching narrative as we know it in interesting ways. First, black actors in whiteface play the roles of the lynchers, the members of the lynch mob, and the lone horseman who attempts to intervene on the victim's behalf, whereas a white actor in blackface plays the role of the mob's victim. Second, the film assigns the roles normally associated with whites and blacks in lynchings to people who are referred to as white-*faced* and black*faced*, as opposed to white and black. In the context of a racialized lynching narrative, whether a historical or a fictional account, whites are the victimizers and blacks are the victims. Thus, the whitened and blackened faces of black and white actors are initially—and I think intentionally—a bit jarring. The unsettling effect of these reversals mimics the instability of relative position that compelled whites' fascination with the minstrel show. With which "face" or body, a viewer might wonder, do I associate the act of racial terrorism that is enacted? The blackened face on the discernible white body? Or the whitened face on the visibly black body? Immediate recognition of who is white or black, what that means, and why it matters suddenly becomes more difficult. Blandon skillfully uses costume against character to unsettle simplistic assumptions about racial identities and the types of performances that define them.

In *The Last Blackface*, such reversals work in connection with suffixes to deny viewers the security of a narrative with a binary structure and, by extension, the security of a binary view of racial identity. The effect of this defamiliarization is the disassociation, albeit a fragile one, of phenotype from a predictable and consistent cultural role. Susan Gubar, in *Racechanges: White Skin, Black Face in American Culture* (1997) discusses *Plessy v. Ferguson* (1896) as a historical example of such disassociation. *Plessy v. Ferguson* exemplified how "culture or social context shapes racial identity without completely replacing biological definitions of race" (14). Gubar argues that Plessy's impersonation of a white person to enter the whites-only carriage, followed by his pronouncement that he was black, undermined the simple association of skin color and racial identity (14). Plessy's method of resistance, however, exposed the limitations of its message. That is, whereas Plessy could choose when, where, and if to expose his blackness, such agency did not extend to his right or ability to function freely as a white person (Gubar 14). Blandon makes a similar point when he employs the suffix -*face* as a synonym for "mask" in *The Last Blackface*. The addition of the suffix -*face* to the adjectives *white* and *black* signifies on the recognizable roles of whites and blacks within a society overwhelmingly organized around hierarchies of race generally. The defamiliarization wrought by the masks themselves and the suffix -*face* disables the visual and cognitive machinery that too easily connects a culturally scripted role to the racial identities of the individuals who perform it. It is interesting that Blandon chose not to allow the whiteface and blackface masks to fully conceal the skin that they disguise. The gap between mask and body can be read as the suggestion that the performance of a culturally constructed role needs to be distinguished from the essence of the individuals who are contained within the regime governed by whiteness, whether as beneficiaries of its privileges or as its victims. The mask is not the essence of the individual. The representation is not the essence of whoever it is purported to represent. We see this when the lone opponent to the lynching, a black actor in whiteface, rides his horse into the midst of the mob and pleads with its members to let the law handle the dispute. He does so on the grounds that what the mob is doing to the victim is characteristic of the behavior of animals, not human beings. His efforts to stop the act of racial terrorism do not succeed. Thus, although we see that the agency of those who resist their containment within the regime of whiteness is limited, so too is the power of the mask that represents the regime's power, for it is possible to move outside of the role that it represents.

As Blandon has acknowledged by defamiliarizing racial categories and as Guerrero has argued, when considering representations of blackness in film, it is not enough to examine only the sorts of binary representations of blackness and whiteness generally and black men specifically that are most commonly associated with the legacy of type. Rather, it is equally important to direct attention to other kinds of evidence that wisdom and profit lie in simultaneously loving and hating black men (Guerrero, "Black Man" 182). Here, though, a correction to Guerrero's language is in order. Bell hooks in *We Real Cool: Black Men and Masculinity* (2004) disputes the use of the term *love* to describe white America's feelings toward black men. She argues that the tradition of nonblack people gazing at black males from an envious perspective is most definitely not a practice informed by love. *Envy* and *desire* are not synonyms for *love*, and it is a dangerous mistake to employ them as such in critical discourse. To do so is to provide white America's long-standing fascination with and fear of black men with an artificially benevolent glaze (hooks, *We Real* xi–xii). As was the case with blackened faces in nineteenth- and twentieth-century minstrel performances, so too the language we use to characterize white America's obsession with black men can disguise the malevolent looking practices that lurk beneath counterfeit covers. Such looking practices are implicated in the cultural systems of surveillance and control that operate within various realms of representation.

Guerrero credits Spike Lee for his attempts to broaden and complicate the image of black masculinity that popular culture sows within the national imagination ("Black Man" 182, 183). So too, S. Craig Watkins cites Lee as an example of someone who has turned the black filmmaker's conundrum to his advantage by exploiting white America's obsession with blackness. Watkins locates the politics of Lee's work in a commercial context wherein the goal is to create products that will appeal to a large market. Lee's oeuvre represents evidence of his struggle to challenge the commercial and critical containment that defines the parameters within which black filmmakers work if they wish to enter the mainstream marketplace. Whereas Blandon's work has not yet entered the mainstream, Lee has had to figure out how both to command the art of filmmaking generally and to negotiate the studio politics that become roadblocks to his ability to produce work of the sort he desires. One such roadblock that filmmakers often find themselves confronting is studios' efforts to censor work. Such censorship takes the form of a filtering process that involves changing scenes or dialogue in an effort to offset the possibility that a film will be perceived as a threat to the status quo. In Lee's case, the transition from independent to commercial filmmaking made him vulnerable not only to the requirements of film studios but also to the expectations of the African American community that he use his craft to counter negative images of African Americans in films (Watkins 107, 113, 116–17).

Although Lee does not, of course, in principle oppose representing African Americans in positive ways, requirements and expectations that he make it his primary goal generate what he calls a "positive image trap" (Watkins 118). A positive image trap compels representations of African Americans that are in keeping with bourgeois notions of respectability but does little to depart from a historical tradition of depicting African Americans as a monolithic, one-dimensional group. This type of censorship, Watkins argues, represents "what Kobena Mercer has described as the 'social engineering' approach to Black cultural production" (118). Lee's challenge as a filmmaker, then, has been to develop projects in which he endeavors to work betwixt and between binary images of blackness and African American people. This has meant finding ways to avoid falling prey to the positive image trap while also avoiding making films that are framed solely by comedic or ghetto-based narratives (Watkins 129). *Bamboozled* provides insight into the ways that Lee has attempted to expose this conundrum and work toward progressive ends within the genre.

In *Bamboozled*, Lee calls attention to historical consistencies in white anxieties about black men and to black men's struggles to liberate themselves from the resultant representational traps. No character in *Bamboozled*, white or black, escapes the consequences of the overwhelming, albeit unintended, success of a modern-day television minstrel show. Rather than creating one figure who models the possibility of thinking and functioning outside the parameters that define the United States as a prison writ large, Lee draws on a range of characters to gesture toward what may well be the impossibility of doing so, at least at this particular moment in history. In this way, Lee leads us toward a more complete understanding of the dynamic of fascination and hate and the paradoxes and contradictions that inform white America's views of blackness and black men as well as of the ways in which black men experience and deal with the forms of containment to which such ways of seeing give rise.

The desire to control the images of black men is a cover for an underlying desire to control the black male body and the perceived threat of its potency and agency. Hooks notes that almost all African American men have had at least once to refrain from expressing themselves as they would like because of a fear, which history tells us unequivocally is legitimate, of being maimed or killed. The white supremacist, capitalist, patriarchal culture of the United States requires black men to govern their thoughts, their expressions, and their behavior to the extent that the prison writ large compromises the possibilities inherent in both thought and action (hooks, *We Real* xii). Many of the richest and most complicated dimensions of black masculine identities have been ignored, distorted, denied, or obliterated within the context of white supremacist capitalist patriarchy generally and sites of cultural production such as film specifically. The enormity of this threat notwithstanding, hooks cautions against viewing all black men as castrated victims. Indeed, she argues, only through the lens of whiteness-inflected looking practices does the image of the castrated black man appear. This is not to say that all black

men have recognized and resisted limited, stereotypical renderings of black masculinity. But it is wrongheaded to assume that all black men are concerned with
earning recognition for their conformity to dominant standards of masculinity.
Even though African Americans have always been angered by white America's stereotypical beliefs and views of black men, their rage has not necessarily precluded
efforts to imagine and to live in accordance with alternative masculine ideals for
black men (hooks, *Black Looks* 89). Although all men are contained by the masculine roles assigned to them within a patriarchal society, black men face a unique
set of limitations and challenges that arise when race and class are thrown into the
prescriptive patriarchal mix (hooks, *We Real* xii). Many of these limitations and
challenges are apparent in *Bamboozled*.

Bamboozled assesses the clarity with which each character sees his position
relative to the white supremacist capitalist patriarchal system within which each
functions and/or from which each tries to escape. The film focuses on the ways
in which racist images dehumanize and in some cases simultaneously reward the
characters whose work gratifies white America's desire to see its fantasies about
black men brought to life. At some level, all of the characters, with the exception
of Dun Witty, the white boss played by Michael Rapaport, recognize and attempt
to address their containment with lesser and greater degrees of success. The paradoxes and contradictions that define their containment and the role of representational practices in structuring that containment become apparent through the
characters' various levels of investment in the patriarchal system. The system's
appeal to, incentives for, and costs for black men determines the ways in which and
the extent to which each character is invested in and contained by it. A gap exists
between each character's awareness of his containment and his ability to mobilize
that awareness with an eye toward functioning more freely within or to escape
altogether from the sector(s) of the prison writ large that contain him.

Bamboozled revolves around the professional cum personal quagmire in which
Pierre Delacroix, a middle-class black man, finds himself. Delacroix is an employee
of a television studio that is pushing to raise ratings. Of all the film's male characters, Delacroix arguably most actively resists both the role constructed for him
and the pressure to conform to stereotypical images of black men. He understands
that although succumbing to both would indicate his acquiescence to the system,
it would also pave the way to his professional success. Thus, he devises an elaborate
plan to resist his containment through the risky machinery of satire. Delacroix's
agenda is complicated by Dun Witty's utter obliviousness to his racism, which
governs his ideas about the type of program that will produce the desired jump
in ratings. Delacroix's goal is to expose Witty's racist agendas while appearing to

follow through on his instructions to develop a hit television show. Delacroix decides to pitch a modern-day minstrel show that will exploit every conceivable stereotype of African Americans. He believes that he can avoid furthering the reach of his boss's racism and banks on his belief that the appallingly racist nature of the minstrel show he proposes will be acknowledged through its rejection.

A provocative layer of the film emerges from Witty and Delacroix's relationship. Just as each is involved in the creation and production of a modern-day minstrel show, so too their respective roles bear a relationship to those of the white blackface minstrel and the black blackface minstrel. For example, Witty thoroughly appropriates the diction, material signs, and behaviors that he interprets as characteristics of an authentic black identity. He does so to the extent that he considers himself to be blacker than Delacroix. Like the white blackface performer, Witty buys into a single image of blackness that he counterfeits through simplistic and reductive performances and exploits through his efforts to capitalize on it. Witty's appropriation and performance of a counterfeit black identity makes Lee's point that the literal blackening of one's face is not necessary in modern manifestations of the minstrel principle. Yet just as nineteenth-century white audiences "subtly acknowledged the greater power of the genuine article" (Lott 115)—performances by real black men—so too does Witty, who envelops himself with images of black celebrities and pieces of African art. Witty satisfies his desire for titillating encounters with blackness and assumes his entitlement, to borrow the title of Greg Tate's book by the same name, to everything but the burden. Moreover, the sexual undertones of Witty's obsessive need to mimic what he imagines to be authentic black behavior become apparent when Delacroix pitches the idea of *Man Tan: The New Millennium Minstrel Show*. In this scene, he argues that the satiric nature of the overt racism of the show will not only be apparent to the audiences but also promote peace, harmony, and racial healing between whites and blacks. Delacroix skillfully builds to the climax of his presentation, marked by the entry of Man Ray and Womack, and draws an unwitting Witty into the plan. Delacroix's seduction is successful according to Witty, who claims that his erect penis is a reliable indicator of the extent to which Delacroix's proposal has turned him on. This scene of seduction mimics those of nineteenth-century minstrel shows and lynchings in which "black men were conjured up for the various delectations of white male audiences," allowing "implicit or explicit appreciation of black male sexuality [to] slip into homoerotic desire" (Lott 120).

In contrast to Witty, Delacroix goes to great extremes to forge a persona that he uses to disassociate himself from things black. Although Delacroix seems to know very little about from what or whom he is disassociating himself, his persona seems devised to send the message, "Whatever THAT is, I am not it." His persona, which is marked in part by an unidentifiable accent that even his parents do not recognize, constitutes a response to the daily acts of degradation that he suffers at the hands of Witty. When late for a meeting, for example, Witty accuses Delacroix of operating on "colored people's time." Witty takes great pleasure in flaunting repeatedly what he perceives as his right to use the word *nigger* despite Delacroix's request that the word not be used in front of him. Although viewers receive a glimpse of Delacroix's repressed desire to smack Witty silly, Witty sees only the reserve and apparent submission of his subordinate. But Delacroix is not as passive as Witty thinks. Rather, Delacroix attempts to employ satire to resist his boss's directive to create a forum in which his complicity would be demanded in the reproduction of stereotypical images of African Americans and African American culture. Unwilling to concede to the demand for his complicity in what he recognizes will be his own degradation, Delacroix instead imitates Witty's ways of seeing and thinking about blacks. Delacroix does so to set in motion the process that he hopes will undermine the arrogant certainty that underscores Witty's counterfeiting of black identity. Like Tommy in John Edgar Wideman's "All Stories Are True," Delacroix's effort to resist his degradation by imitating the perspective of its source makes for interesting comparisons with the performances of the first black blackface minstrel, William Henry Lane.

Lane, better known as Master Juba, was the only black minstrel man to perform in white theaters in the 1840s (Lott 113). Juba became famous for what he called "imitation dances," in which he first imitated white blackface performers and then claimed to be imitating himself (Gubar 147). Lott remarks on the irony and significance of the imitation dances, which he reads as instances when white blackface performers were mocked by those on whose images they were capitalizing in counterfeit form. Whatever momentary agency the black blackface dancer achieved, imitations of imitations provide a caustic reminder of "minstrelsy's fundamental consequence for black culture, the dispossession and control by whites of black forms that would not for a long time be recovered" (Lott 115). Whereas the counterfeit nature of the white blackface minstrel is certain, Juba's imitation dances destabilized the reliability of his performance by worrying the line between the counterfeit and what merely seemed to be counterfeit. A white audience's desire to experience an authentic rendition of blackness is necessarily interrupted—if not thwarted altogether—by a performance in which the dancer capitalizes on the hypervisibility such desire affords him while protecting the privacy of the authentic self that the claim of imitation obscures.

The protection of an authentic self notwithstanding and of which Lee affords us barely a glimpse, Delacroix's imitation is risky because his visibility and the material benefits that it affords him are at stake. Yet Delacroix is cognizant that visibility in the eyes of white America comes at the cost of conformity to stereotypes of black men as animals, brutes, rapists, and murderers or as comic figures whose sole pleasure is to entertain, please, or pacify white audiences. He sees this as a risk worth taking because it affords him a rare opportunity to work a system that affords visibility only to those black men who represent themselves as white America imagines them to be (hooks, *We Real* xii). Craig Smith's discussion of visuality in "Darkness Visible: The Politics of Being Seen from Ellison to Zebrahead" sheds light on the nature of the risky terrain of the new millennium that Delacroix attempts to navigate. Smith uses the term *visuality* to describe the contemporary state of hypervisibility in which many black men are caught. Smith contrasts the visuality of black men today with the invisibility on which Ralph Ellison focused more than half a century ago in *Invisible Man*. As Smith sees it, the invisibility that Ellison addresses throughout his novel offers a less accurate description of the condition that affects perhaps the largest segment of the African American population today. Now, he contends, "[i]nvisibility has evolved into an equally deformative, equally symptomatic visibility which is constructed, still, in order to control and contain the discomforting difference of America—to manage, that is, the American 'racial unconscious'" (2). Lott defines the American racial unconscious as "a structured formation, combining thought and feeling, tone and impulse, and at the very edge of semantic availability, whose symptoms and anxieties make it just legible" (33). The visuality that Smith claims characterizes more recent approaches to containing black men is not only a condition but also a "social practice that enables American racialism, the system of organizing human possibilities and limits, character and essence according to a hierarchical scheme of racial value knowable, readable, discernible in the epidermally visible" (3). That is, visuality shapes what Smith calls "structures of containment," or what I call the prison writ large, by organizing the ways in which black males are seen "within strictly delineated categories, . . . within a frame which appears to offer compensatory interest after centuries of aversion, but which, in effect, performs a coercive act of ideological re-negation" (C. Smith 3). Whereas visuality produces an image of black masculinity as pathological, "innately violent, aggressively sexual, loudly inarticulate, aggrieved, and resentful," contexts in which it is operative also allow "so-called model minorities and the black middle class" to coexist with "neoconservatives and postliberals" in what might best be termed a probationary manner (C. Smith 3). The guise of such inclusiveness distracts us from the role that visuality plays in perpetuating the containment of black men and thereby obscures oppressive projects such as the one that Witty assigns Delacroix.

However difficult it is to do, many black men have found ways to resist the personal and professional impact of such visuality and the attendant distortion of black men's images (hooks, *We Real* xiii). Delacroix's desire to resist precisely these things certainly drives him to employ satire with an eye toward his and others' emancipation from the dehumanizing effects of racist images. Such emancipation, however, relies on the television audience's willingness as well as its ability to recognize satire. In the absence of such recognition, the modern-day minstrel show that Delacroix proposes simply reproduces the effects of historical images, obliterating the audience's view of the humanity of the black male actors Delacroix recruits to perform in blackface. Delacroix's plan to satirize the images and ideas that structure his and other black men's containment fails because Witty and the television audience empty them of satire. Delacroix's plan backfires and heightens his visibility because the show's ratings make it a smashing success. The violent and dehumanizing effects of blackface are exposed, although not in the liberating ways that he imagined. His act of resistance appears to have failed. But which moment in the film marks this failure? The failure of Delacroix's effort to resist the machinations of whiteness is apparent when Man Ray steps from behind the blackface mask and strips away the safe aura wrought by his seemingly counterfeit representation of blackness.

In this scene, Delacroix is the only person other than Man Tan/Ray who is not wearing blackface. Hereafter, we do not see Delacroix again without his face blackened, which suggests that he too has been contained by this mode of representation. After receiving word that Man Tan/Ray has donned neither his costume nor the burnt cork grease, Delacroix immediately pays the actor a visit. When Delacroix asks Man Tan why he is not yet ready to go on stage, he asserts that his name is not Man Tan but rather Man Ray and declares, "I'm not playing myself no more." Man Ray's declaration at once conjoins and distinguishes him from Delacroix. Both have assumed new names to forge a space for themselves in the entertainment realm of the white supremacist, capitalist, patriarchal economy in which each hopes to reap material rewards for his participation. To different degrees, both have deluded or played themselves into thinking that they could participate without getting burned. Delacroix's chosen moniker indirectly acknowledges his recognition that to play oneself is to willingly leave oneself open to the possibility of crucifixion. As he says to Man Ray of his insistence on not wearing blackface, "It's your funeral." At the same time, though, like Master Juba, both Man Ray's and Delacroix's adopted personas afford them the possibility if not the guarantee of maneuvering within the liberating space between what is real and what is counterfeit. However, over time Delacroix loses sight of what Man Ray comes to see more clearly: both are playing or imitating themselves as others, such as Witty, would see them.

There is no way of knowing, based on Delacroix's and Man Ray's performances, which attributes are counterfeit and which merely seem counterfeit. Thus, although each plays himself in response to efforts to exert mastery over the images of black people and black cultural practices, both Man Ray's and Delacroix's performances constitute efforts to prevent such mastery from becoming absolute. In Man Ray's case, his efforts seem successful at first. He emerges literally from the jaws of minstrelsy, takes the stage sans blackface, and begins to dance. The audience is silent. They do not know how to respond when the "fakery evaporate[s]" and they are left with no choice but to deal with Man Ray's act "of unsettling authenticity" (Lott 113). Screeching "Stop Dancing! Stop Dancing!" Witty can no longer cope with Man Ray's display of talent when he rejects the mask and reveals the man behind it. If, as Lott suggests, the "primary purpose of the mask [was] as much to maintain control over a potentially subversive act as to ridicule" (113), then Man Ray's refusal to appear in blackface constitutes an outright rejection of such control. Ironically, Man Ray's overt act of resistance is the ultimate test of whether Delacroix has completely lost sight of his commitment to realizing what he hopes would be the subversive possibilities of the minstrel show. Heretofore, Delacroix's unblackened face suggested that he was still playing himself as a means of resistance. But like the whitefaced perpetrators of the violence in Blandon's film, Delacroix assumes a role that even he—especially he—never imagined when he promises the audience that he will deal with Man Tan/Ray's case of "coonitis" by taking him out back, whipping him, and if necessary cutting off his foot. Delacroix's invocation of such historically loaded punishments and acts of torture as whipping and dismemberment to reassure the audience that the black male dancer who stepped out of the role is under control, suggests that he, like the Mau Mau who eventually murder Man Ray, has been trapped by the rules of his own game. The violence of the final scenes of *Bamboozled* is arguably gratuitous because the film so thoroughly makes apparent the nature, function, and effects of the imagic violence represented throughout the rest of the film. If there is a place in the film when Lee becomes caught in the lockstep of his own dance, it is here. If there is a charge to be laid against Lee, it is that the ultimate annihilation of almost every black male character in the film reveals its slippage in and out of the empty space of representation because it resorts to the familiar technique of selling the extermination of black men as entertainment (Guerrero, "Black Man" 183). The violence around which *Bamboozled*'s narrative revolves escalates to a climax marked by the annihilation of the black male victims. Such annihilation results from Lee's failure to represent an alternative space within which black masculine agency can thrive beyond the confines of the white supremacist, capitalist, patriarchal realm.

Lee's exposure and interrogation if not resolution of such paradoxes and social contradictions provide a benchmark for the consideration of the popular and controversial film *Barbershop*. Whereas *Bamboozled*'s strength is that Lee does not veer disingenuously toward simple means of resolution, *Barbershop*'s weakness is that it does exactly that. And whereas *Bamboozled* is marked by brief moments of slippage out of the empty space of representation, *Barbershop* is marked by its brief but nonetheless significant forays into it. *Barbershop* bears out Lee's observations and conclusions because its narrative reveals many of the paradoxes and social contradictions that lead to the bamboozlement of all of the characters in Lee's film. The challenges and conundrums that confound Delacroix and others also confront the black men in *Barbershop*. However, although *Barbershop*'s formulaic narrative gestures tentatively toward the richness and significance of black masculine spaces, in the end it misses its opportunity to fully convey their value as sites in which the nurturing of alternative masculine identities takes place. It is arguably too easy for a mainstream audience to miss the humanity of the figures whom the film envelopes in characteristics of type. The film only occasionally allows such figures space in which to protest, as Ellison once put it, "Watch out there, Jack, there're people living under here" ("World" 123–24). Rather, order is restored within the narrative when the values and standards that govern the formation of white, patriarchal, masculine identities are recuperated. Therefore, although certain characters, particularly Calvin and Eddie, stand on the edge of the empty space of representation, in the end they cannot entirely escape the lockstep created by the combination of comedy and criminality that dominates the narrative. Ultimately, then, *Barbershop*, a Cube Vision production, begs the question of what vision lies behind this project. Does Ice Cube, who portrays Calvin, like Man Ray/Man Tan, play himself by avoiding ventures into less typical terrain? Does his play in this regard account for the seemingly drastic shift between his earlier adoption in the rap music industry of a hard-core gangsta type and the strikingly different roles that he now accepts? A closer look at *Barbershop* suggests that Ice Cube's professional vacillations and his role as Calvin may signify something other than evidence that he has bought into the same system that his earlier work as a rapper and an actor arguably opposed.

A brief turn to Richard Wright offers insight into this way of conceptualizing Ice Cube's play relative to the legacy of type that *Barbershop* appears at first glance to perpetuate. Wright's short story, "The Man Who Lived Underground," suggests that to come out on top in the games black men must play aboveground, they must go underground to acquire insight into the nature and function of the system that defines the parameters of such games. Noting the degree to which violent fantasies infiltrate contemporary African American popular culture, Paul Gilroy suggests that something may be gained by casting our critical eyes backward to Wright's creative explorations of various forms of compensatory resistance (xiv). Gilroy also calls attention to the astute ways Wright addresses the degree to which "[b]lacks and whites enjoy radically different forms of consciousness and are sundered from each other even when they occupy the same spaces" (xv). With Gilroy's comments about Wright's work in mind, it would be very easy to condemn Ice Cube for participating in projects that reproduce images of black men that in turn perpetuate the legacy of type. However, "Cube Vision" may signify the recognition of and possibly the concession to the different ways in which blacks and whites are conscious of their own and each other's respective places in society. Approaching *Barbershop* with this double vision in mind offers a way of conceptualizing performances that exploit the naïveté of a white perspective for the amusement of blacks who see the world from other points of view. Whereas white America's perspectives are often characterized by a lack of awareness of the doubleness of the black perspective, the same cannot be said of black perspectives in relation to the limitations of white ones. The subversive potential of black perspectives is invisible through the lens of the white perspective and is thus mobilized relatively easily.

The importance of seeing things differently and of finding ways to exploit the possibilities and the risks inherent in invisibility are central to "The Man Who Lived Underground." Gilroy describes Wright's story as a meditation "on the characters and dynamism of black masculinity—enacted, feared, celebrated, worried over, lived, and beheld both by outsiders and initiates" (xiv). Wright theorizes about the different ways that black men and whites—especially white police officers—see themselves and understand their relationships with one another. The narrator of the story is Fred Daniels, a black man whose name we do not learn until well into the story. Readers meet Daniels in the first lines of the story when he is looking for a place to hide. He has escaped from a police interrogation room, where he was forced to sign a confession stating that he had murdered a white woman (Wright 71). He chooses to hide in a sewer system, to which he gains access when torrential rains cause a manhole cover to lift (19). Daniels's journeys through the underground tunnels lead him to a psychic place from which he develops a new way of understanding how the aboveground world works and where he learns to see himself as a man (Baker, *Blues* 160). Houston A. Baker Jr. characterizes Daniels's unique angle of vision as a "threshold perspective," characteristic of one who transgresses boundaries to "secure a distinctive outsider's point of view" (*Blues* 160). Daniels negotiates the invisible terrain of the underground world, which affords him the perspective of an "unseen seer" and enables him to recognize the absurdities and contradictions of life in the aboveground world (Baker, *Blues* 160). His observations of an audience of black people seated in the reserved section of a movie theater lead to his understanding of the extent to which he had heretofore allowed those absurdities and contradictions to determine his view of himself as something less than a man. In the theater, he hears a chorus of voices and is initially unable to discern whether they are "joyous or despairing" (29). When he realizes that the voices are in fact joyous, he suppresses an impulse to tell the crowd to stop laughing. He is disgusted that the people in the theater "were laughing at their lives . . . shouting and yelling at the animated shadows of themselves" (30). Although he resists the urge to alert the patrons to the error of their ways, he leaves the theater believing that the crowd had somehow been tricked as easily as children into a zombielike state where they were "sleeping in their living, awake in their dying" (30). In the end, it becomes apparent to Daniels that his disgust is misplaced. He begins to grasp that like whites who perform in blackface, he too has been completely taken in by illusions about black men (Wright 29–30). This accounts for his failure to consider that the patrons' laughter may be what Ellison referred to as "a profound rejection of the image created to usurp [their] identity" ("Change" 55). Whereas the black patrons laugh because they recognize the gap between what Ellison calls "the shadow and the act" ("Shadow" 278), Daniels's blindness with respect to the authenticity of his role results from his failure to differentiate between shadow and act.

This failure arises, Ellison tells us, when people confuse the portrayal of African Americans in Hollywood films with the real actions that give rise to such representations. As he puts it, "In the beginning was not the shadow, but the act, and the province of Hollywood is not action, but illusion. . . . [T]he anti-Negro images of the films were (and are) acceptable because of the existence throughout the United States of an audience obsessed with an inner psychological need to view Negroes as less than men" ("Shadow" 276). Ellison's "Change the Joke and Slip the Yoke" (1958) also offers insight into the sorts of contradictions with which Daniels wrestles as he makes his way through the theater, with which Delacroix wrestles as he watches his plan of resistance unfold in ways other than he had imagined, and which shape the contrary instincts that inform *Barbershop*. What Daniels and perhaps Delacroix fail to grasp, though perhaps Ice Cube and crew do, is what Ellison calls "the joke at the center of the American identity." Half of the joke arises from the "white man's half-conscious awareness that his image of the Negro is false

[and] makes him suspect the Negro of always seeking to take him in, and assume his motives are anger and fear—which very often they are" ("Change" 55). The other half of the joke arises because African Americans find it amusing that whites "can be so absurdly self-deluded over the true interrelatedness of blackness and whiteness" and therefore view whites as hypocrites who boast of having a "pure identity while standing with [their] humanity exposed to the world" ("Change" 54–55). The laughter and joy that Daniels and Delacroix find so bewildering are in fact part of a complex system of masking that arises as a response to the joke that Ellison identifies.

Although it is at times questionable as to whether Ice Cube's roles as an actor allow him to slip the yoke, in *Barbershop* his performance as Calvin definitely allows him to contribute to changing the joke. That is, the "Cube Vision" that informs *Barbershop* grows out of the ways in which its narrative and images become means of compensatory resistance. As we know from his rap of yore, Ice Cube is not blind to—though some would argue that he has been complicit in reproducing—the sorts of containment with which black men contend every day. Yet he participates in a film that solicits its appeal to a mainstream (white) audience through a narrative and characters that conform perfectly to the images that come to us through the legacy of type. The film banks—literally—on the assumption that black audiences will see past the recursion of a narrative that takes shape around the story of black male criminals beguiled by their own stupidity (the shadow) to the act, which is the use of the narrative to dance within the confines of the nation's and the industry's lockstep. It employs this recursive device to make visible a story that traces the growth of black male characters whose ethics and respect for themselves and other black males allow the film to teeter on the edge of the empty space of representation. Although *Barbershop* revolves around a series of bumbled ventures on the parts of a series of characters and some of their identities conform perfectly to images passed down through the legacy of type, others brush against such images but in the end veer subtly away from them.

Calvin, Ice Cube's character, is a thirtyish black man who works in and runs the barbershop that his father passed down to him. Calvin is married, and he and his wife are expecting a baby. We first meet Calvin working in the music studio that he has set up in the basement of his home. We learn from his wife that he has invested money that he ought not to have invested in the studio as well as in other failed projects. But Calvin has big dreams. Although he does not aspire to Oprah's level of wealth, he dreams of purchasing for himself and his wife a house like the one she uses as a guesthouse. Such a vision, he realizes, is not likely to be attained from working in a barbershop while engaging in make-it-big experiments on the side. Calvin initially lacks an understanding of and respect for his place in the community where he lives and works. On the contrary, he views the barbershop's ghetto location as a roadblock to its and thus his success. In Calvin's mind, as is also the case for Jimmy, the college-educated barber in Calvin's employ, the barbershop is a means to an end. He does not appreciate its significance to the people who work there or its function for those in the community at large. He does not see that it represents a safe space for those who enter. Indeed, his behavior at times compromises the integrity of the barbershop, which others revere as a fraternal site wherein black men remind and affirm one another's worthiness as human beings. Instead, Calvin sees the barbershop as an inherited burden, a sign of his father's failure to accumulate and pass on material wealth and a sign of his father's and his failure to be men.

Calvin's view of what it means to be the owner of a barbershop is interesting given that such ownership was once a sure sign of a black man's success. As Melissa Harris-Lacewell discusses in *Barbershops, Bibles, and BET* (2004), the majority of black entrepreneurs have historically been barbers or hairstylists. Prior to emancipation, black males constituted the majority of barbers, their customers were primarily wealthy whites, and the owners of barbershops were among the most prosperous entrepreneurs. In part, this was because the service nature of the work gave them a monopoly on it: whites were reluctant to engage themselves in work of a service-oriented nature and felt entitled to be served by blacks (164). Later, as Harris-Lacewell explains, the great migration of southern blacks to urban areas created a new market for barbers, and the shops attained a new significance in black communities. Barbershops became sites where information was exchanged and distributed, often through newspapers that the barbers sold. However, newspapers were neither the only nor the most important source of information. The shops were places wherein black folk gathered to discuss matters of immediate concern, such as employment opportunities and whether there was merit in migrating to urban areas (166). Today, as Bryant Keith Alexander notes in "Fading, Twisting, and Weaving: An Interpretive Ethnography of the Black Barbershop as Cultural Space" (2003), barbershops remain very important cultural sites within the black community where men gather to socialize and to engage in intellectual exchanges about a wide range of issues (105). In the black barbershop, the sharing of different forms of cultural knowledge is a means through which the space becomes dynamic and alive as it is created and re-created by the discourses of the people who inhabit it. The lives, narratives, experiences, opinions, and relationships of the black men in a barbershop bring the past into conversation with the present (B. K. Alexander 106). In the shops, black men interact with each other in ways that allow them to make sense of the world and their place in it. The shops are places from which they leave with more than a haircut: they leave having affirmed their place in a community of black men who, whether they encounter each other elsewhere or not, sustain each other through the provision of and payment for a service, through the intimacy of the exchange, and through conversation and critique that takes place beyond the parameters of the white gaze.

Calvin, however, is oblivious to all of this as he strives to create a lifestyle that conforms to a particular model of respectability—he is legitimately employed, he is married, he discourages cursing, and he aspires to some degree of class mobility to escape what he views as the containment of the ghetto. What he lacks is an awareness of and respect for his father's investment in people, as Eddie puts it, and thus for the immaterial riches that define his current locus. The limitations of Calvin's character, like Delacroix's, call attention to the hollowness of a model of respectability that is void of the consciousness that comes with recognition of and respect for one's place in the history and day-to-day activities of one's community. What makes this film so interesting is that it calls attention to such hollowness through characters who on the one hand conform to comic and criminal types and on the other hand articulate black masculine perspectives that push against the limitations of such types.

Viewed through the lens of patriarchal masculinity, black men who do not conform to the model of respectability to which Calvin subscribes appear as deficient failures who lack what it takes to "realize the ideal" (hooks, *We Real* 14). This way of looking at black men has historical precedent. Prior to emancipation, black men were denied status and respect relative to their contributions to the economy in the form of slave labor. A man's ability to reap the benefits of his labor to support his family was the mark of manhood. Black men's labor was not recognized. Neither, therefore, was their manhood, according to white definitions. In the absence of such recognition, black men were perceived and represented as being lazy and unmotivated. Stereotypes of black men as being unwilling to work were invoked as justification for denying them the opportunity to do so, creating a vicious cycle that trapped black men between perception and representation. That is, representations of black men as a slothful class of workers arose as a consequence of denying them the opportunity to live up to the terms and requirements that defined patriarchal masculine identities (hooks, *Black Looks* 90). As hooks puts it, "It has served the interest of racism for white people to ignore positive aspects of black life. . . . It was vital to white male self-esteem to belittle unconventional black masculinity, saying that these men were castrated" (*We Real* 12). Such perspectives eclipse representations of alternative masculine identities and ideals that become the substance of "revolutionary manhood" when they are afforded space within the texts that shape the national imagination. hooks's remarks direct us to the complex ways in which black-focused films both draw on and resist images of black men as seen through the lens of whiteness (hooks, *We Real* 11–14).

Barbershop gives us insight into how black men have resisted such images in ways that have little to do with white ways of looking. As did Walker in her search for mothers' gardens, several of the male characters in the film direct their gazes inward to the place where, however far they have to go to find it at times, the whole-ness of their souls and psyches remains intact. Although Delacroix failed in his efforts to reach this place, at least until it was too late, Calvin comes closer to finding it. Ironically, as Walker discovered on her search for "the secret of what has fed that muzzled and often mutilated, but vibrant, creative spirit that the black woman has inherited," Calvin and other black men are led by characters whose traits make them seem the most "wild and unlikely" guides for such a journey toward the site from whence the secret can be excavated (Walker, "In Search" 239).

In contrast to Delacroix's workplace, Calvin's barbershop is a refuge for black men in addition to being the hub of the action in the community. The people Calvin encounters in his workaday world guide him toward a redefinition of the respectability and wealth for which he yearns but which exceed his grasp because he has bought into the belief that his value as a man depends on the money that he has rather than on his work ethic, integrity, or values (hooks, *We Real* 18–19). Like the ATM thieves whose buffoonish behavior provides the standard against which Calvin's transformation is measured, he initially believes that money, regardless of the means through which he acquires it, will buy him a ticket into the game, which in his view is being played and won beyond the boundaries of the Chicago ghetto in which his barbershop is located. Calvin's perspective is consistent with a historical connection between "money making and patriarchal authority" that logically compelled many black men to covet "equal pay for equal work—which was the vision of basic civil rights" and thus "the economic power to provide for themselves and family" (hooks, *We Real* 15).

One alternative to buying into a system that equates money with masculine authority is to adopt a hustling ethic. Such an ethic allows one to resist co-optation within a system of work in which a man's blackness means that his patriarchal man-hood will always be denied. To find a hustle is often akin to finding or at least search-ing for some degree of agency within a dehumanizing system, even if that means upholding the structures that dehumanize (hooks, *We Real* 19). Robin D. G. Kelley, in *Yo' Mama's Disfunktional: Fighting the Culture Wars in Urban America* (1997), associates such contrary instincts with graffiti artists, rap musicians, break-dancers, and athletes who "invest their time and energy in creative expression" in their hustle as ways of escaping demeaning, unfulfilling wage work. The efforts of such individuals exemplify "how young people have turned the labor of play into a commodity" (*Yo'* 57). Kelley disputes the notion that the terms *work* and *play* are binaries. Instead, he argues, there exist "dialectical links between work and play within the context of capitalism" (*Yo'* 75). That is, because play is associated with pleasurable activities, the extent to which its execution requires hard work is often forgotten or overlooked. Activities that represent solely a leisure form for some become arenas in which to mobilize entrepreneurial impulses and exercise some degree of control over one's own labor. Kelley points out that although African American urban youth have had some success at turning the activities at which they are skilled and in which they take pleasure into cash-making opportunities, nothing they do or produce undermines capitalism or benefits the entire black community; then again, Kelley notes, it is not intended to. When their work circulates representations that lend support to racist beliefs and/or is mobilized against minorities by those who buy into the belief that anyone can escape any situation if they work hard enough, the nature and function of structural racism are easily overlooked or denied (*Yo'* 45–46).

Other ways of escaping wage labor stem from need and deprivation and often have dire consequences. During the 1980s, urban conditions and opportunities deteriorated in ways that exacted enormous costs for city dwellers. Permanent job losses, military-style police presences in inner-city areas, and the erasure of job programs for youth led to the growth of an underground economy in which young people were actively involved in selling the new wave of drugs that included PCP and crack. The increased levels of violence that accompanied the growth and development of the crack economy notwithstanding, many young black people found that selling crack was the only and/or the most profitable venture available (Kelley, *Yo'* 46–47). Whatever the potential and likely negative implications for black communities and for the peddlers themselves, an ethic lies behind such activities. This ethic is framed by the notion that what one does is less important than the money one gets by doing it. It is an even more diluted version of the ethic that governs Calvin's decisions. Calvin's ethic has been stripped of the respect for and responsibility to self and community that transform work and money from signs of patriarchal authority to means of support and sustenance for those who are denied such authority.

A similarly diluted ethic drives the ATM thieves' obsession with gaining access to the money that they believe is inside the machine they have stolen. The film reveals both the impotency of the ethic that underlies their hustle, which is their undoing, and the debilitating allure of that which tempts Calvin. In their places, the film offers a model for a more liberating form of hustle and a black masculine identity that is respectable in its own right and on its own terms. Ironically, Eddie, the chicken-eating, finger-licking senior barber whose humor and mannerisms situate him neatly within the parameters of type that shape the film's comedic frame, guides Calvin toward a new way of looking at himself, other black men, and the community. Throughout the film, the stereotypes to which Eddie conforms are displaced by a mature, masculine perspective that he offers and that enables Calvin to remember the standards by which his father measured his and others' worth as black men. Eddie reminds Calvin that his father used the barbershop not only as a means to make a living but also as a site from which to offer other black men the wherewithal to view themselves as men and to reclaim what others attempted to destroy. It is not a coincidence that Eddie, who has lived through some of the most significant decades in the struggle for civil rights, reminds Calvin and all of the other barbers in the shop that the barbershop is a site of creativity in which barbers are not only artists but "all-around hustlers." Eddie knows and tries to impart the knowledge that the haircuts that black barbers craft for their customers serve a function beyond mere aesthetics. The haircuts and the context in which they are given define the process through which the construction of black masculinity takes place in the barbershop (B. K. Alexander 120). As Bryant Keith Alexander explains,

> The recrafting of Black masculinity in [the] barbershop is one that is done within community by and with other Black men. It is done through the buzz of clippers, the drone of televisions, or the smooth grooves of soft jazz. The construction is done within talk—laughing, joking, and engaging the intimate and not so intimate aspects of shared communities. The construction is done with delicate razors—controlling coifs, straightening hairlines, and defining lips by shaping mustaches, jaw lines, and beards. . . . It is a site where the cultural and racial familiarity of Black male bodies is acknowledged as meaningful. (120)

During the course of a haircut, black men experience a rare and unacknowledged moment of intimate, sanctioned, masculine contact (B. K. Alexander 120). Such contact is not sexual. Rather, the intimacy stems from the knowledge that underscores the function of the service. Both barber and customer know that "a Black man who knows and understands the growth pattern of Black hair and the sensitivity of Black skin—is caring for another Black man" (120). The provider and beneficiary of a haircut participate in this act of "sanctioned trust" that constitutes "a symbolic representation of the meaningfulness of the black barbershop as a site for cultural exchange and maintenance" (120). As we see in Calvin's shop, the physical and discursive intimacy that defines how the black men engage with one another is contrary to "the stoic images of Black masculinity that we see on television; or the rough, mean, and/or aggressive images that we [usually] see in film; or the violent, sexualized, and sometimes ineffectual images that we are expected to take as real" (120). The images of the men who gather in Calvin's shop are in keeping with those that Alexander associates with black men in black barbershops generally: "smiling faces, brothers engaged in friendly exchanges, negotiating space and intention" as they seek sustenance from the space in which they find themselves beyond the reach of the surveilling white gaze (B. K. Alexander 120). Although Calvin is oblivious to all that the barbershop represents, Eddie is not.

In one of the most powerful scenes in the movie, Eddie carefully shaves the face of a customer with pearl-handled, initialed blades lovingly taken from their case for the purpose of this demonstration. He narrates the process as he goes, thereby linking his craftsmanship to his sense of history, to his knowledge of himself as someone important within that history and to the community of people whose lives are informed by it. "If you want to be somebody," Eddie tells his audience of mostly black men, "it take respect to get respect." On this occasion, Calvin remains conspicuously on the margins of Eddie's attentive audience and on the periphery of this intimate exchange between black men. Later, in the conversation in which Calvin confesses to Eddie that he has sold the shop to a loan shark who plans to turn it into a gentlemen's club, Eddie reminds Calvin of the historical connection that his action is disrespecting, negating, severing. Eddie tells Calvin that the barbershop is a place where a black man means something and where something as simple as a haircut can change the way a man feels on the inside. Calvin witnesses this firsthand when Lamar steals a haircut, only to return to pay for it after landing a job. The job, Lamar tells Calvin proudly, will enable him to put his daughter into a "real day care" instead of leaving her with a crackhead relative, which had been his only alternative. Whatever the comic role that Eddie plays, then, the film does not allow that role to define Eddie's essence. This is not to say that, viewed through the lens of whiteness, Eddie's performances as comic and criminal throughout the film will not be taken as his essence. But as Eddie's comments suggest, the emphasis ought to be on the liberating effects of the black masculine gaze when its agent learns to sever it from the whiteness that threatens to subsume it. Eddie offers those willing to look a chance to see the men behind the masks.

It seems, then, that this Cube Vision production "slips the yoke" of mainstream filmmaking by confronting those who view it exclusively through the lens of whiteness with the punch line of their own joke. The film offers its audiences a choice. We can look at and laugh at *Barbershop*. There are no surprises here, only familiar representations of black men whose performances do not depart drastically from what whites have always expected to see when blacks take the stage (or screen, as it were). Eddie, the ATM thieves, Lamar, Ricky—comics and criminals— all are present in the heterogeneous forms that cycles of white lore have carried into the twenty-first century. If we avoid looking for the men behind the masks, that is all we will see when we view *Barbershop*. The alternative is to acknowledge the other ways of seeing to which the gaze that defines this product of Cube Vision directs us. This alternative gaze takes us inside the barbershop, beneath the screen from which Ellison's friend Jack cries out ("World" 123). This gaze takes us behind the mask that is *Barbershop* to the barbershop where the voices of black men mean something. In the barbershop, the film suggests, there is no yoke because in this place, if but for a moment, the joke is irrelevant. It is not that comedy and criminality are absent from this site of black fraternity, for humor is as central to the discourse of the barbershop as is the dialogue between men who struggle to understand where personal responsibility and systemic violence and racism begin and end when it comes to understanding black men's involvement with the criminal justice system. But in this place, what whites see when they look at black men matters not. For in the barbershop, like the mirrors that hang from its walls, black men fill the empty spaces left by the representations that reflect the legacy of type. They do so by mirroring images that return what the masks have stolen, revive what may have been forgotten, and restore what may have been thought lost. In this place, the love that is undeniably absent from the violence of the legacy of type is strikingly and unabashedly present. In this place, if only for the time it takes a man to get a haircut, lockstep becomes dance.

Guerrero reminds us that figures such as Sergey Eisenstein and Charlie Chaplin once speculated that film would permanently alter the ways in which people "perceive, understand, and communicate with one another" in progressive ways (*Framing* 2). Regrettably, Eisenstein and Chaplin's predictions have not fully been realized for African Americans and other minorities. Rather, film production throughout the twentieth century played a significant role in furthering the subordinating, marginalizing, and dehumanizing practices that preserved "the white-dominated symbolic order and racial hierarchy of American society" (*Framing* 2). Figures as diverse as the three whose works I discuss in this chapter, along with many others, continue to seek ways to use their craft to stay in the struggle to relieve or eliminate the containment wrought by representational practices in popular culture. Films such as *The Last Blackface, Bamboozled,* and *Barbershop* remind us that ideologies of "racial domination and difference can never be permanently fixed in place" (Guerrero, *Framing* 2). Those involved at all levels in the making of black-focused films remind us in both encouraging and discouraging ways that these films constitute sites of "perpetual contestation, struggle, and consequently change" (Guerrero, *Framing* 3). It is critical, therefore, that analyses of representations of African Americans not perpetuate images of blacks as being "mere victims of Hollywood's conjurings" (Guerrero, *Framing* 3). Rather, our analyses of representations of African Americans need to take into account "the dialectical push of Hollywood's cultural construction and domination of the black image and the pull of an insistent black social consciousness and political activism" (Guerrero, *Framing* 3) that becomes legible in many black-focused films. For this reason, Guerrero ultimately revives Eisenstein and Chaplin's optimism regarding the possibilities to which the trajectory of black films in the late twentieth century seem to point, suggesting that "in spite of the proscriptions and containments of the dominant film industry, this new wave of films and filmmakers holds out renewed hope for the future of a liberated black cinema" (*Framing* 4). There are other realms of popular culture to which we ought also to direct our analysis to enable a better understanding of the ways in which black men resist and at times become complicit in domination as practiced through representational practices. The realm of rap music is rife with examples of figures attempting to navigate their way through a system that promises freedom—at a price. I turn in the final chapter to this realm.

"HOLLER IF YA HEAR ME"
Black Men, (Bad) Rap(s), and the Return of the Black Brute

The drums sounded the warning
    Oppressors are coming
    Oppressors are coming
And when slavers discovered
How much we communicated
With music they could not understand
They took up our drums
But not our rhythm

—T. J. REDDY, "A POEM FOR BLACK RHYTHMETICIANS"

We have seen how the association between criminality and black masculinity is the legacy of historically consistent efforts to control and manipulate images of black men. The persistent and pervasive presence of this association in popular culture furthers the exploitation and distortion of images of black men that each turn of the white lore cycle carries forward. Black men's containment within the prison writ large is reinforced not only by the presence of stereotypical images but also by the absence of images that represent them as heterogeneous, complex human beings. As we saw in chapter 2, the advertising industry capitalizes on binary representations of black men as comic entertainers and/or criminals while posturing as an integrated, egalitarian space. We saw in chapter 3 how the image of the black brute is immediately and ruthlessly mapped onto black athletes when they violate what is always their probationary status as celebrities. We saw in chapter 4 how makers of black-focused films have diligently attempted to interrupt the association between black masculinity and criminality by exposing, complicating, contextualizing, and correcting reductive representations of black men. The preceding chapters indicate that the efforts of individuals as diverse as Dennis Rodman and Spike Lee have worried but not yet altered the trajectory of the legacy of type that followed black men into the twenty-first century. However, this is not to characterize their efforts to critique, expose, correct, and confuse historically consistent representations of black men as failed acts of resistance. As Robin D. G. Kelley notes of social movements more broadly, "Unfortunately, too often our standards for evaluating social movements pivot around whether or not they 'succeeded' in realizing their visions rather than on the merits or power of the visions themselves. By such a measure, virtually every radical movement failed because the basic power relations they sought to change remain pretty much intact. And yet it is precisely these alternative visions and dreams that inspire new generations to continue to struggle for change" (*Freedom* ix). Many rap opponents have fallen into the trap that Kelley describes. That is, they frequently condemn the genre and the artists outright without pausing to consider what visions may underscore what opponents perceive as valueless and/or dangerous cultural products. The histories of African American literary and musical traditions indicate that it may be unwise to turn away from the examination of rap even when—perhaps especially when—the form seems to be misguided, offensive, or regressive. For forms that were once condemned have often been later recognized as valuable contributions to the struggle for change and freedom. Unfortunately, the backlash against and calls for censorship that have plagued rap throughout its history suggest that debates about its value (or lack thereof) occur within a space of representation that, like film, is only partially utilized.

The images and narratives that have caused public moralists and rap's opponents to demonize the genre are often compelling, ironic, and most important audible efforts to appropriate, exploit, and/or critique the perception that an umbilical connection exists between race and criminality. As such, the focus in this final chapter is twofold. First, I briefly rehearse the arguments that disregard the "merits or power" of the visions of young black men such as the late Tupac Shakur, whose name and image have become synonymous in the eyes of some of rap's opponents with all that is wrong with rap generally and young black men specifically (Kelley, *Freedom* ix). Second, I argue that opposition to rap is often symptomatic of the extent to which the traumatic effects of historical acts of violence against black men continue to haunt the national imagination (Walcott, "Images"). In particular, uncritical opposition to rap is frequently articulated as a response to the invocation of the black brute in this contemporary theater of type. Given the extent to which the returning figure bears witness to the legacy of violated black male bodies, it is not surprising that its insistent presence appears to haunt white America and to compel calls for the eradication of the genre and the voices that speak it.

As I suggested in the introduction, in white-focused cultural arenas, the historical antecedents that are recalled by the mapping of criminality onto the black male image are rarely if ever acknowledged or recognized. Overt assertions of the association between black masculinity and criminality are inhibited by the demand for political correctness. However, far from being a sign of progress or genuine change, political correctness demands that overt expressions of racist attitudes toward and views of black men be silenced or, more commonly, articulated in code. Political correctness of this nature does not challenge the foundation on which such attitudes and views rest but merely encourages the denial that underwrites efforts to disguise these attitudes. Explicit statements that connect black masculinity to criminality are no longer necessary, then, because the connection is repeatedly affirmed by the recursion of images that enhance the efficacy of the disciplinary methods that structure the prison writ large. The silence and denial fostered by the deceptive benevolence of politically correct climates enable white America to hide its racism in full view.

So it is that rap music becomes a venue within which artists appropriate and recirculate familiar languages and images of social injury, only to be held responsible for the genesis and importance of those languages (Butler 96). Judith Butler links the irony of this process of blame to a hegemonic desire to hide the complicity of the figure of power (white America) in the construction and dissemination of such languages and images behind masks that depict integrity and concern for the greater good (78). Such masking enables the powerful to define, to identify, and to punish forms of expression that have been produced and employed in injurious ways. The figure of power, then, assumes and exercises its ability to demarcate "the line between the domains of the speakable and the unspeakable" (Butler 77)—that which is heard and that which is "scene" (Baker, "Scene" 39)—and to remake and sustain those lines. Thus, languages and images of injury—in this case, those that criminalize black men—are named by a figure of power that deploys its power to denounce the rights of disempowered figures to exercise similar powers, resistant or not, through language, images, and their effects.

Butler calls attention to two of the ways that rap artists respond to and use languages and images of social injury. On the one hand, many struggle to reclaim the right to define the contexts within which languages and images of social injury mean and matter so that they might be deployed to further an agenda of agency and liberation (77). Ice Cube and Tupac provide us with excellent examples because of the rigor with which each has exposed the origins of the practices to which injurious languages and images give legitimacy. A good deal (but not all) of their work reflects their efforts to reenact injurious words and images in revisionary, aesthetic contexts. As Butler explains, within such contexts, rappers

> both *use* the word [and the image] and *mention* it, that is, make use of it to produce certain effects but also at the same time make reference to that very use, calling attention to it as a citation, situating that use within a citational legacy,

making that use into an explicit discursive item to be reflected on rather than a
taken for granted operation of ordinary language. Or, it may be that an aesthetic
reenactment *uses* that word, but also **displays** it, points to it, outlines it as the
arbitrary material instance of language that is exploited to produce certain kinds
of effects. (99)

No consensus exists about whether it is truly possible to empty injurious words
or images of the meanings attached to their legacies. However, many people have
tried to do so. Regrettably, rap opponents fail to recognize such attempts as explorations of how words or images "become the site[s] for the power to injure" (Butler
100) and sites in which the injured appropriate power. This is not to say that the
broader cultural contexts in which rap and rappers circulate do not at times obvi-
ate the political significance or impressiveness of their efforts. Nor is it to deny
that injurious languages and images may be received in ways that do not "over-
come their degrading meaning" but rather "recirculate their degradation" despite
efforts to afford them new significations (Butler 100). However, it is impossible
and unproductive to discuss the merits or power of rap as though these traits exist
as binary opposites to languages and images of social injury. To do so limits the
ability to understand how and why rap functions as a site in which black men find
ways to identify the nature of their containment, to complain about it, to voice
their resistance to it, and at times to become complicit in exactly the practices they
criticize. Even—and maybe especially—voices that seem to be obscured by scenes
of black male criminality need to be heard and considered on their own terms. If
rap does nothing else, it provides many young black men with a site within which
their voices are audible.

Eithne Quinn takes note of the risk and the burden that rap artists assume in
their efforts to speak and to be heard when she unpacks the multiple implications
of the "rap on gangsta." Gangsta rappers get an especially bad rap, Quinn argues,
because they are unduly blamed for problems that they did not create. At the same
time, gangsta rappers "*beat* the rap" because their performances of hyperbolic,
masculine personas are lucrative ventures of the sort from which most black youth
are generally excluded (37). Further, rappers "*take* the rap" by becoming the voice
for black youth and the targets of antirap critics (37). The challenges brought by
this burden notwithstanding, it should be clear by now that rappers did not invent
the images of black men that dominate white America's imagination and the texts
mediated by those images. However, rappers have profitably lured white America
into a space where it is willing to pay handsomely to be confronted by the images
of black men that remain at the center of its fantasies and fears. Some sectors of

white America have reacted to these confrontations in ways that indicate the extent to which the legacy of type haunts the national imagination and compels the need to exorcise the specter of the past in the various forms it reappears. Rap's images of black men as thugs and criminals are particularly troubling specters because their presence denies white America the sanctuary it desires from its violent past and its pervasive legacy (Jordan).

The hysteria around the subject of rap, race, and criminality thus marks an important and especially volatile moment in the turning of the white lore cycle. Although rap has brought important issues to the forefront, it has not transformed the United States from what Toni Morrison calls a racial house into a Home. As discussed in chapter 1, Morrison defines a *Home* as a nation from which the ideologies and practices that structure the prison writ large are absent. However, rap is helping to transform the prison writ large into a place where the sounds of black men's voices call racism and its malevolent effects out of their hiding places. Rap has contributed to the transformation of the United States into a racial house by carving "away accretions of deceit, blindness, ignorance, paralysis, and sheer malevolence embedded in raced language" and raced images (Morrison, "Home" 7). The images and sounds of rap haunt the racial house of the United States by making alternative ways of seeing and thinking about familiar images of and ideas about black men available and perhaps inevitable. In rap, representations of black men bearing far more than traces of their historical antecedents return in spectacular and audible forms. Although individual celebrities in other arenas, such as sport, have performed the role of the black brute, never has it been exploited for profit and pleasure to the extent that has been the case in rap. The figures of thugs or gangstas—America's worst nightmares, as Tupac once called them—return in rap as speaking subjects. As history has shown, when black men speak beyond the parameters of acceptability delineated by white America, their voices are demonized, what they say is more often than not pathologized, and calls to eradicate them become louder (Perry 95). The rapper who bears witness for those who lack a platform of stardom finds himself a more visible subject within the disciplined structure of the United States and increasingly subject to the technologies of surveillance that are integral to the panoptic power structure of the prison writ large. His testimony becomes a trap, albeit one that is not absolute in its effects (Perry 113).

As we have already seen, a peculiar combination of fascination, fickleness, fantasy, and fear defines white America's relationships to spectacles as diverse as the minstrel show, lynched black bodies, athletics and athletes, and black-focused films. So too, white America's responses to rap music are driven by the familiar sense of attraction and repulsion that manifests itself in the desire to consume and to destroy the object of this fear and desire. Antirap arguments that peaked during the 1990s are symptomatic of white America's persistent fear of blackness and black men and its efforts to mask the deleterious effects of its policies and practices on the resources and opportunities available to them. Rap has been attacked from all angles and scapegoated on the basis that it fosters violence, sexism, and criminality. By focusing attention on rap, opponents deflect attention away from the equally prevalent levels of violence, sexism, and racism in American culture generally and in other forms of popular culture specifically. Such deflection shifts attention away from the ideologies, institutions, and practices that give rise to such problems and criminalizes the mostly black male individuals who produce rap. Antirap debates often lack a critical tone because they tend to dehistoricize and decontextualize violence, sexism, and racism. Moreover, rap's critics often attach responsibility for the production and resolution of such problems to groups or individuals that have rarely benefited from ideologies, institutions, and practices that purport to exist for the greater good.

Efforts to censor rap have come from public moralists and defenders of so-called family values such as Dan Quayle, Bob Dole, and C. Delores Tucker. In contrast to rap's opponents, critics such as Michael Eric Dyson dismiss claims that rap is responsible for increasing levels of moral corruption and the decline of family values. Dyson argues that the term "'family values' is a code for a narrow view of how families work, who gets to count as a legitimate domestic unit, and consequently, what values are crucial to their livelihood" (*Between* 183). Moreover, he continues,

> To be sure, there have been severe assaults on American families and their values, but they have not come mainly from Hollywood, but from Washington with the dismantling of the Great Society. Cruel cuts in social programs for the neediest, an upward redistribution of wealth to the rich, and an unprincipled conservative political campaign to demonize poor black mothers and their children have left latter-day D. W. Griffiths in the dust. Many of gangsta rap's most vocal black critics (such as Tucker) fail to see how the alliances they forge with conservative white politicians such as Bennett and Dole are plagued with problems. Bennett and Dole have put up roadblocks to many legislative and political measures that would enhance the fortunes of the black poor they now claim in part to speak for. Their outcry resounds as crocodile tears from the corridors of power paved by faith. (*Between* 183–84)

The practice of blaming black rappers for social problems that have been and remain pervasive throughout American history and American society simply constitutes another manifestation of the tendency to demonize black men in discussions of the welfare state, incarceration rates and prison programs, the war on drugs, and male violence toward women (Perry 27). Assertions that hip-hop causes or encourages violence divert attention away from the violence wrought by social and economic inequities and disparities (Perry 96). As Mikal Gilmore contends in *Rolling Stone*, "rap gave voice and presence to truths that almost no other form of art or reportage was willing to accommodate.... [I]f hardcore rap were to disappear tomorrow, [the social problems for which rappers are blamed] would still exist" (81). In short, the United States is indisputably violent, but hip-hop did not make it so.

Demands to censor the lyrics and in some cases to stop the production and distribution of rap altogether and gangsta rap in particular deflect attention from the insights that rap and its creators provide into mainstream American culture and the complex ways in which rappers are situated relative to it. Dyson makes this observation when he writes that "gangsta rap's greatest 'sin' may be that it tells the truth about practices and beliefs that rappers hold in common with the mainstream and with black elites. This music has embarrassed mainstream society and black bourgeois culture. It has forced us to confront the demands of racial representation that plague and provoke black artists. It has also exposed our polite sexism and our disregard for gay men and lesbians. We should not continue to blame gangsta rap for ills that existed long before hip-hop uttered its first syllable" (*Between* 186). Blind resistance to the genre reflects white America's reluctance to examine its beliefs and practices and their effects. It also reflects the fear and loathing of black men's agency, sexuality, and autonomy that have always existed at the root of American race relations. Opponents too often overlook the fact that hip-hop culture generally and rap music specifically offer youth a place from which to form alternative identities and regain social status in communities where traditional institutional support systems have deteriorated, along with the concrete indicators of their presence (Rose 34). 2 Live Crew's Luther Campbell and Tupac Shakur once forthrightly acknowledged what many critics will not—that their participation and success in the rap music industry offered them a legal means of making a living (and a good one) in places where the possibilities for upward mobility are limited at best. Campbell, for example, wrote to the *New York Post* in response to claims that he was broke and selling answering machine messages for five dollars apiece: "Under no circumstances am I doing bad.... If I do go broke, you and other writers like you will be the first ones that I will come rob" ("2 Live Crew Star" B6). Similarly, on the title track from *Strictly for My N.I.G.G.A.Z.*, Tupac addresses his critics when he raps, "Pick up my shit or I'll be back doin' stickups/I better see five stars next to my picture." Both Campbell and Tupac point directly to the irony implicit in much of the criticism about rap when they argue that critics ought not to be afraid of rap artists who have found a means by which to support themselves well but rather should fear those whom poverty and unemployment force to commit crimes to put food on their tables and roofs over their heads. Implicit in Campbell's, Tupac's, and Gilmore's statements is their recognition of the ways that capitalism structures a cycle of containment in which black men often must choose between being the victims of its oppressive effects or becoming complicit in the system that produces such effects. Opponents to rap too often ignore the internal critiques or performative aspects of the oppressive forces in many rap narratives that seem to glorify "that which ails the community" (Perry 96).

Yet rap, like the African American aesthetic tradition of which it is part, is full of examples of efforts to identify, critique, and resist the containment wrought by white America's ways of seeing black people generally and black men specifically and by white America's engagement with and manipulation of various forms of black cultural production. Chuck D says as much on Public Enemy's 1988 CD, *It Takes a Nation of Millions to Hold Us Back*, at the beginning of "Prophets of Rage":

> *With vice I hold the mike device*
> *With force I keep it away of course*
> *And I'm keepin' you from sleepin'*
> *And on the stage I rage*
> *And I'm rollin'*
> *To the poor, I pour it on in metaphors*
> *Not bluffin', it's nothing we ain't did before.*

Even rappers whose work does not reveal an explicit effort to engage in a political critique of mainstream society often perform the hypermasculine role of the black brute that frightens white America (Perry 28–29). Imani Perry links this role to a legacy of resistant performances in which black folks have found ways to side-step the rules that regulate social relations (29). Perry also locates the practice of exploiting stereotypes within the context of the black literary tradition, in which language, storytelling, and especially metaphor enable transcendence (64). The invocation of the black brute in the form of the thug or gangsta is a key example of how rappers appropriate and exploit demonized and pathologized constructions of blackness and black men and use them to enact a form of black empowerment that operates through white America's fear. Although such performances do not undermine the system of capitalist exploitation, they turn the manipulation of stereotypes through image and metaphor into empowering acts that become items for consumption (Perry 64, 48).

Other critics, such as Tricia Rose, locate rap within performative traditions, including slave dances, blues lyrics, jazz, Mardi Gras parades, and Jamaican patois, that combine pleasure with ingenious and frequently disguised critiques of the powerful. Rose writes,

> Under social conditions in which sustained frontal attacks on powerful groups are strategically unwise or successfully contained, oppressed people use language, dance, and music to mock those in power, express rage, and produce fantasies of subversion. . . . These cultural responses to oppression are not safety valves that protect and sustain the machines of oppression. Quite to the contrary, these dances, languages, and musics produce communal bases of knowledge about social conditions, communal interpretations of them and quite often serve as the cultural glue that fosters communal resistance. (99–100)

In the antebellum United States, for example, the use of drums raised the fear and ire of many slaveholders to the point that talking drums were frequently banned on plantations for fear that slaves might use them to generate and communicate insurrection (G. Jones 91; Webber 217). John Miller Chernoff explains in *African Rhythm and African Sensibility: Aesthetics and Social Action in African Musical Idioms* that "in traditional African music, [drum] rhythms themselves are a specific text. When the earliest European travelers described drum-signaling between villages, they assumed that the beating was a code. In reality, the drums actually speak the language of the tribe" (75). Patricia Washington and Lynda Dixon Shaver point to similarities between rap music and the blues when they note that both genres are primarily verse and secondarily music, both evolve from an African American oral tradition, and both describe "pain, struggle, and survival despite periods of hopelessness" (167).

So too, jazz, which represents one of the most important U.S. cultural contributions to the world, invoked antagonistic and fear-driven reactions in the 1920s for many of the same reasons that rap does now. Kathy Ogren, in *The Jazz Revolution: Twenties America and the Meaning of Jazz* (1989), reminds us that jazz was greeted with both criticism and praise. Its worst critics "dismissed it as noise" and deprecated its lower-class black origins, while jazz fans, in contrast, considered the music both "exciting entertainment" and "an antidote for repressive industrial society" (7). Indeed, Ogren contends, "the circumstances under which it was performed embodied social change. . . . Americans shared a common perception that jazz had transforming qualities that could last beyond the time of a song and the space of a cabaret act. For many Americans, to argue about jazz was to argue about the nature of change itself" (6–7). Gayl Jones makes a similar argument when she cites Kimberly Benston's claim that "jazz music engages European-American culture in a revolt" that threatens "Western history and civilization" and posits that perhaps the "Western artist *should* legitimately hear and respond to [jazz] as a battle" (47). And Thaddeus Russell, in "Is Rap Tomorrow's Jazz?," cites early claims that jazz was "killing . . . people," driving others insane, and causing others to lose their religion (1). Jazz also was maligned on the grounds that it was "an impediment to integration" (2). The campaign against jazz, as is so often the case with the campaign against rap, was compelled in part by the fact that it departed "from the norms of 'respectable' culture" (2). Yet precisely this departure ultimately led to jazz's distinguished place in American and world culture. That whites have always viewed black folks and cultural productions with disdain seems to have escaped the observations of rap's opponents. Just as civil rights leaders denounced jazz as antithetical to the struggle for full citizenship, so too contemporary black leaders such as Jesse Jackson and Cornel West claim that "music companies and rappers made it easy for whites to 'view black bodies and black souls as less moral, over-sexed and less intelligent'" (Russell 2). The connection that they fail to articulate is that the fear-driven prohibitions against the use of the talking drums, the form and nature of the blues, and resistance to both the form and content of jazz are replicated in today's debates about and responses to rap music. The twin notions persist that the genesis of criminality and violence coincided with that of rap and that black males are responsible for such problems. To be sure, the ways in which rap artists have both flaunted for profit and challenged the criminalized image of the black male in American culture have not by any means been entirely (or at times at all) progressive. Yet the debates that surround rap clearly demonstrate that the genre's creative manipulation, reclamation, and reinterpretation of injurious language and images previously controlled and manipulated by white America have struck a familiar nerve.

It is important to distinguish between the images of black men that circulate through rap and those that come to us through news broadcasts. As Perry argues, a difference exists between a person who reacts with violent rage in response to the conditions in which he (or she) lives and one who performs such rage with an eye toward enlightening others about its underlying causes and effects (125). Such a distinction, however, is contingent on an audience's willingness and ability to read the performance of black criminality—regardless of whether this performance seems intended as a critique—as evidence of persistent racial and class inequities in the United States and as a product of their brutal effects. In this regard, Perry rightly

> rejects a politics of respectability with regard to hip hop that implicitly says, "look at how white people are seeing us," or, "look at how this facilitates racism," because there is no need to facilitate it. Even when the vast majority of our public representation showed the clean-cut, straitlaced African American, the image of the black brute did not disappear. Also, in hip hop, the double voice resides in the fact that this character who is so easily cast into white night terror fantasies, also says something complex about his psychology, emotions, and life. One wonders if a white male listener hears it. (125–26)

To fully appreciate what some rappers do or try to do requires a departure from evaluative guidelines that seek clear evidence that political critique is or is not present. Such guidelines are contrary to grasping how rap is situated vis-à-vis blackness and whiteness and how it departs from other black artists' efforts to negate "the construction of blackness as demonic or depraved" (Perry 47). These guidelines provide little in the way of insight into the politics of rap because the hip-hop generation simultaneously opposes and revels in the role of Other into which black men are cast. Perry defines this positioning as "a radical commitment to otherness, which confounds those ... whose political standing comes out of either a civil rights or black power tradition" (47). What Perry identifies as a "radical commitment to otherness" is reflected in the recursion of and the response to the image of the black brute in rap (47).

As I alluded earlier, the return of the black brute transforms the racial house, or prison writ large, into a haunted space. The hysteria that defines antirap debates is driven not only by the return of the black brute image in rap but also by the fact that the figure has returned with a voice. The black brute who speaks poses a threat to the infrastructure of his own containment. The fear and antagonism the figure's voice inspires in some sectors of white America are symptomatic of what Rinaldo Walcott characterizes as the unresolved cultural trauma that is a product of America's violent history ("Images"). Although the middle passage is the birth site of such trauma, lynching and police brutality are among the residual effects of white America's refusal to revisit or fear of revisiting psychic sites of trauma. Such refusal, reluctance, and/or fear forestalls understanding how whites and blacks have been situated as victims, victimizers, or heroic figures within such loci (Walcott, "Images"). The black brute's return in rap narratives and rappers' personas may be read as an effort on the part of young black men to resolve a conscious or unconscious but nonetheless painful identification with a history of black male victimage that complicates the celebration of the black male as a heroic survivor of and participant in the struggle for full citizenship. So too, white America's refusal to hear what the men behind the masks are trying to articulate indicates that it has not acknowledged, let alone dealt with, the lingering effects of the evildoing through which whiteness has repeatedly asserted its power (Walcott, "Pedagogy" 135–37). Vehement, uncritical opposition to rap is but one place in which we are or ought to be reminded that those who do not put their dead to rest are doomed to be haunted by the myriad ways in which traumatic histories return (Walcott, "Images"). The residue of such trauma and violence inhabits the figure of the black brute in its recursive appearances in vernacular forms such as rap. Uncritical opposition to rap reveals the lingering effects of cultural trauma that are played out in white America's fraught relationship with rap music generally and with the figure of the black brute specifically (Walcott, "Struggle" 138).

The recursion of the black brute recalls not only the marked and commodified slave's body but also the spectacle and violation of the lynched body. The return of the black brute in rap raises the specter of racialized and sexualized violence that governed the relationships between white and black men both prior to emancipation and during the Jim Crow era. The specter of the black brute recalls the trauma wrought by both the imagined figurations of violence and the literal violence that defined the axis around which turned and around which were negotiated the practices that governed how black and white men were to behave and thus their relationships to each other. On the one hand, the hysteria and furor around the production and consumption of rap forces into view white America's deeply embedded fear of the black male Other. On the other hand, black men's invocation of the "haunt" in rap lyrics and their performative inhabitations of the black brute figure are indicative of their conflicted positioning "within late modern capitalist behavior-orienting practices" (Walcott, "Struggle" 139–40).

The black brute, then, is a "symbolic formation . . . of black manhood and the hauntological conditions of black manhood in the postslavery and postmodern era" (Walcott, "Struggle" 140). In his "hauntological" approach to the many formations of black masculinities, Walcott addresses the many forms that circulated within a range of representational realms in the 1990s. He notes the extent to which such apparatuses, and in particular gangsta rap, reveal the "consolidation of a hard black masculinity [that] sits alongside the 'endangered black man' thesis" (142). The irony is that "if black men are indeed 'the hardest' of the 'hard,' they also seem to be the easiest victims in North Atlantic society—that's the discourse of endangered" (143). Walcott contends further that this "irony of hard, yet victim and therefore endangered, flashes up . . . because black men suffer from the crises of the undermining of patriarchy in postliberation society in ways that continually reference the haunting of slavery" as well as the violence of Jim Crow (143). The return of the black brute in the form of a subject who speaks—often of his own death or the deaths of other black men—provides a striking example of the extent to which "Black masculinities are frequently tied to an axis of life and death" (143). Indeed, Walcott goes so far as to argue that representations of and a seeming obsession with black male deaths in 1990s rap not only traversed the divide between heterosexuality and homosexuality but also signified a form of necrophilic desire. This desire is articulated in the discursive practice of "[f]ucking the dead in hip hop," which plays itself out in the articulation of "revenge fantasies" or elegies of "homeboy love" in addition to the seemingly "erotic charge that [narratives about] taking another's life" seem to carry (144). The hardness of this configuration of black manhood is the element that is at stake in homoerotic, necrophilic engagements depending on whether one is the hard one or the endangered black man (the pussy) in the scenario ("Struggle" 140–44).

The queer position in which Walcott locates the black male rapper and the hardness that is embodied in the figure of the black brute recall the homoeroticism of the ritualized lynchings of black men. As I discussed in chapter 2, lynching rituals enabled white men to appear hard while satisfying their desire to take the hard black brute into themselves through touch, taste, and smell. The compensatory act of emasculating the signifier of hardness from the dead or dying black male body was an act of transference, a refusal to remain a pussy in the violently homoerotic, necrophilic encounter. The compensatory act of castration was the sign of the white lyncher's disavowal of his own relative softness. Thus, the return of the hard black brute in rap narratives and rappers' personas "raises the specter of slavery and postslavery permutations of the exploitation of black male bodies given release in service of capital" or white male desire (Walcott, "Struggle" 147). In Walcott's scenario, we see again how the black brute is perceived and received in familiar ways: with wonder (signified by the desire to consume the hardness of the black male) and ridicule (signified by the conflicting desire to destroy his ability to speak, to circulate, and to reproduce himself). The black brute's uninvited return in the spectacularly loud for(u)m of rap brings up the legacy of type and violence in a differently configured form through which he demands that white America confront the history and its legacy that his presence signifies.

Thus, the haunting return of the black brute is usefully read in relation to Houston A. Baker Jr.'s discussion of early scenes of American violence in which black male figures had no opportunity to speak. In "Scene . . . Not Heard," Baker discusses the challenges that African Americans have faced in their struggles to affect or inflect hegemonic versions of history with their voices and their images. Baker's comparison of rap with the African American slave narrative offers astute insight into the struggles for interpretive and discursive power that revolve around the signifier of the black brute. Baker characterizes the slave narrative as a "classic site of what might be called the 'scene of violence' in American discourse" (38). According to Baker, this scene has played itself out in an infinite number of forms in American history, but "in slave narratives and Afro-American history in general, it shapes itself according to a unique logic of sound and silence, agency and powerlessness" (38). Playing on the notion of being seen but not heard, Baker argues that the slave narrative's efficacy was compromised by readers' refusal to interpret the narrative as a "lyrical repudiation of the master's exclusive right to meaningful being in the world" (41). The narratives' effect was limited by the fact that white readers had the exclusive say regarding the narratives' meaning. Such prerogative rendered slave narratives and their authors scenic but not audible. Baker associates such "scening" with the literal objectification and silencing of black men today. He contends that the term *scening* still accurately describes white America's efforts to construct and to control the images and voices of black men (Baker 38–44). The return of the black brute, then, in a form that demands to be heard and not just scene exemplifies what Alice Walker implies when she argues that ancestors' signatures are made clear in more than the biological lives of black folks today ("In Search" 243).

Some sectors of white America have attempted to claim similar entitlement to interpretive prerogatives of rap lyrics, rap artists' personas, and their agendas. The resultant tension provides evidence for Rose's claim that "[r]ap music, more than any other form of black cultural expression, articulates the chasm between black urban lived experience and dominant, 'legitimate' . . . ideologies regarding equal opportunity and racial inequality" (102). The chasm to which Rose refers might also usefully be imagined as a frontierlike space. Although it marks the political, ideological, social, and economic divides in the United States, it also represents a site where we can grapple with the meaning of some of the most creative, troubling, complex, and controversial discussions and representations of black men and the black male experience that we have seen to date. The notion of a frontier captures better than that of a chasm the possibilities inherent in the divide to which Rose calls our attention. Whereas, according to *Webster's Third New International Dictionary of the English Language* (1981), a chasm marks an "irreconcilable division, separation, or difference," a frontier connotes a "new or relatively unexploited field

that offers scope for large exploitative or developmental activity." The notion of a
frontier seems a more apt way to characterize the tension-fraught cultural spaces
within which white America and blacks manage and contest their relationships to
one another and their places in the various U.S. hierarchies.

James C. Scott, in *Domination and the Arts of Resistance: Hidden Transcripts*
(1990), claims that the activities that take shape within such spaces structure "a zone
of constant struggle between dominant and subordinate" (14). Out of these sites
may arise hidden transcripts, which have two components: first, they are specific to
particular social sites; second, they may include speech acts as well as gestures and
practices "that confirm, contradict, or inflect what appears in the public transcript"
(14, 4). Rap produces and responds to the tensions that such spaces create. It also
furthers black men's efforts to speak about, speak to, and speak against the various
means by which the prison writ large is structured and supported. Cultural critics
share the onus for hearing and helping others to hear those voices as a way of coun-
tering the silencing effect of uncritical responses to rap music and rap artists that
overlook, dismiss, misunderstand, or misrepresent the resistant characteristics of
rap. We need to find ways to make sense of rap artists' perspectives on what it means
to be black and male in the United States and thereby to interrupt the constancy
of the legacy of type that is worried each time black men insist on their right to be
heard rather than relegated to a scripted role in the scene of American violence.

Michel Foucault's juxtaposition of genealogy with what he terms "effective history" is usefully applied as a means to that end. Genealogy, Foucault explains, "is
gray, meticulous, and patiently documentary" ("Nietzsche" 139). Its role is to record
histories "of morals, ideals, and metaphysical concepts" and "the concept of liberty
or of the ascetic life" ("Nietzsche" 152) in ways that genealogical records come to be
viewed as acceptable representations of events. The limitation of such representations stems from their static, tangible nature, which can never adequately capture
dynamic, mutable, and intangible conceptualizations and experiences. Rather, they
compensate by forcing multiplicities into inadequately nuanced forms. In contrast, an effective history refuses the "certainty of absolutes" by representing events
in ways that liberate their "divergence and marginal elements" ("Nietzsche" 153).
As Foucault puts it, these types of representations function as effective histories by
introducing discontinuity into systems, dividing emotions, dramatizing instincts,
multiplying bodies, and setting them against themselves ("Nietzsche" 152–54). An
effective history draws nuances and uncertainties out of their hiding places and
creates opportunities to reverse "relationship[s] of forces," to usurp power, and to
appropriate words and images and turn them against those who had previously
used them in injurious ways ("Nietzsche" 154). Effective historians reconfigure

historical narratives centered on bodies that have been imprinted and/or destroyed by, among other things, traditional history's "grand view," which prioritizes distance rather than proximity to individual narratives and the people who embody them. In contrast, effective histories (re)produce dominant narratives and reshape events with an eye toward inverting power relations, if only temporarily, by exposing, evading, and/or subverting the incongruous narratives on which social hierarchies are founded and maintained. Effective historians merge historical experiences of physical and social bodies into narratives that are altered by more recent experiences and perspectives. They therefore thrive in frontier spaces such as that which exists between the lived experiences of black men and hegemonic views of them and do so by forcing conflicting representations into an ongoing contest (Fiske, "Black Bodies" 187–89).

Rap's frequent emphases on the minute and often contradictory details of hegemonic discourses, its aggressive inversion of those discourses, and its use of African American autobiographical and historical narratives situate the genre uniquely to interfere with traditional history's grand view, which is necessary to uphold the supporting logic of American racism and its effects. Although it is important not to lose sight of the ways that the rap industry enables young black men to profit from complicity in their oppression, it is equally important to promote hearings for rap artists whose artistic work merits critical analysis and/or resists co-optation by the keepers of public transcripts who would use them to further the project of constructing black males as delinquents rather than politically astute raptivists. [1] A number of rap artists, including Ice Cube and Tupac Shakur, represent excellent examples of 1990s rappers whose work situated them as effective historians. They employed their work to call attention to, to critique, and to reconfigure the relationships between the points of view of panoptic eye(s) and those of black men. They articulated such perspectives through language and images and body and song, engaging in a battle in which nothing less than the physical and psychic freedom of black men is at stake. Although the work of all rappers merits such consideration—although of course some materials take us further than others—I want to discuss the ways in which each invokes the black brute in ways that enter into conflict and conversation with the transcripts and territories from which black men's voices are so frequently excluded.

Rap's deep bass sounds, profanity, references to violence, and explicit—often angry—calls for change bring to the forefront white America's fear of black males, whom it associates with the black brute. Lindon Barrett notes one of the reasons that the black brute is such a haunting presence: "[W]hen black people in large numbers have become relatively assertive in their pursuit of a fair share of the good things in life ... white people have proved themselves ready for violence" to the extent that many "resist fully imagining that those 'fans' of gangsta rap 'rooted in the ghetto' are acutely aware of 'another [way of] life' and, what is more, are often fully cognizant of their violent, though 'reasoned' disbarment from it" ("Dead Men" 312). The right to control, to represent, to define, to use, and to abuse black men is at stake in the often deadly battle in which the police, critics, politicians, moralists, and rap artists are engaged. Ice Cube's "Who Got the Camera?," a track from his 1992 CD *The Predator*, captures the potentially fatal effects of scenes of violence in which black men have been and continue to be violated and silenced. "Who Got the Camera?" opens with a collage of voices intended to represent both white and black speakers. A female dispatcher's voice opens the song with the repeated phrase, "See if there's a black and white that can do a traffic light." The dispatcher's voice repeats the phrase increasingly quickly until the words blur together and it sounds as though she is asking, "See if there's a black and white that can do a drive-by." The lyrical shift produced by the technologically manipulated dispatcher's voice signifies on the ways in which the anticrime rhetoric masks racist, often homicidal agendas aimed at black males. That is, the shift inverts the tendency to define drive-by shootings as crimes associated with black male delinquents. In this way, Ice Cube links the notion of a drive-by to actions of police brutality that represent institutionally prescribed and premeditated patterns of aggressive behavior toward black males. This move unmasks the injurious language usually used against black men and redirects it so that its effects more precisely locate the respective roles of police and black men in scenes of violence.

"Who Got the Camera?" goes on to relate the story of a black man who is pulled over by the police after doing a U-turn on the grounds that there "was a robbery and the nigger looked just like you." The narrator relates his subsequent beating by the officers, whose agenda Ice Cube combines with the narrator's in the chorus:

> *Oh please, oh please, oh please, just gimme just one more hit*
> *Oh please, oh please, just gimme just one more hit*
> *Who got the camera?*

He also notes that the presence of a crowd of witnesses offers him little in the way of protection unless one of them has a camera on hand to record the events. In the narrator's story, the presence of witnesses seems to have a minimal effect on the outcome of the beating. Indeed, he feels quite certain that if "the crowd weren't around they would've shot me." By invoking the relative importance of a camera compared to a crowd of presumably African American witnesses, Ice Cube addresses the irony of the vast impact of the Rodney King case. As George Church put it in the 11 May 1992 issue of *Time*,

> To an extent that whites can barely even imagine–because it so rarely happens to them–police brutality to many blacks is an ever present threat to their bodies and lives.
>
> Indeed, few things more vividly illustrate the extent to which whites and blacks live in different worlds than their reactions to police brutality. A white who was sickened by the tape of King's beating would probably have said to himself something like, Look what they're doing to that poor guy. A black would be almost sure to say, My God, that could be me. . . .
>
> [In the Rodney King case], many blacks apparently hoped, it would be different. After all, this was not merely the word of a black with an arrest record against the word of one or more cops: this time there was hard evidence in the form of a tape on which the jurors, like hundreds of millions of TV viewers around the world, could actually see the beating. (25–26)[2]

Black men, in other words, are well aware of the very real possibility that they will be victims of police brutality at least once during their lifetimes and that there is not likely to be anyone with a camera rolling.[3] Another very real possibility also exists: police officers who perpetrate such violence may never be held accountable for their actions.[4] "Who Got the Camera?" therefore makes a succinct point about the value—or lack thereof—assigned to African American autobiographical accounts in the absence of a video text.[5]

One would think that it would be considerably more difficult (though, as the King case proved, far from impossible) to make a video fit the parameters of the public transcript. Yet Elizabeth Alexander, in "'Can You Be BLACK and Look at This?': Reading the Rodney King Video(s)," notes the ways that the video representation of the King beating was manipulated in the courtroom to support the Los Angeles Police Department's version of the events that transpired the night of the beating. Her description of the language used to describe Rodney King coheres with that employed in a review of a rap concert that Rose discusses and that I mentioned earlier in this chapter. According to Alexander, in the first trial in Simi Valley, "a language of black male bestiality and hypervirility, along with myths of drug abuse and 'superhuman strength,' was deployed" (93). She elaborates, "The defense in the Simi Valley trial employed a familiar language of black bestiality to construct Rodney King as a threat to the officers. The lawyers also slowed down the famous videotape so that it no longer existed in 'real time' but rather in a slow dance of stylized movement that could as easily be read as self-defense as a threat. There was neither the sound of falling blows nor screams from King or from witnesses on the slowed-down tape" (109).⁶ The closing lines of "Who Got the Camera?" offer a similar critique of the ways that transcripts of African American experience are at risk of distortion when whites take advantage of their prerogative to publicly interpret such transcripts:

> Fuckin' police gettin' badder
> But if I had a camera the shit wouldn't matter.
> Y'all done did it this time, uh
> Who the fuck got my nine

On the one hand, Ice Cube acknowledges the importance of the video recording in the King case—almost certainly the only reason that the officers were asked to explain, let alone held accountable for, their actions. On the other hand, the agents of the public transcript manipulated the video text in the criminal justice system and in the media to reinforce the image of African American males as dangerous and threatening brutes. Their manipulation compromised the video's potential to bridge the gap between the African American lived experience and "ideologies regarding equal opportunity and racial inequality" (Rose 102) to which I referred at the beginning of this chapter. As George Cunningham claims, "the present[,] with its linear and progressive possibilities," coexists with recursive moments that tell us who we are on the basis of past events. In the case of black men, Cunningham argues, such recursive moments are almost always figured as violated bodies (134). It makes sense, then, when Ice Cube suggests in the closing lines of the song that, like it or not, a gun may offer black men a more reliable form of insurance against the very real risk that they will at some point be the victim of police brutality. However, in "Who Got the Camera?," Ice Cube situates a black man's firsthand account of a violent incident in place of the official (white) representation of it. In so doing, Ice Cube restores hermeneutic power to the black male autobiographical subject in his song and provides him with a voice and a means of escape from the scene of American racial violence (Baker 38). In "Who Got the Camera?," then, the black brute returns on or in the ultimate figure of masculine authority—the white cop. Through Ice Cube's performance of an autobiographical account, the accosted black subject enters the official body/narrative and asserts the hard truth about routine violations of black men's bodies. This penetration, however, constitutes an unwelcome denial of the sanctuary that unspeakable acts of violence have historically secured.

Although Ice Cube's track is a relatively straightforward example of a narrative of black men's encounters with the police, Tupac Shakur's efforts to redefine and reclaim the persona of the black brute were anything but straightforward. Whereas I have discussed but one example from Ice Cube's oeuvre, the rest of this chapter takes a more comprehensive look at the complex ways in which Tupac constructed a forum for the black brute's return on his body. Tupac, who was shot and killed in Las Vegas in September 1996, employed the genre and his body to redeem the figure of the black brute, to rescue the figure from a site of victimization, and to call for change within the prison writ large. Yet Tupac's tattooed body, music, and death have been misrepresented as at best forms of regressive activism and at worst misguided acts of youthful rebellion. This is not to suggest that Tupac's behavior did not at times warrant such criticism. He certainly had at least his fair share of legal problems. In 1992, he was involved in a fight in which a stray bullet killed a six-year-old boy. In 1993, he was charged with but later acquitted of shooting at two off-duty police officers. And in 1995 he served eight months in prison on Rikers Island after being convicted of two counts of sexual abuse involving a female fan in a Manhattan hotel room in 1993 (F. Alexander and Cuda 54). It is important that, as critics, we try to prevent our engagements with his artistic projects from being tainted by our knowledge and feelings about his personal shortcomings, which often seemed to contradict his political vision. Those who view Tupac and his work in that light err by falling prey to the assumption that "what these wayward citizens require to extricate themselves from their inevitably violent lives and circumstances is an epiphanic moment in which they acknowledge the distinction between an ill-chosen, unappealing self-performance and a more authentic self-performance deferred, often fatefully, by the other" (Barrett, "Dead Men" 313). Proponents of such views include Mumia Abu-Jamal, political prisoner and author of books and essays concerning the containment of black men in the United States. Abu-Jamal characterizes Tupac's lifestyle and art as regressive forms of activism that signaled the movement from "revolutionary to thug . . . in one generation." Abu-Jamal views Tupac's death as a lost opportunity to "influence millions to go toward a revolutionary, as opposed to a materialistic, 'gangsta' direction." Similarly, the founder of Def Jam Records, Russell Simmons, attributes Tupac's death to misguided, youthful rebellion and claims that it "was just that rebelliousness for the sake of it, that wild Rock n' Roll side of him that did this" (F. Williams 104). Darrell Dawsey concurs with Simmons, suggesting that "perhaps if the brother had chilled a bit more, he would have lived a bit longer" (38).

In contrast to critics such as Abu-Jamal, Simmons, and Dawsey, Greg Tate's understanding of black genius might have been written with Tupac in mind. Indeed, Tate captures precisely the nature and results of effective histories generally and the legacy of Tupac's work specifically, stating, "To live is to defy the logic that all we're supposed to do is stay black and die. To leave in your wake artistic legacies, documents, abstract bodies of work and knowledge, conceptual paradigms, aesthetic philosophies and methodologies, signature styles, mythic identities, is to increase confusion exponentially" ("He" 116–17). Unfortunately, like the readers of slave narratives to whom Baker refers, Tupac's critics and many of his fans often failed to consider how Tupac attempted to recontextualize historical and stereotypical representations of the thug and the notion of thug life. In fact, Tupac defied the logic that is supposed to dominate the curriculum vitae[7] of a young black male by using his music and his tattoos to imagine the criminalized young black male as a revolutionary figure, a liberator, and a martyr modeled on the image of a black Jesus, whom Tupac saw as a saint for thugs and gangstas.[8] If Tupac is ever to be laid to rest, it is critical that we hear him by considering his body, his work, and his death vis-à-vis the frontier space and the sacred and secular contexts in which he clearly located himself. Regrettably, the ways in which and the degree to which Tupac situated himself betwixt, between, and across these contexts have received insufficient critical attention. Tupac's political concerns and the forms of representation through which he articulated them point to his sophisticated understanding of the relationships between the structure of the prison writ large, racial and class oppression, political activism, thug life, and rap music. Yet Dan Quayle once declared with respect to Tupac's 1991 CD *2Pacalypse Now*, "There is absolutely no reason for a record like this to be published. . . . It has no place in our society" ("Pac's Theme," *Strictly for My N.I.G.G.A.Z.*). Quayle's view of Tupac's work— and, by logical extension, of Tupac himself—represents just one of an extensive list of dismissals that convinced Tupac that for him and for those about whom he cared most there was to be no room at any American inn.

Tupac grew up living the life of an impoverished, urban nomad for whom his mother, former Black Panther Afeni Shakur, did her best to provide a religious foundation, an education, and an understanding of the everyday issues with which he, as a black male, would have to contend. As Tupac puts it in "Souljah's Revenge," a track on *Strictly for My N.I.G.G.A.Z.*,

> Momma told me "Don't let 'em fade me.
> . . . Don't let 'em make ya crazy."
> Game is what she gave me.

Given his background, the ten-year-old Tupac's response when the Reverend Herbert Daughtry of the House of the Lord Church in Brooklyn asked the boy what he wanted to be when he grew up is not surprising: "I'm gonna be a revolutionary" (bandele 29). In keeping with his childhood ambition, Tupac described himself as a "hybrid cross of 'a black panther and a street hustler'" known and criticized for his glorification of thug life, for his criminal record, for surviving acts of violence, for his tattoos, and of course for the form and content of his music (Mitchell-Bray 103). Daughtry seems to have been correct when he suggested at a memorial service for Tupac that his early aspirations toward revolution might explain the course of his life (A. White 2). But to acquire a better understanding of Tupac's life, critics must engage in the work of effective historians, which entails both reread-ing texts that white America constructs and uses to perpetuate images of black males as criminals and, in Tupac's case, drawing on his music and tattoos to grasp what he attempted to articulate in response to such representations. Because he is no longer with us, it is especially important to try to hear what he so diligently endeavored to convey through the many scenes in which he was implicated and in which he sought room to speak.

Marsha Mitchell-Bray argues that Tupac's image as a thug overshadowed what she terms his "secondary role[s] of intellectual, philosopher, [and] social activist" (103). She attributes the dominance of his thug image to a lack of respect among young black men for "intelligence, philosophical insight, social activism or formal training, of which Shakur had an abundance" (103). In other circles, the emphasis on Tupac's thug image to the exclusion of the other components of his persona constituted a way of silencing him. Critics' responses to his thug image deflected attention away from the political and aesthetic value of his work and from his attempts to recontextualize the notion of thug life. Whereas Tupac has been criti-cized for failing to recognize and to respect the line between art and life, theory and practice, those lines may have been clearer to Tupac than to anyone.[9] As Tupac accurately predicted, citing earlier revolutionaries such as Malcolm X, "I'm going to die in violence. . . . All good niggers, all the niggers who change the world, die in violence. They don't die in regular ways. Motherfuckers come take their lives" (qtd. in Shaw 173). That clarity of vision notwithstanding, it seems apparent that Tupac considered the risks of crossing those lines to be worth taking given all that lies at stake if one respects them. As Sharon Holland suggests, "Black mas-culinity becomes meaningful, at least theoretically, when it is able to articulate for the culture a participatory system of mourning for us all" (388). In Tupac's case, his "claim to the truth of [his] *eventual* death" is supported by the fact that "statistically, being black and male means that he will die before he lives" (Holland 388–89). Nonetheless, as he once put it, "I'm not on no bullshit or anything, I'm gonna change the rules in this rap game. . . . I'ma shake up the whole Congress" (D. Smith T6). Tupac capitalized on the rap game by exploiting its potential as a political arena in which it was possible, appropriate, and—in Tupac's eyes—essential to disrupt the sanctity of the cultural, legal, and ideological paradigms that structure a prison writ large for black men.

Notwithstanding the risks, Tupac undertook the work of an effective historian by producing narratives of events about which he hoped that his audiences would theorize by reading them "through their diverse mediations" (Spillers 459). Tupac's death was indisputably a tragedy. However, rather than reading his death as evidence of the pathology of thug life, critical energy is more productively invested in reading and rereading the bodies of work that he produced. In particular, we need to better hear how and why he identified thug life as a site of integrity and activism. To that end, I offer a reading that I hope will not constitute an abuse of my interpretive prerogative and will help reconcile what are mistakenly assumed to be contradictions between Tupac's invocation of and devotion to thug life and his closely related invocation of and improvisation on three of the most sacred texts and figures in western culture—the Bible, Moses, and Jesus Christ. One of the most interesting but unrecognized acts of political imagination involving Exodus structures the relationship between Tupac's tattoos and his resistant praxis.

Tupac's comparison of himself and other black men who hustle to Jesus and Moses is also in keeping with an African American worldview that does not recognize a dichotomy between the sacred and the secular. As Geneva Smitherman explains, "[W]hile the secular style might be considered the primary domain of the street, and the sacred that of the church, no sharp dichotomy exists, but [rather there is] a kind of sacred-secular circular continuum" (93). Smitherman notes that the "most striking example of this merging of sacred and secular styles is in the area of black music, where lyrics, musical scores, and singers themselves easily float in and out of both worlds" (93). She emphasizes that "the traditional black church's other-worldly orientation is balanced by coping strategies for *this* world. And, like the traditional African God, the black American God is viewed not only as Someone Who dwells on High but One Who also inhabits this mundane earthly world" (92). That continuum makes Tupac's claim that "I've been blessed by God, and God walks with me" and his description of God as "a nigga that knows where I'm coming from" seem less at odds with thug life as he understood it (D. Smith T7).[10]

Wilson Jeremiah Moses, in *Black Messiahs and Uncle Toms: Social and Literary Manipulations of a Religious Myth* (1993), claims that "old prophetic traditions no longer occupy a central position in Afro-American life" (15). Moses links the absence of such traditions to the erosion of folk traditions, illusions, and values wrought by African Americans' inundation in postindustrial culture (15). The extent to which Tupac's work is underwritten by intertexts of African American religious and cultural traditions generally and the messianic tradition specifically suggests that their erosion is by no means complete. Indeed, as Moses asserts, one of the most important functions of the African American messianic tradition is to reconcile the contradictory experiences of "oppression by American social institutions, and immersion in the mainstream of American messianic culture. Ironically, it represents both a rejection of white America and a participation in one of its most sacred traditions" (14). Tupac's invocation of the Bible, Moses, and Jesus Christ functions similarly in that the rap artist's work draws its resonance from this sacred tradition as it critiques the effects of racist ideologies and practices.

Accordingly, I locate Tupac's body and/of work within the conceptual framework of typology that Theophus Smith, in *Conjuring Culture: Biblical Formations of Black America* (1994), defines as "the hermeneutic (interpretive) tradition that links biblical types or figures to postbiblical persons, places, and events" (55). On many occasions, Tupac declared his allegiance and compared himself to a black Jesus, defined as a saint for thugs and gangstas, whom Tupac distinguished from killers and rapists (D. Smith T7). In an interview with *Vibe*, for example, he claimed, "I got shot five times and I got crucified in the media. And I walked through with the thorns on, and I had shit thrown on me, and I had the word thief at the top. . . . I'm not saying I'm Jesus, but I'm saying we go through that type of thing every day. We don't part the Red Sea, but we walk through the 'hood without getting shot. We don't turn water to wine, but we turn dope fiends and dope heads into productive citizens of society. We turn words into money—what greater gift can there be? . . . I believe God blesses those that hustle" (*Tupac Shakur* 98). Tupac's alignment of himself with a black Christ coheres with his claim that his work would land him "on the cross . . . crucified for keeping it real" (D. Smith T7). His comparison of the struggles of young black males to the feats and deeds of Moses also falls within a long history of African American identification with and bias toward the stories of the Old Testament.

Despite the frequency with which slave narratives include scathing indictments of the use of Christianity to justify the enslavement of African Americans, the Bible, especially the Book of Exodus, played a fundamental role in shaping how slaves and ex-slaves configured freedom in their lives, their culture, their literature, and their music. As Theophus Smith argues, the significance of the Exodus figure tended to be the inverse of what it was for Puritans. For white, European Christians, America signified a promised land; African Americans, in contrast, saw and experienced America as another Egypt and associated themselves with the Hebrew slaves held in bondage under the pharaoh. Smith makes the point that the "slaves' inverse identification evinces an improvisational propensity . . . for variations and transformations of the available Euro-Christian materials and resources" (64). Accordingly, the exodus of the Hebrew slaves from Egypt provided African Americans with a "figural vision of . . . emancipation" that became "the paradigm for subsequent strategies and acts of political imagination" (63). According to Smith, "almost all blacks in America—past and present—have identified Egypt with America, Pharaoh and the Egyptians with white slaveholders and subsequent racists, and blacks with the Israelite slaves" (71).[11] This Old Testament bias results in a tendency to draw Jesus (who was crucified after being found guilty of treason) into an Old Testament context in which he is conflated with Moses (whom God chose to deliver the Hebrews even though he had murdered an Egyptian) into a single "*ideal* of all that is high, and noble, and perfect, in man" (35).[12]

Without a doubt, the industries and activities in which Tupac participated situated him on a twentieth-century auction block of sorts by exploiting both his blackness and his maleness as a valuable commodity. The tattoos with which Tupac framed his body were one means by which he improvised on the Exodus figure and positioned himself as a speaking subject on the continuum that stretches between a culture with which many people associate criminal behavior and all that is sacred in western culture. I employ the term *frame* to characterize the relationship between Tupac's tattoos, his body, and the identity that he uses both to produce. This notion of a frame is in keeping with Jean Comaroff's claim that the body itself functions as a "tangible frame of selfhood in individual and collective experience, providing a constellation of physical signs with the potential for signifying the relations of persons to their contexts" (qtd. in Steiner 431). Tupac employed tattoos as signs to adorn his social body; to render its surface "the common frontier of society, the social self, and the psychological individual"; and to function as a language through which "the drama of socialization is enacted" (Steiner 431). He used tattoos to signify on both past and present forms of containment as well as on bodily texts that bespeak suffering. He did so by richly inscribing his flesh with messages of resistance to being scene but not heard and with calls for what he foresaw as revolution. In this manner, he located himself within a tradition where human bodies have served as sites for the inscription of genealogical historical processes while using his body to articulate an effective history (S. White and White 126).

Hortense Spillers's distinction between body and flesh is useful in terms of understanding the relationships among containment, abuse, and resistance to which Tupac's tattoos speak. According to Spillers, the distinction between body and flesh is the central one between captive and liberated subject-positions. In that sense, before the "body" there is the "flesh," that zero degree of social conceptualization that does not escape concealment under the brush of discourse, of the reflexes of iconography. Even though the European hegemonies stole bodies—some of them female—out of West African communities in concert with the African "middleman," we regard this human social irreparability as high crimes against the *flesh*, as the person of African females and African males registered the wounding. If we think of the "flesh" as a primary narrative, then we mean its seared, divided, ripped-apartness, riveted to the ship's hold, fallen, or "escaped" overboard. (457)

What Spillers terms the flesh is what Shane White and Graham White discuss as the surface of black bodies on which in "freedom, as in slavery . . . the struggle between black and white was often cruelly etched, and on which the record of that struggle may be read." White and White cite as an example the story of an ex-slave named Sandie who mutilated his body and threatened to commit suicide in front of white witnesses who were attempting to return him to bondage after the burning of documents attesting to his freedom. The authors relate how, many years later, Sandie, by then a successful farmer renowned for his physical strength, still bore the signs of his struggle for freedom on his flesh (125–26). According to White and White, "Within a social context that denied blacks any kind of discursive access to the public world, we can sense Sandie's determination to control his own fate, to write his own script, as it were. . . . Given Sandie's inability to document his freedom by producing the lost emancipation papers, he was compelled, by the limitations faced by a free black in a slave society, to inscribe that freedom on his body, and in the most dramatic of ways" (126).[13] Although the inscriptions on Sandie's flesh were not audible per se, in important respects their longevity countered the erasure characteristic of genealogical histories. However, as Foucault contends, "The body manifests the stigmata of past experience and also gives rise to desires, failings, and errors. These elements may join in a body where they achieve a sudden expression, but as often, their encounter is an engagement in which they efface each other, where the body becomes the pretext of their insurmountable conflict" ("Nietzsche" 148). Tupac's intricately related tattoos and the varying degrees and types of attention afforded them situated his body as the site of a conflict of the sort that Foucault identifies.[14]

The largest of Tupac's tattoos were the thug life, which stretched across his abdomen, and the EXODUS 1811, which covered most of his upper back. Although Tupac's thug life tattoo was photographed frequently and has been mentioned

disparagingly by almost everyone who has written about him, the EXODUS 1811 tattoo was rarely photographed and, to my knowledge, has never been discussed. On
the one hand, it would seem obvious to attribute the lack of attention to the EXODUS
1811 tattoo to the fact that it was so rarely photographed. On the other hand, such
an explanation does not account for why photographers ignored it in the first
place, given its size and the fact that it was situated as prominently on Shakur's
body as the thug life tattoo. As Robert Rawdon Wilson asserts in "Tattoos: Play
and Interpretation," "Back tattoos are always especially striking. The area of skin
to be covered is larger than any other part of the body and permits more detailed,
integrated images. It is also a part of the body that the tattooed person cannot normally see. Hence back tattoos are literally designed for others to see. They are often
flagrant . . . but they are also the tattoos most likely to make aesthetic claims" (75).
The lack of attention given to the EXODUS 1811 tattoo is even more mystifying given
the rich nuances of its relationship to the thug life tattoo. By discussing Tupac's
thug life tattoo in isolation from both EXODUS 1811 and his music, critics confined
Tupac to the scene of American violence and obscured—indeed, erased—the evidence of his efforts to define, to advocate, and to engage in his method of theorizing the ways that black men live and die. He used his tattoos to bring into closer
proximity rap music, the hustling ethic that for him was inextricably linked to thug
life, his sense of his Christlike role as one both chosen and willing to bring about
change during his short time on earth, and the Judeo-Christian God's revolutionary approaches to social and political transformation. What seem at first glance to
be unrelated sacred and secular referents for each tattoo function together to free
Tupac's body from the texts of genealogical history by articulating resistance to the
notion that knowledge is anything more than perspective (Foucault, "Nietzsche"
153, 156). Both the tattoos and critics' responses to them (or lack thereof) make
sense in light of John Fiske's claim that visual texts (such as tattoos) and verbal
responses to such texts (such as those of both fans and opponents of rap) share
a complex relationship. That relationship is characterized by movement "up and
down the social and discursive hierarchies, as they oppose or endorse each other's way of knowing" (*Media Matters* 133). Tupac's tattoos denote one interstitial
locus at stake in what Foucault refers to as "the hazardous play of dominations"
("Nietzsche" 148). In Tupac's case, he reincarnates the black brute as a thug and
positions it at the crossroads of sacred and secular discourses.

The verse Exodus 18:11 is part of an elegy to God for liberating the Israelites
from slavery. The verse relates how God dealt with the Egyptians "in just that matter in which [the Egyptians] were presumptuous against" the children of Israel. The
Black Panther slogan, with which Tupac obviously would have been quite familiar,

"Defend our communities by any means necessary," might just as easily have been God's motto as he liberated the Hebrew slaves (Smitherman 83). Like God's eye-for-an-eye approach to effecting change, Tupac, in addition to turning his words into money, used his flesh and his rhymes to call attention to the ways in which whites have been presumptuous against blacks, to reassign blame accordingly, and to demand that people rethink their assumptions about the issues with which he was concerned but which he did not create. He did so by constructing an image of himself as a thug who was also a revolutionary, a martyr, and a saint—that is, a black Jesus who was willing to suffer so that others might lead better lives.

Tupac's critics, however, mistakenly and reductively interpret frequent references to thug life as his attempt to advocate criminal lifestyles as opposed to a hustling ethic. Michael Datcher, for example, suggests that when Tupac "scrawled thug life across his torso, he was writing a painful treatise on the limited possibilities of his life. A dissertation that he researched by imitating bullshit niggas masquerading as men who learned their ideas from bullshit niggas before them. thug life became his mantra. He repeated it each time he made a choice to ignore the brilliance that threatened to make him feel good about himself" (35). In one sense, Datcher was correct. Tupac, a frequent user of acronyms, claimed that thug life stood for "the hate you give little infants fucks everybody" (Dyson, "Holler" 115). He certainly had firsthand knowledge of the relationship between racial hatred and the social and economic implications for African American people. He queried the causes and consequences of being both poor and black in the United States in a posthumously released track, "I Wonder If Heaven Got a Ghetto," which appears on *RU Still Down [Remember Me]*. However, Tupac also envisioned and articulated a definition of *thug life* that exceeded the limits that critics imposed on its meaning. As Tupac asserts in "Pac's Theme," "I was raised in this society so there's no way/You can expect me to be a perfect person cuz I'm a do what I'm a do." Tupac's point is that if there is no place in Quayle's version of "our" society where Tupac and other young black male subjects can be heard and not scene, then alternative spaces must be forged. Ironically, Tupac's success in the industry meant that the much-maligned space in which he functioned enabled him to buy into—even though he chose not to—a Dan Quayle style of respectability. Rightly or wrongly, therefore, Tupac suggests that young black males living in the United States today often have little choice but to embrace the hustling ethic, to "get over" by whatever means necessary, sometimes in the manner in which others have been presumptuous against them. As one young fan of Snoop Dogg put it, "You gotta take what's yours. If you want to get out of the projects, which always there are people trying to keep you in, he's saying you gotta take that chance" (qtd. in M. Quinn 76). This fan implies that "violence might be one way out of the ghetto, since it is a form of violence which keeps you there" (M. Quinn 76). As Holland astutely argues, "thug life represents a coming back from the dead, as black youth recognize not just their relative invisibility in the culture at large, but also perceive an active hatred of them that is systematic (this is what the universal and capital 'U' implies). These words etched in the flesh take on a life of their own and resonate even after Shakur's death—Still/Here" (392).

By invoking Exodus 18:11, Tupac reminds us of the violence to which the angry, merciless brutelike God of the Old Testament resorted to free the children of Israel. Tupac then draws on this sacred precedent to back (literally) his call for black men to engage in an equally persistent uprising against the dominant society. He justifies the need for such violence in his song "Words of Wisdom," which appears on *2Pacalypse Now*:

> Killing us one by one
> In one way or another
> America will find a way to eliminate the problem
> One by one
> The problem is
> The troubles in the black youth of the ghettos
> And one by one
> We are being wiped off the face of this earth
> At an extremely alarming rate.
> And even more alarming is the fact
> That we are not fighting back
> . . . .
> Niggas what are we going to do?
> Walk blind into a line or fight
> Fight and die if we must like niggas.

In "Soulja's Story," also from *2Pacalypse Now*, Tupac echoes Ice Cube's point in "Who Got the Camera?," talking about the conundrum in which black males find themselves all too often:

> . . . just cause I'm a young black male . . .
> Cops sweat me as if my destiny is makin' crack sales
> . . . .
> Keep my shit cocked, cause tha cop's got a glock too
> What tha fuck would you do?
> Drop them or let 'em drop you?

On at least one occasion, as Tupac recalls in "Soulja's Story," he "chose droppin' tha cop," a choice that in 1993 saw him arrested in Atlanta for allegedly shooting two off-duty cops who were hassling a black motorist, although the charges were later dropped (F. Williams 104). But Tupac's lyrics also indicate that he advocated the use of discursive weapons to lay claim to space within the public transcript, to wage war, to effect history, and to create an effective history. That is, he was aware of and capitalized on rap music's usefulness as a way to circulate knowledge about and mobilize resistance to scenes of American violence in which African American males are implicated as silenced victims.

In *2Pacalypse Now's* "Young Black Male," for example, Tupac raps, "I try to effect by kicking the facts ... cuz I ain't equipped to stop how I look." The consequence of "kicking the facts," he explains in another track from *2Pacalypse Now*, "Violent," is that critics

> ... claim that I'm violent
> Just cuz I refuse to be silent
> These hypocrites are havin' fits
> Cuz I'm not buying it
>
> . . . .
>
> I'm Never Ignorant
> Gettin Goals Accomplished
>
> . . . .
>
> This time tha truth is gettin told
> Heard enough lies
> I told 'em fight back
> Attack on society
> If this is violence
> Then violent's what I gotta be.

Capturing the severity of the threat that critics (whom he likens to police officers in "Souljah's Revenge") pose to hearings for black men generally and for him specifically, Tupac uses "Violent" to call attention to the hypocrisy that underscores such efforts to silence him:

> You wanna censor something
> Motherfucka censor this! My words are weapons
> and I'm steppin to the silent
> Wakin up the masses
> But you claim I'm violent.

In this regard, Tupac echoes other cultural critics when he contends in "Violent," "If you investigate you'll find out where it's coming from/Look through our history, America's the violent one." Fighting in the form of writing rhymes, then, is a concept central to Tupac's thinking. Both his tattoos and his music speak to his awareness of the relationship between the policing of African American discourse and art and the policing of black bodies. Tupac's emphasis on and use of his flesh to (re)produce effective histories, his subversion of hegemonic discourses in his lyrics, and his invocation of the past to make sense of the present make him an ally in the struggles of other young black men.

Tupac's EXODUS 1811 and thug life tattoos also suggest that his work is informed by an African American messianic tradition that "has always been related to motifs of vengeance and retribution" (Moses 226). Theophus Smith emphasizes the long history of the messianic tradition within which I locate Tupac's work, writing, "The transformation of encounters with ethnic violence into ritual occasions for identification with Christ and his suffering or passion extend from the period of slave religion in the United States to the King movement of the 1960's" (184). Tupac's incorporation of messianic myths in his work speaks to the tradition's longevity. His work also reflects the black jeremiad tradition. Moses uses the term *jeremiad* to describe the "constant warnings issued by blacks to whites, concerning the judgment that was to come for the sin of slavery" (30). An important part of this tradition grew out of black abolitionist David Walker's *Appeal*, published in 1829 in response to Jefferson's racial theories. A significant component of Walker's *Appeal* was its second article, "Our Wretchedness in Consequence of Ignorance," in which Walker criticized blacks whose behavior situated them "in league with slave holders" and was indicative of their failure "to know and act in accordance with their best interests" (qtd. in Moses 41). Walker attributed such complicity to blacks' belief in their inferiority. Tupac at times gestured toward the issue of black men's complicity in their oppression. His invocation of the East-West rivalry on the cover of *Makaveli: The Donkilluminati: The 7 Day Theory* invoked the nihilistic behavior that occurs within the rap community. It is unfortunate that he did not live long enough to further explore the tensions that surrounded the art form at which he excelled and in which he believed as a medium of political expression. We likely would have benefited from his additional insights into the recording industry, which in many ways encouraged disunity rather than solidarity among young black men. Tupac seemed to have begun to shift his focuses toward the latter.

Tupac's work also reflects a tension in the messianic tradition between the "apocalyptic version of the [messianic] myth, derived from the Book of Revelation," and the "sacrificial version, derived from the Sermon on the Mount" (Moses

229). Tupac's firsthand knowledge of the violent consequences that hustlers too frequently suffer and his accurate foresight regarding his death led him to prepare a body of work resembling apocalyptic texts warning that the time for change, resurrection, and redemption was near.[15] For example, Tupac's prophecies of his untimely and violent demise in both his music and his interviews suggest that he, like Christ, was resigned to the fact that his body and blood would constitute the inevitable cost of what he believed to be his mission on earth. That mission, as he put it in "Words of Wisdom," was to be a spokesperson for the masses and the lower classes. On 7 September 1996, Tupac was marked by stigmata that for the second time in his short life took the form of multiple bullet wounds. Like Christ, Tupac died from those wounds on a Friday—13 September 1996. As with other celebrities who have died, Tupac's passing fostered numerous theories based on numerological, biographical, and artistic evidence that he faked his death to add substance to his claims that he would be crucified for his stands. Proponents of such theories expect that Tupac will someday return to bear witness to the redemption of his followers. Clues involving the number seven in both his work and his life led some hopeful fans to speculate that Tupac's second coming would occur in 2003—seven years after his death—in time to fund a candidate of his choosing for the next presidential election. Tupac's posthumously released *Makaveli: The Donkilluminati: The 7 Day Theory*, also added a good deal of fuel to the fires of second-coming theories. For example, the lyrics of many of the songs on this CD have been read in a manner akin to the Book of Revelation; the executive producer of the CD is listed only as Simon, another name for the apostle, Peter, who both helped Christ to carry his cross and was the first witness to Christ's resurrection (Luke 24:34; 1 Cor 15:5); and, most interestingly, its cover depicts Tupac nailed to a cross inscribed with the names of urban centers from both eastern and western parts of the United States. The names of the cities allude directly to the East Coast/West Coast rivalry between rappers on which some people have blamed Tupac's death. But the issues with which he was concerned and for which he was willing to die suggest that he intended the album cover and music to reference problems far more complex than a rivalry that took shape around geographic loci and loyalties. The classism, racism, and sexism that produced the environments within which Tupac sought to effect awareness, resistance, and change are not the product of a world divided by geographic differences but rather are the product of a nation that more than 140 years after emancipation continues actively to seek ways to contain African American people generally and black men in particular.

Tupac's construction of himself in the image of a black Christ was geared toward goals that exceeded the relative importance of a single individual. His work suggests that he wanted his biblical imagery and his representation of himself as a black Jesus to be heard, interpreted, and employed in ways that would positively affect black communities sooner rather than later. Christ's preaching, biblical scholarship suggests, contains no evidence that he foresaw a resurrection for himself; rather, he envisioned a collective resurrection of believers willing to forgo temptation so that they might be delivered from evil after his death (Metzger and Coogan 647). Likewise, Tupac took advantage of the crosslike pedestal on which he foresaw his fame and fortune ultimately situating him to call in his unique way for a resurrection of both community and nation.

Efforts to secure a hearing for rap and its artists do not preclude the fact that rap and its various agents seem at times to be complicit in the sorts of containment that they have a stake in undermining. Contradictions of course exist between the political agendas with which many rap artists purport to be concerned and the products into which such agendas are shaped prior to their release into the cyclonic configurations of market, culture, and ideology. To hear the narratives and positions that rap makes audible does not require that we explain away contradictions, profanity, misogyny, and violence. As I stated in the introduction, my concern has been to seek coherence in places in which none may be assumed to exist. This focus has left untouched other subjects—particularly those related to black women, rap, and the formation of black masculinity—despite their importance. The project of disrupting the legacy of type and the huge role it plays in reinforcing the structure of the prison writ large remains unfinished. As we have seen, white America has made an art of manipulating the images of black men to suit social, political, and economic agendas that share the goal of containing African American men. Like prisoners, athletes, and filmmakers, rap artists have responded in myriad ways by forging creative avenues of resistance by which they attempt—sometimes successfully, sometimes not—to reclaim some of the power and agency that are up for grabs in the zones of struggle between dominant and subordinate (Scott 14). The untimely deaths, criminal records, and violent-sounding products of more than a few rap artists suggest that the "chasm between black urban lived experience and dominant, 'legitimate' . . . ideologies regarding equal opportunity and racial inequality" has only begun to be bridged (Rose 102). But bridged it must be, for various forms of the prison and the battlegrounds that encompass them abound where black men labor to expose and to resist in myriad ways the forms of containment within which they function.

CONCLUSION

Throughout this book, I have argued that for black men the United States functions as a prison writ large. I have discussed the nature and function of particular forms of containment to which black men are subject by focusing on figures, both real and fictional, whose containment arises from the hypervisibility and/or invisibility, silence, and violence wrought by hegemonic representations of black men. I have approached the figures as enigmatic texts that demand to be recognized and to be read on their own terms. I have attempted to give these texts room to speak by hearing what they have to say in ways many of them have been denied in other contexts. I have not done so, however, without risk. As I have suggested earlier, the practice of close reading necessarily involves the participation of a party external to the text in the construction of its meaning. In this case, that party happens to be a white female assistant professor of English who is, no less, Canadian. I am cognizant of the fact that these factors may have affected my readings of the texts and that, however careful I have been to avoid doing so, I may have abused my prerogative as a reader to determine what a text means or is meant to say.

Houston A. Baker Jr., in "Scene . . . Not Heard," calls our attention to historical abuses of such prerogative with respect to slave experiences and slave narratives in ways that resonate with my concern here. Baker refers to an instance when a slave master killed one of his slaves and was asked to account for the death. The master explained that "if one slave refused to be corrected, and escaped with his life, the other slaves would soon copy the example; the result of which would be, the freedom of the slaves, and the enslavement of the whites" ("Scene" 39). Baker reads the master's testimony as a powerful reassertion of his fear that to recognize a slave's "'uncorrected' right to speech or action" was to risk becoming enslaved (39). Baker also notes the conspicuous silence of the slave, which functioned as a reminder of the fact that "it was unthinkable for a black person to offer testimony against any white act whatsoever" (39). Further, Baker notes, "even when blacks were permitted to tell their stories, the *interpretation* of their narratives—no matter how effective a slave's oratory—was the exclusive prerogative of their white-abolitionist employers" (40). The solution that Baker offers to readers who wish not to exploit their interpretive agency is to "[p]ipe to the spirit ditties of no tone" (41), thereby acknowledging that much is said between the lines and engaging themselves as effective readers in the hermeneutical practice of overhearing. In the case of slave narratives specifically, Baker contends "what is overheard by effective readers is a lyrical repudiation of the master's exclusive right to meaningful being in the world" (41). Throughout this book, I have sought to overhear my primary texts and thus to make audible assertions that have been silenced within racialized scenes of American violence.

Accordingly, I have focused not only on how black men are contained through representational practices but also on some of the ways that African American men resist subjection within the prison writ large. My discussions of specific sites and forms of African American men's containment and resistance have been informed by Alice Walker's invocation of the notion of "contrary instincts" in "In Search of Our Mothers' Gardens." Walker reminds us of Virginia Woolf's assertion that a gifted woman born centuries ago "would have been so thwarted and hindered by contrary instincts . . . that she must have lost her health and sanity to a certainty" (235). Walker argues that evidence of "contrary instincts" is apparent through the tradition of African American women's writing. As a case in point, she discusses Phillis Wheatley's work, in which the author's struggles with "contrary instincts" are apparent. Such instincts underlay, for example, Wheatley's poetic construction of liberty in the form of a golden-haired goddess, an image that made her for many years the subject of ridicule.[1] On behalf of critics who criticized Wheatley for such expressions, Walker issues an apology: "We know now that you were not an idiot or a traitor; only a sickly little black girl, snatched from your home and country and made a slave; a woman who still struggled to sing the song that was your gift, although in a land of barbarians who praised you for your bewildered tongue" (235–37). Walker's apology stems from her recognition of the ways that Wheatley's life experiences, along with the historically contradictory social, economic, cultural, and political organization of the United States, informed the contradictions apparent in the poems through which she expressed her worldviews. Implicit in Walker's apology is a critique of responses to contemporary cultural productions, behaviors, and experiences of African Americans that do not reflect a similar sensitivity to the possibility that they too may be informed by "contrary instincts." It seems to me, therefore, that Walker's critique has relevance in the context of black men's sometimes bewildering cultural productions and equally bewildering self-representations.

Black men's ways of seeing, being seen, and making themselves heard in the contemporary United States often are clearly informed by contrary instincts that are overlooked or employed as grounds for dismissal of the importance of their work in both academic and nonacademic forums. Yet, just as in Wheatley's case, these contrary instincts inflect black men's work in ways that inspire critical responses with the potential to be as damaging as those for which Walker apologizes. Indeed, the question that critics have cynically asked of Wheatley—"How could she?"— is asked of black men whose behavior and cultural productions deviate from a deceptively linear and obtusely marked path to resistance, change, equality, and freedom. "How could they?" is asked of black prisoners whose criminal actions are taken as a reflection of a criminal essence. "How could they?" is asked of rap artists who seem at times to victimize themselves through purportedly resistant language and actions that seem only to degrade themselves and other members of their communities. "How could they?" is asked of professional black athletes who violate the rules of the many different games in which, as both black men and athletes, they are forced players. "How could they?" is asked of black working-men who bend their lives, if not their views of themselves and their lives, to fit the hegemonic parameters within which they have learned to get by from day to day. I cannot help but wonder if it is not wiser, more astute, more critically productive, and more compassionate to approach the evidence of contrary instincts in black men's lives and cultural productions, as does Walker of Wheatley, with the questions "How could they not?" and, "Since they did, what of it?" That is, given the degree to which distorted images of black men shape the prison writ large, is it not reasonable to expect that black men's work as prisoners, artists, and athletes will be laden with contradictions, will create further contradictions, and will sometimes seem as distorted as the contexts out of which it arises (C. Johnson and McCuskery xix)? And if such expectations are unreasonable, then is it not worthwhile for critics to direct attention to overhearing what is being said in and around the rough edges delineated by contrary instincts?

Ralph Ellison, in "The Little Man at Chehaw Station: The American Artist and His Audience," offers a paradigm within which to envision the resultant critical scenario. Ellison begins that essay by relating an incident that took place when he was a music student at Tuskegee Institute in the 1930s. After a less-than-stellar trumpet performance before a panel of faculty members, Ellison sought comfort from another of his teachers, Hazel Harrison. Instead of offering him sympathy, however, Harrison gently admonished Ellison, reminding him that, "You must *always* play your best, even if it's only in the waiting room at Chehaw Station, because in this country there'll always be a little man hidden behind the stove" (4). Although he is initially frustrated by Harrison's offer of a riddle in lieu of sympathy, Ellison eventually conceptualizes "the little man at Chehaw Station" as "the enigma of aesthetic communication in American democracy" (6). The "little man," he explains, represents the characteristics of a cultural production (and, I would add, of an experience, a behavior, a representation, a story, a memory) that makes it possible—indeed, necessary—for critics as well as consumers, academics, and policy makers to engage with any of these forms in the spirit of "antagonistic cooperation; acting, for better or worse, as both collaborator and judge" (Ellison, "Little" 7). The enigmatic quality of a form appeals to the audience's experiences and emotions to make them sympathetic to those of the artist while leaving room for the audience to reckon with the art form. The little man thereby inducts into the critical realm what Ellison calls "new dimensions of artistic truth" ("Little" 7). Whereas the chaos that the little man has the potential to precipitate risks being condemned "as a source of confusions, a threat to social order, and a reminder of the unfinished details" of the United States, it remains an integral component of the "American scene and language" that "goads its users toward a perfection of our revolutionary ideals" ("Little" 4–8).

The realization of "revolutionary ideals" is complicated by the clever irony underlying Miss Harrison's association of a metaphor as complex as the little man with Chehaw Station, a simple "whistle-stop" yet also "a point of arrival and departure for people representing a wide diversity of tastes and styles of living" (Ellison, "Little" 15). The ironic locus of the little man leads Ellison to argue that "the mystery of American cultural identity contained in such motley mixtures arises out of our persistent attempts to reduce our cultural diversity to an easily recognizable unity" (15–16). In a much broader context than Walker, Ellison calls attention to the ways that contrary instincts function in the United States as a major impetus to efforts to ameliorate the unease that accompanies diversity. Such efforts take the form of contests of civility, piety, and tradition that Ellison views as the "improvised moral equivalent for armed warfare" (16) and that take forms such as wars of words, clashes of style, or the designation of victims as scapegoats. As Ellison puts it, "We stand, as we say, united in the name of these sacred principles. But, indeed, it is in the name of these same principles that we ceaselessly contend, affirming our ideals even as we do them violence" (17). Ellison fears that such conflicts could forever stand in place of less violent, more viable modes of coexisting in a nation founded on abstract ideals and principles ("Little" 15–17). But for the reliable, albeit disturbing, presence of the little man, Ellison's fears would seem well founded.

The little man reminds us that such contests have multiple dimensions. As concerted as are efforts to resolve through oppression the unease apparent in the contrary instincts that structure racial hierarchies in the United States, so are the efforts to mobilize that unease in the form of emancipatory paradigms.

My concern throughout *Lockstep and Dance* has been to explore texts through which black men have endeavored to develop the latter. The question that remains is whether it is possible to claim that any of the figures or texts to which I have directed my attention are revolutionaries or are revolutionary. Again, I look to an essay by Alice Walker for an answer. In "Duties of the Black Revolutionary Artist," Walker contends that in an ideal world, black artists would write in isolation from political and social debates and without regard for their color. For my purposes here, I would add that in an ideal world, black people would be able to make music or films, to play sports, or go to work and return home each day without having to think about who they are or what color they are. However, the racial organization of the United States denies such freedom in ways that force African Americans to be constantly on the lookout for "*what is Bull and what is Truth*, what is practical and what is designed ultimately to paralyze [their] talents" (Walker, "Unglamorous" 133–34). To undertake, in whatever form, searches for what is bull, what is truth, and what constitutes a trap is, I think, to lay the foundation for revolution. And just what exactly is revolution?

According to Walker, revolutions are concerned with "the least glamorous stuff" ("Duties" 135), such as making history more accessible by rewriting its narratives in a simpler form or reciting them orally. Revolutions look backward as well as forward to remember the lessons, deeds, misdeeds, and images of yesterday in forms that resonate today while gesturing hopefully toward tomorrow. Arguably most important, revolutions rely not on artists for flattery but rather on representations of men and women as they are. As Walker explains, a "man's life can rarely be summed up in one word; even if that word is black or white. . . . One should recall that Bigger Thomas was many great and curious things, but he was neither good nor beautiful. He was real, and that is sufficient" ("Unglamorous" 135–37).[2] Walker's assertion leads me to wonder if I may have found the answer to my question.

At the heart of revolution is the little man at Chehaw Station who mediates the transition of abstract, ideal principles from their symbolic forms to forms that enact and sometimes mobilize social actions. Those social actions accord with ideals that in turn "insist upon being made flesh" (17), thus spurring the artist, the prisoner, the filmmaker, the athlete, the musician, and countless others to find ways to make those ideals concrete (Ellison, "Little" 17–18). John Edgar Wideman. Robby. Tommy. Richard Wright. Ice Cube. Rodney King. Tupac Shakur. Latrell Sprewell. Dennis Rodman. Fred Daniels. Revolutionaries all? Not because they dream of demolishing the prison writ large. Not because they speak the unspeakable so that we might see the unseeable. Not because they attempt to change the rules that govern play on the inside. Not even because some of them died trying. But perhaps, evidence of contrary instincts notwithstanding, each is a revolutionary because, under the tutelage of the little man, he shows us, in great and curious ways, how to spot the truths, the bull, and the traps that inhabit the mundane. And perhaps each is a revolutionary because he directs us also to the little man who leads those willing to follow into the lower frequencies of their lives, their stories, their songs, their games, their memories, and even their deaths, where everything that we see and hear is real, even if it is not good or beautiful. It is real because it may have affected the person who exposes it. It is real because other people have been affected by it. It is real because the forms through which the person does the exposing are themselves real. And that is sufficient to warrant serious critical attention. The nature of critical attention is necessarily clarified by hindsight concerning past responses to African American lives and literary and cultural productions. Likewise, it benefits from our knowledge, appreciation, and consideration of the degree to which the objects of our attention may be underscored by contrary instincts.

In Wheatley's case, temporal distance contributed to critical blind spots in the reception of her work. Today, other kinds of distance among critics, academics, policy makers, and the contemporary African American male experience—social, cultural, economic, geographic, racial, gendered—pose risks to our ability to overhear the effects of contrary instincts on black men's worldviews and the mediums through which they express them. These other kinds of distance leave open the door for cultural and critical responses to black men's behaviors, activities, performances, and cultural productions every bit as violent as those once directed to Wheatley's work. I have borne such risks in mind as I have attempted, for better or worse, to do some business with the little man in each chapter. The little man first led me to study containment and resistance in African American men's lives and representations of them. The little man guided me—inspired me, even—as I sought, through close readings of Wideman's, Blandon's, Lee's, Wright's, Tupac's, and others' work and of representations of Sprewell and Rodman, to see and hear "order in apparent cultural chaos" (Ellison, "Little" 23). The little man guided me as I set out to find my way to the "real" men whom I expected eventually to locate behind various forms of aesthetic gesturing. In the end, however, the little man showed me that what I was looking for all along, the essence of the works on which I have focused, was to be found not in the often "comic clashing of styles, but in the mixture, the improvised form, the willful juxtaposition of modes" that kept me engaged throughout (Ellison, "Little" 23–24). Thus, as Wideman says of Reuben in his novel by the same name, as complicated as it may be to react responsibly and nonviolently to experiences and cultural productions that look like someone has deliberately thrown in "shit that makes no sense at all and just [left] you to deal with it" (35), it is integral that we look closely at whatever it is about them that keeps us coming back.

NOTES

Introduction

1. The Black Codes were a set of laws enacted between 1865 and 1866 in the southern states. According to A. Leon Higginbotham Jr., these laws were "designed to regulate the lives of the southern African American population. These Black Codes were principally aimed at maintaining the inferior and subordinate status of the newly freed African Americans, especially through labor relations" (232 n. 36).

2. Wahneema Lubiano, in her introduction to *The House That Race Built: Black Americans, U.S. Terrain* (1997), employs the word *public* "without a race adjective because the operation of racism is so thoroughgoing that even those individuals who are its objects are not exempt from thinking about the world through its prism" (vii). Although I employ a race adjective, I use the term *white America* throughout this book to refer to a national consciousness that is similarly pervasive and infectious throughout the United States. It is important to note, as Dylan Rodríguez points out, that white America is not all white: "The contemporary hegemony of law and order, its materialization into a 'way of life,' is based on a discursive and material expansion of civil society's normative whiteness, to the extent that 'nonwhites' or 'people of color' have increasingly invested in the protection of this sanctified property interest [in whiteness]: the sustenance of civil society and its reproduction on a scale of globalized magnitude as the United States of America" (25).

Chapter 1

1. Dylan Rodríguez describes how a similar methodological conundrum inflected his relationship with Viet Mike Ngo, who is imprisoned in Soledad Prison in California (29): "Ngo suggests that our attempt at 'collaborative work' is radically insufficient, and that there can be no authentic relation of integrity or equity between those inhabiting the formal and opposed categories of free and unfree. He is, instead, momentarily solaced by the hope that my pedagogical appropriations of his intellectual work (though such appropriations must often go anonymous and unaccredited to minimize further endangerment of the imprisoned) are somehow relevant to his political desires, visions, and fantasies" (33).

2. Wideman uses the word *unbearable* in ways that he credits to his mother. As he explains, "'Unbearable' is my mother's word. She uses it often but never lightly. . . . Unbearable is not that which can't be borne, but what must be endured forever" (*Brothers* 181).

3. Wideman makes the same point in a slightly different way when he writes, "The worst things [Robby] did followed from the same impulse as the best. He could be unbelievably dumb, corrupt, selfish, and destructive but those qualities could keep him down no more than his hope, optimism, his

refusal to accept a dull, inferior portion could buoy him above the hell that engulfed black boys in the Homewood streets" (195).

4. Wideman explores the effects of his failure to decompartmentalize his life via a description of a trip to Maine with his wife, Judy, and Robby. On the drive, Robby has "a good ole nigger ball" listening to "black music on the radio" (28). Wideman recalls how he felt shame and anxiety because although it was music that they had grown up "hearing and loving and learning to sing in Mom's living room . . . you were doing it in my new 1966 Dodge Dart, on the way to Martha's Vineyard and Maine with my new white wife in the backseat. Didn't you know we'd left Pittsburgh, didn't you understand that classical music volume moderate was preferred in these circumstances? Papa's got a brand-new bag. And you were gon act a nigger and let the cat out" (*Brothers* 28). Wideman's discomfort in this situation stems from his inability to reconcile the gap between the place that he calls home and the very different space to which he thought he had escaped. His insistence that it is easier to live as though he were two people renders him unable to reconcile the chaos that Robby's presence in the car brings to Wideman's neatly compartmentalized life. Wideman recalls his experience at college when a white male student challenged him about what constituted "real blues" (29). Wideman responded angrily to the challenge and then wondered why that "smart ass white son of a bitch [had] so much power over me." He answers these questions by recognizing that "[f]our hundred years of oppression, of lies, had empowered [whites] to use the music of [black] people against him" (32). Wideman senses the ways in which white "power, the raw, crude force," mocks and diminishes him (32). In other words, this white boy denies Wideman's identity by undermining one important way in which the he sees himself—that is, Wideman's belief that he "*was* the blues" (28).

5. Describing an occasion on which he took his wife, mother, and children to visit Robby, John Wideman notes his ironic feelings as he accompanies his family through the parking lot to the prison: "I fall in behind them. Far enough away to be alone. To be separate from the women and separate from the children. I need to say to whoever's watching—guards, prisoners invisible behind the barred three-story windows partitioning the walls. These are my people. They're with me. I'm responsible. I need to say that, to hang back and preside, to stroll, almost saunter, aware of the weight, the necessity of vigilance because here I am, on alien turf, a black man, and I'm in charge. For a moment at least these women, these children have me to turn to. And I'm one hundred percent behind them, prepared to make anyone who threatens them answer to me. And that posture, that prerogative remains rare for a black man in American society. Rare *today*, over 120 years after slavery and second-class citizenship have been abolished by law. The guards know that. The prisoners know that. It's for their benefit as well as my own and my family's that I must carry myself in a certain way, make certain rules clear even though we are entering a hostile world, even though the bars exist to cut off the possibility of the prisoners seeing themselves as I must see myself, striding free, in charge of women and children, across the official lot" (44).

6. Rubin "Hurricane" Carter makes a point similar to Robby's, writing, "The penitentiary was geared to making the black inmates rise to the heights of their own incompetencies—even in the protection of themselves" (164).

7. Wideman's sense that "each visit's rooted in denial, compromise, a sinking feeling of failure" stems from his concern that suppressing the "rage, the urge to fight back doesn't rise from a truer, better self" (191). Rather, he worries that the suppression denies "not the instinctual core of my being but an easily sidestepped, superficial layer of bravado, a ferocity I'd like to think is real but that winds up being no more than a Jonathan Jackson, George Jackson, Soledad-brother fantasy, a carryover from the

Old Wild West, shoot-em-up days as a kid. . . . Maybe I needed to imagine myself in that role because I knew how far from the truth it was. Kidding myself so I could take the visits seriously, satisfy myself that I was doing all I could, doing better than nothing" (191).

8. Morrison cautions against the risk of converting a racial house "into a palace" where racism does not hurt or where "coexistence offers the delusion of agency" (4).

Chapter 2

1. As Robyn Wiegman puts it, "Caught there, within the framework of a subjectively reductive sexualization, the phallicized black male displays the anxieties and contradictions underlying the 'logic' and disciplinary practices of white masculine supremacy; in reducing the black male to the body and further to the penis itself, white masculinity betrays a simultaneous desire for and disavowal of the black male's phallic inscription. To put this another way, the white male desires the image he must create in order to castrate, and it is precisely through the mythology of the black male as mythically endowed rapist that he has effectively done this. In the process, the creation of a narrative of black male sexual excess simultaneously exposes and redirects the fear of castration from the white masculine to the black male body, and it is in the lynch scene that this transfer moves from the realm of the psychosexual to the material" (98).

2. According to a *USA Today* article, the advertising campaign "earned higher-than-average popularity and effectiveness scores when measured for Ad Track, *USA Today*'s consumer poll of national ads. It was particularly popular among young adults 18–24: 45% said they liked the ads 'a lot.' Of that same group, 43% of them also said they believed the campaign was effective" (Wells 14B).

Chapter 3

1. I take this example from Wideman's novel, *The Lynchers*, which is the story of a group of black men who devise a plan to lynch a white police officer. Although all of the men in the group embrace the idea of the lynching and participate in the construction of the plan, it serves different functions for each man. For some, engaging in the construction of a narrative about the lynching of a white man provides the wherewithal to play the game by continuing to get up each morning and go to work each day. For other members of the group, only the literal execution of the plan would make them feel as though they had won the game into which they had been forced as black men. For all, however, the game remains to be won or lost, and each must determine the best way to make sure that he comes out on top.

2. In *Philadelphia Fire* (1990), Wideman indirectly addresses the complexities of the games in which black men find themselves implicated when he describes what typically happens when a game of basketball lasts beyond the hours of daylight: "If you keep playing, the failing light is no problem. Your eyes adjust and the streetlamps come on and they help some. People pass by think you're crazy playing basketball in the dark, but if you stay in the game you can see enough. Ball springs at you quicker from the shadows. Pill surprises you and zips by you unless you know it's coming. Part of being in the game is anticipating, knowing who's on the court with you and what they're likely to do. It's darker. Not everything works now that works in daylight. Trick is knowing what does. And staying within that

range. You could be blind and play if the game's being played right so you stay out past the point people really seeing. You just know what's supposed to be happening. Dark changes things but you can manage much better than anyone not in the game would believe. Still there comes a point you'll get hurt if you don't give it up. Not the other team you're fighting then, but the dark, and it always wins, you know it's going to win so what you're doing doesn't make sense, it's silly and you persist in the silliness a minute or two, a pass pops you in your chest, a ball rises and comes down in the middle of three players and nobody even close to catching it. You laugh and go with the silliness. Can't see a damn thing anymore. Whether a shot's in or out. Hey, O.T., man. Show some teeth so I can see you, motherfucker. Somebody trudges off the court. You all can have it. I can't see shit. The rest laugh and give it up too. You fade to the sidelines. It's been dark a long time at the court's edges" (39). In this passage, Wideman speaks to the tactics that black men employ to function as freely and with as much dignity as possible in environments that are designed to deny them such opportunities.

3. Though largely anecdotal, University of Washington English Professor David Shields's *Black Planet: Facing Race during an NBA Season* (1999) provides a fascinating look at the racial conversation over the course of a season during which he watched and studied the Seattle Supersonics.

4. Nelson George explains in *Elevating the Game: Black Men and Basketball* (1992), "Of America's major professional sports only boxing maintained a consistent level of African American participation in the 1900s. In large part that's because the spectacle of black men fighting each other was quite familiar to whites. Battle royals, where for prize money a dozen or so black men were blindfolded, ushered into a ring, and told to fight until one man was left standing, were extremely popular" (14). Ralph Ellison describes a battle royal early in *Invisible Man*. The battle takes place on the day that the narrator graduates from high school: he and some of his schoolmates are forced to participate to entertain the "town's big shots" (17). The battle takes place on a "gleaming space of polished floor" inside a "big mirrored hall" (17–18). The boys (all black) are blindfolded and are required to fight with one another. After the fight, the floor is electrified and covered with "coins of all dimensions and a few crumpled bills" (26). The boys do not know at first that the floor has been electrified and that their painful scrambling for the money constitutes yet another form of entertainment for the men who have gathered to watch.

5. The reference to basketball players as "cagers" stems from this period, during which "Roman Colosseum-like barrier[s]" separated athletes from spectators (George 7).

6. Nelson George contends that manifestations of the black aesthetic in basketball are not always physical but are always aggressive: "Verbal intimidation on the court (a.k.a. 'the selling of wulf tickets') is a large part of the operating dynamic. Wulf tickets are intended to demoralize opponents by demeaning their intelligence, judgment, self-respect, manhood, and overall claims to humanity. Words like 'sucker,' 'turkey,' 'lame,' along with a constantly evolving variety of others, usually compounded by some artfully articulated obscenity, are employed to undermine the thin-skinned. Like 'the dozens,' a verbal trial by insult practiced among blacks for generations, these taunts are essential to the game's component of one upmanship and to psychological combat. . . . In fact, most black ball expressions are about elevating oneself by embarrassing others" (xvi). Trash talking assumes physical as well as verbal forms. As Phil Taylor notes in *Sports Illustrated*, "You don't have to open your mouth to talk trash. There are ways to get a message across nonverbally, as Atlanta's Dikembe Mutombo does by wagging his finger after blocking a shot" (8). The NBA has attempted to increase its control over this aspect of the game as well by making it possible for a player to receive a five-hundred-dollar fine and a technical foul if he is caught trash talking.

7. Shropshire notes the lack of consensus regarding the nature of the Sprewell incident: "The greatest variation in the telling is the level of provocation and the degree to which Sprewell 'cooled down' before" returning to the practice floor and threatening Carlesimo again (81).

8. As Shields notes with respect to the prevailing tendency to deny the obvious, "I'm struck by the fact that in all matters of human communication, when someone makes a point of announcing that something isn't so, it often means that it in fact is so; in matter of human communication relating to race, when someone makes a point of announcing that something isn't so, it means almost without exception that it in fact is so" (10).

9. Lhamon states, "Lore cycles perform a mediating function. They keep culture traveling and mutating even while they monitor the positional relationships in the originally textualized scenes. Once a taboo line is fixed and challenged, the lore cycle that accrues around it may move the line back and forth, accepting or proscribing behavior; or, the allowable play along the line itself may broaden or attenuate. But its own inertia tends also to maintain the line. Lore cycles exist to draw and redraw the line. A lore cycle gives itself power by moving the line slightly. This is cultural gerrymandering, and it is quite political. There are exact illustrations of this in minstrelsy, which has repeated motifs of *walking the line*, reinforcing the image with such vivid vernacular as 'walk chalk' and 'walk jawbone'" (79).

10. As Barrett puts it, "What Rodman exposes as indispensable to the NBA is its 'struggle over the relations of representation,' and systems of representation and desire, as Judith Butler adeptly demonstrates, mirror one another in a 'strangely necessary' relation" ("Black Men" 108).

11. It is interesting to read the proximity of Romijn's hand to Rodman's ear in relation to a newspaper advertisement for the BMG Marketing Group that appeared in the *Village Voice* in April 1998. BMG's ad depicts the back of a black man's shaven head on which sits a set of headphones. The caption for the ad, inscribed across the man's head, reads, "When you've got them by the ears their hearts and minds will follow." Such subtle images speak to white America's ongoing concern with gaining control of the bodies, hearts, and minds of African Americans.

12. The cover to which I am referring appeared on newsstands. *GQ* subscribers received magazines that depicted Rodman poised behind the model, his hands in a no-foul gesture, and the likeness of his hands painted on Romijn's bare breasts. The different covers speak to the editors' cognizance that confronting the general public—in this case, nonsubscribers—with such an obvious allusion to interracial sex posed a greater risk of negative repercussions than offering it to an already committed audience of regular subscribers. In other words, the editors were unwilling to bank on general audiences' preparedness to respond neutrally, let alone favorably, to the image of a black man with his hands on a white woman's body.

13. *GQ*'s restoration of racial and sexual order illustrates a pattern to which Lindon Barrett refers when he claims that "market-driven colonizations of desire (and representation) . . . reduce desire in all its material, imaginary, and symbolic manifestations to a narrow set of calculable, idealized civilities and affabilities ultimately resolving themselves in 'the heterosexual domestic space . . . as an inviolate sanctum'" ("Black Men" 108).

Chapter 4

1. Aaron Blandon understands the notion of bringing something into the light as follows: "It's about presenting what is not readily served at the popular table, the perspectives, issues, and folks

NOTES TO PAGES 103–44   171

whose views are not normally shown. However, another meaning is intended as well; it is probably sooner understood by cinematographers and directors. . . . [S]hooting into the light, with the subject between the camera and the light source, is more difficult and requires a different care when making exposures, but it gives you greater possibilities for how you can show the subject" (Blandon).

2. The abundance of black-focused films made since 1990 would allow rich discussions of the ways in which and the extent to which each ventures into the empty space of representation. I sought not to engage in an exhaustive study of a multitude of films but rather to explore examples of the patterns of representation with which this book is concerned. For a more comprehensive look at contemporary black-focused film, see Reid's *Black Lenses, Black Voices: African American Film Now.*

Chapter 5

1. I take the term *raptivists* from Charise Cheney's essay "Representin' God: Rap, Religion, and the Politics of a Culture." Cheney uses the term in reference to rap artists who "use rap music as a forum for politicking" (1).

2. Fiske, in *Media Matters*, accounts for such different perspectives in his discussion of "situational logic": "Rodney King's behavior was categorically different in white and Black discourse. Discourse is, of course, continuous with social experience, so discursive differences are always social ones. African Americans knew instantly the trouble that Rodney King was in merely by seeing him surrounded by cops; the brutal beating that followed, was, in light of their experience, the logical and predictable outcome. Many whites, however, with their quite different social experience, were unable to see that situated 'logic' and thus had to look to King's behavior for an explanation. The defense lawyers capitalized on this and turned much of the trial into an investigation of what Rodney King did rather than what the police officers did. For them, the beating could be made to make sense only through white categorizations of Rodney King's behavior" (135).

3. Fiske relates the story of an incident in Detroit in which a black motorist, Malice Green, was pulled over and beaten to death by police officers: "But there was no video of the scene; the incident was made known verbally both through literacy (the media) and oralcy among African Americans, but the inopportune absence of a camera prevented its hypervisualization. It could not, therefore, become a media event with its own hyperreality" (*Media Matters* 137).

4. The Los Angeles riots that followed the first trial and acquittal of the police officers who had beaten King stand as evidence of the black community's anger about what seemed both then and now to be a fact of African American life that white America has a vested interest in barring from the public transcript. Such anger was also apparent in St. Petersburg, Florida, in October 1996, when police declared a seventy-two-hour state of emergency after a white police officer shot and killed a black driver. The ensuing riots led to police ordering black youth to stay off of the streets and to restricted gun and gasoline sales. City leaders were surprised at the riot that took place. As one official put it, "The feeling was that things had greatly improved, but we could have been wrong" ("Crackdown"). In contrast, the riot came as no surprise to black people living in the area where the riots took place. As one African American woman told reporters, "The police harass you for nothing. . . . People have got fed up. That's what they should have burned down, the police station and everyone inside" ("Crackdown"). Further north, according to a June 1998 *Village Voice* article, black motorists refer to the New Jersey Turnpike as "White Man's Pass." "Since 1988—and possibly long before that—state police have been

'engaged in a program of racial targeting' on the New Jersey Turnpike, according to court documents in a pending case against 19 black men and women who, in a joint motion, claimed they were illegally targeted, stopped, searched, and arrested by troopers on the turnpike in Gloucester County between January 1988 and April 1991. Allegedly, the troopers target blacks, especially those driving luxury cars such as BMWs, Mercedes-Benzes, and Lexuses. The state police assert that it is a trumped-up conflict and deny they practice such a policy; if anything, they insist, their actions amount to nothing more than aggressive enforcement of traffic regulations. But for blacks, who experts say are nearly five times more likely than whites to be stopped on the turnpike, it is a case of constantly being picked on" (Noel 39–40). Efforts on the part of members of the New Jersey-based organization Black Cops against Police Brutality to get state troopers to police themselves have led to group members being "threatened with arrest by the Turnpike Authority if they violate 'restrictions on filming, photographing and videotaping on the turnpike'" (40). Despite the potential that agents of the public transcript will manipulate video and photographic texts in ways that adversely affect African American defendants, the production of such texts continues to represent at least something of a threat.

5. Hazel Carby, in *Race Men*, offers a compelling example of how even radical lyrics taken from rap songs can be distorted and made to uphold rather than to subvert the public transcript. In reference to a scene in the film *Grand Canyon* (1991), she writes, "[M]usic becomes *the* prime vehicle for representing a cultural war which has encoded within it the political potential for a larger civil war. The rap group NWA (Niggaz with Attitude) is pitted against [Warren] Zevon in a symbolic enactment of [director Lawrence] Kasdan's narrative of race and nation which is about to unfold: a liberal white suburban male confronts a 'posse' of young black urban males. The musical battle both produces and accompanies the wider class and racialized meanings of the scene, meanings which in turn both produce and confirm ideological beliefs about the 'problem' of the inner city, of what is wrong with America. The skewed perspective of this cinematic confrontation is revealed in the unequal editing of the musical 'war.' In contrast to the verbal and musical fragments of NWA's 'Quiet on the Set,' the audience hears coherent narrative selections from the Zevon lyrics. We do not hear sequential sections of a verse, or even complete sentences, of the NWA lyrics; the narrative coherence of 'Quiet on the Set' has been deliberately disrupted" (172–73).

6. Fiske notes that the "success with which race was silently recoded into place in the geographic dislocation of the trial was repeated as the defense's verbal discourse referred to every physical aspect of Rodney King's body except its race. They consistently described him in terms of his weight, height, strength, and masculinity. Time and again he was put into discourse as a 250-pound, six-foot-three-inch man with the physical strength to throw off police officers and withstand Taser guns, batons, and boots. He was repeatedly likened to a bear—a neat analogy in which racism could be simultaneously denied and exploited" (*Media Matters* 141).

7. I employ the term *curriculum vitae* to refer to Tupac's body of work because its literal meaning, the "course of a life," and its use as a term to describe academic résumés effectively capture the important ways in which Tupac interwove theory and personal experience to yield a legacy of praxis.

8. Greg Tate, in "He Is Truly Free Who Is Free from the Need to Be Free," argues that "Jesus must be the black man's patron saint because we do the martyr thing so prolifically" (116–17). For a discussion of other African American uses of the black Christ figure, see Sundquist 81–83 (Nat Turner), 592–623 (W. E. B. Du Bois). Countee Cullen's lengthy poem, "The Black Christ" (1929), also provides an important example of how black artists employ the Christ figure to speak to black men's physical and psychic suffering.

9. Examples of such criticism include Kevin Powell's statement in *Rolling Stone* that Tupac's work "crosses the line from art and metaphor to real-life jeopardy" (51) and Ivan Solotaroff's comment in *Esquire* that "the line between art and life was erased in his mind" (86).

10. In "Words of Wisdom," from *2Pacalypse Now*, Tupac defines his use of the controversial term *niggas*: "When I say niggas it is not the nigga we are grown to fear / It is not the nigga we say as if it has no meaning / But to me / It means Never Ignorant Getting Goals Accomplished, nigga."

11. Theophus Smith makes particular note of the extent to which African Americans' religious and political productions draw on the book of Exodus. Indeed, he claims that in the "Afro-American figural tradition it appears that all corporate liberation efforts can be configured, in the manner of ritual performances, as dramatic reenactments of Exodus, and their readers envisioned as approximate types of Moses" (67). Smith's claim is supported by both Levine, who states that the "most persistent single image the slave songs contain is that of the chosen people" (33), and James Weldon Johnson and J. Rosamond Johnson, who claim that it "is not possible to estimate the sustaining influence that the story of the trials and tribulations of the Jews as related in the Old Testament exerted upon the Negro" (20). Eddie S. Glaude Jr. also notes the importance of Exodus to African Americans: "[A]lthough Exodus was a sacred text, it was not understood only in religious terms. The history of the story and its broad application across a disparate field of political engagements suggest that it was also interpreted in this-worldly and historical terms as a model for resistance and, perhaps, revolution" (3).

12. Olguín discusses the frequency with which Chicano prisoners tattoo images of Jesus Christ on their bodies and explains that the icon "problematizes the juridical category of 'criminal' by linking convicts to Jesus Christ, the prototypical victim" (186). Further, Olguín notes how some convicts' tattoos of Christ bear a resemblance to the convicts' faces, thereby "elaborating the likeness of a never-before-seen-figure such as Jesus Christ on the very real and constantly visible convict's body" (187). For the "differently literate Chicano [prison] audience[s]," such conflation assumes the power of "a collective autobiography, a testimonio" (187).

13. Olguín's explanation of the nature and function of tattoos on Chicano prisoners supports Spillers's and White and White's points about inscribed bodies. Olguín writes with respect to the symbolic use value of tattoos in prison, "they represent a form of capital, cultural capital, that all can share—even those without tattoos.... *Tatuajes*, rather than simply modeling the exotic difference of the 'other,' instead expose the dialectical forces at work in the articulation of difference even as these texts produce a counterhegemonic Ideology of difference. The Convict Body in general, and especially the brown, *Tatuaje*-marked *text* of the Chicano Convict Body, make manifest their challenge to the underlying subtexts: that is, the peonage and proletarianization of the racially marked Chicano people after 1848, and the concurrent commodification of the 'convicted' brown body (not to mention the convicted 'Black male suspect') at the twilight of chattel slavery. Thus, the transgression articulated through vernacular writing rituals such as *Tatuteando* (rather than through more easily coopted literary forms of writing) becomes the ontological basis of the new (or old) counterhegemonic Chicano Subject" (175).

14. Wilson argues in "Graffiti Become Terror: The Idea of Resistance" that a "tattoo carries many messages—affiliation, disaffiliation, exfiliation, anger, alienation, empathy, and (like the well-known knuckle tattoos) both hate and love—all of which can be 'read,' or semiotically decoded, as opposition to a given culture, regime, or discipline. A willful energetic exercise in self-symbolization, a tattoo may suggest a sociopathic personality, or merely a carnivalesque one. In all events, it identifies a person who claims a certain identity, usually in the face of social convention, and who exists in opposition to convention" (276). Although I do not agree with Wilson's categorical assertion that all tattoos fly in

the face of social convention, Tupac's complex tattoos lend themselves to readings that decode thickly textured narratives of opposition to racial and class oppression.

15. Generally speaking, apocalyptic texts are those that may include a "survey of history often leading to an eschatological crisis in which the cosmic powers of evil are destroyed, the cosmos is restored, and Israel (or 'the righteous') is redeemed." Apocalyptic texts may also reveal previously unknown or hidden things (Metzer and Coogan 34).

Conclusion

1. Henry Louis Gates Jr. argues that the "peculiar history of Wheatley's reception by critics has, ironically enough, largely determined the theory of the criticism of the creative writings of Afro-Americans from the eighteenth century to the present time" (*Figures* 79).

2. The real, Walker asserts, "is what is happening. What is real is what did happen. What happened to me and happens to me is most real of all" ("Unglamorous" 138). Walker refers to the artist as "he" until the last line of this essay: "The artist then is the voice of the people, but she is also The People" ("Unglamorous" 138). Although Walker does not explain her sudden shift, it is in keeping with the other acts of feminist recovery that she undertakes through the volume.

WORKS CITED

"2 Live Crew Star Gives Press Bad Rap." *Edmonton Journal* 22 Nov. 1999: B6.

Abu-Jamal, Mumia. "2Pacalypse Now." 13 Sept. 1996 <<http://www.mumia.org/index3.html>>.

AC Delco. Advertisement. *Ebony* May 2001: 133.

Alexander, Bryant Keith. "Fading, Twisting, and Weaving: An Interpretive Ethnography of the Black Barbershop as Cultural Space." *Qualitative Inquiry* 9.1 (2003): 105–28.

Alexander, Elizabeth. "'Can You Be BLACK and Look at This?': Reading the Rodney King Video(s)." *Black Male: Representations of Masculinity in Contemporary American Art.* Ed. Thelma Golden. New York: Whitney Museum of American Art, 1994. 90–110.

Alexander, Frank, and Heidi Siegmund Cuda. *Got Your Back: The Life of a Bodyguard in the Hardcore World of Gangsta Rap.* New York: St. Martin's, 1998.

Allen, Ernest, Jr. "Making the Strong Survive: The Contours and Contradictions of Message Rap." *Droppin' Science: Critical Essays on Rap Music and Hip Hop Culture.* Ed. William Eric Perkins. Philadelphia: Temple UP, 1996. 159–91.

Als, Hinton. "GWTW." *Without Sanctuary: Lynching Photography in America.* Ed. James Allen et al. Santa Fe: Twin Palms, 2000. 38–44.

Andrews, William L. "The Literature of Slavery and Freedom: 1746–1865." *The Norton Anthology of African American Literature.* Ed. Henry Louis Gates Jr. and Nellie Y. McKay. New York: Norton, 1997. 127–36.

Bad as I Wanna Be: The Story of Dennis Rodman. ABC. 8 Feb. 1998.

Baker, Houston A., Jr. *Blues, Ideology, and Afro-American Literature: A Vernacular Theory.* Chicago: U of Chicago P, 1984.

———. "Scene . . . Not Heard." *Reading Rodney King/Reading Urban Uprising.* Ed. Robert Gooding-Williams. New York: Routledge, 1993. 38–48.

Baldwin, James. *The Evidence of Things Not Seen.* 1985. New York: Holt, 1995.

———. *The Fire Next Time.* 1962. New York: Vintage, 1993.

———. "Going to Meet the Man." *Going to Meet the Man.* 1965. New York: Vintage, 1993. 228–49.

Bamboozled. Dir. Spike Lee. DVD. New Line Cinema, 2000.

Bandele, Asha. "Meditations in the Hour of Mourning." *Tough Love: Cultural Criticism and Familial Observations on the Life and Death of Tupac Shakur.* Ed. Michael Datcher and Kwame Alexander. Alexandria: Alexander, 1996. 25–30.

Barbershop. Dir. Tim Story. DVD. Metro-Goldwyn-Mayer Pictures, 2002.

Barkin, Jesse. "Gone but Not Yet forgotten." *National Post* 1 Dec. 1998: B11.

Barrett, Lindon. "Black Men in the Mix: Badboys, Heroes, Sequins, and Dennis Rodman." *Callaloo* 20.1 (1997): 106–26.

———. "Dead Men Printed: Tupac Shakur, Biggie Small, and Hip-Hop Eulogy." *Callaloo* 22.2 (1999): 306–32.

Best Buy. Advertisement. *Sports Illustrated* 1 Sept. 2003: 41.

Bickley, Dan. *No Bull: The Unauthorized Biography of Dennis Rodman.* New York: St. Martin's, 1997.

Blandon, Aaron. E-mail to Linda Tucker. 17 July 2005.

BMG Marketing Group. Advertisement. *Village Voice* 28 Apr. 1998: 36–37.

Booker, Christopher B. *"I Will Wear No Chain!": A Social History of African-American Males.* Westport: Praeger, 2000.

Boskin, Joseph. *Sambo: The Rise and Demise of an American Jester.* New York: Oxford UP, 1986.

Boyd, Todd. *Am I Black Enough for You?: Popular Culture from the 'Hood and Beyond.* Bloomington: Indiana UP, 1997.

———. "The Game Is to Be Sold, Not to Be Told." *Basketball Jones: America above the Rim.* Ed. Todd Boyd and Kenneth L. Shropshire. New York: New York UP, 2000. ix–xii.

———. "Mo' Money, Mo' Problems: Keepin' It Real in the Post-Jordan Era." *Basketball Jones: America above the Rim.* Ed. Todd Boyd and Kenneth L. Shropshire. New York: New York UP, 2000. 59–67.

———. "Preface: Anatomy of a Murder: O.J. and the Imperative of Sports in Cultural Studies." *Out of Bounds: Sports, Media, and the Politics of Identity.* Bloomington: Indiana UP, 1997. vii–ix.

Boyd, Todd, and Kenneth L. Shropshire. "Basketball Jones: A New World Order?" *Basketball Jones: America above the Rim.* Ed. Todd Boyd and Kenneth L. Shropshire. New York: New York UP, 2000. 1–11.

Branch, G. E., III. "Sprewell: 'I Wasn't Choking P.J.'" *USA Today* 9 Mar. 1998: 5C.

Brundage, W. Fitzhugh, ed. *Under Sentence of Death: Lynching in the South.* Chapel Hill: U of North Carolina P, 1997. 1–20.

Brunt, Stephen. "NBA Labour Dispute Offers a Lesson in Tactics." *Globe and Mail* 19 Dec. 1998: A32.

Butler, Judith. *Excitable Speech: A Politics of the Performative.* New York: Routledge, 1997.

Caponi, Gena Dagel. "The Case for an African American Aesthetic." Ed. *Signifyin(g), Sanctifyin', and Slam Dunking: A Reader in African American Expressive Culture.* Ed. Gena Dagel Caponi. Amherst: U of Massachusetts P, 1999. 1–41.

Carby, Hazel V. *Race Men.* Cambridge: Harvard UP, 1998.

Carter, Rubin "Hurricane." *The 16th Round: From Number 1 Contender to Number 45472.* 1974. Toronto: Penguin, 1991.

Cheney, Charise. "Representin' God: Rap, Religion, and the Politics of a Culture." *North Star* 3.1 (1999). 8 Nov 1999 <<http://cypress.barnard.columbia.edu/~north/volume3/cheney.html>>.

Chernoff, John Miller. *African Rhythm and African Sensibility: Aesthetics and Social Action in African Musical Idioms.* Chicago: U of Chicago P, 1979.

Chevy Malibu. Advertisement. *Ebony* July 2001: 46.

Chevy Trucks. Advertisement. *Ebony* Apr. 2001: 164.

Christian, Barbara. "The Race for Theory." *Within the Circle: An Anthology of African American Literary Criticism from the Harlem Renaissance to the Present.* Ed. Angelyn Mitchell. Durham: Duke UP, 1994. 348–59.

Christmas, Walter. "Advertising Jim Crow." *Classes and Mainstream* Sept. 1949: 54+.

Church, George L. "The Fire This Time." *Time* 11 May 1992: 22–29.

"Crackdown, Call for Calm: 72-Hour State of Siege after White Police Officer Kills Black Driver." *Edmonton Journal* 26 Oct. 1996: A5.

Cullen, Countee. "The Black Christ." *My Soul's High Song: The Collected Writings of Countee Cullen.* Ed. Gerald Early. New York: Anchor, 1991. 207–36.

Cunningham, George P. "Body Politics: Race, Gender, and the Captive Body." *Representing Black Men.* Ed. Marcellus Blount and George P. Cunningham. New York: Routledge, 1996. 131–54.

Datcher, Michael. "Troubled Flight." *Tough Love: Cultural Criticism and Familial Observations on the Life and Death of Tupac Shakur.* Ed. Michael Datcher and Kwame Alexander. Alexandria: Alexander, 1996. 34–37.

Davis, Angela Y. "Race and Criminalization: Black Americans and the Punishment Industry." *The House That Race Built: Black Americans, U.S. Terrain.* Ed. Wahneema Lubiano. New York: Pantheon, 1997. 264–79.

Dawsey, Darrell. "No Time for Tears: A Eulogy for Tupac." *Essence* Dec. 1996: 38.

Degree Antiperspirant. Advertisement. *Sports Illustrated* 7 Apr. 2003: 87.

Du Bois, W. E. B. *The Souls of Black Folk.* 1903. New York: Vintage, 1990.

Dyson, Michael Eric. *Between God and Gangsta Rap: Bearing Witness to Black Culture.* New York: Oxford UP, 1996.

———. *Holler If You Hear Me: Searching for Tupac Shakur.* New York: Basic Civitas, 2001.

———. *Open Mike: Reflections on Philosophy, Race, Sex, Culture, and Religion.* New York: Basic Civitas, 2003.

———. *Reflecting Black: African-American Cultural Criticism.* Minneapolis: U of Minnesota P, 1993.

Ellison, Ralph. "Change the Joke and Slip the Yoke." *Shadow and Act.* 1964. New York: Vintage, 1972. 45–59.

———. *Invisible Man.* 1952. New York: Vintage, 1990.

———. "The Little Man at Chehaw Station: The American Artist and His Audience." *Going to the Territory.* New York: Vintage, 1986. 3–38.

———. "The Shadow and the Act." *Shadow and Act.* 1964. New York: Vintage, 1972. 273–81.

———. "The World and the Jug." *Shadow and Act.* 1964. New York: Vintage, 1972. 107–43.

Feschuk, Dave. "Call Him What You Want, Worm's a Winner." *National Post* 21 Jan. 1999: B12.

———. "Sprewell's, Ahem, Dialogue with Fans Consists of Four Letters and 10 Grand." *National Post* 25 Nov. 1999: B11.

Fiske, John. "Black Bodies of Knowledge: Notes on an Effective History." *Cultural Critique* 33 (Spring 1996): 185–212.

———. *Media Matters: Race and Gender in U.S. Politics.* Minneapolis: U of Minnesota P, 1996.

———. "Surveilling the City: Whiteness, the Black Man, and Democratic Totalitarianism." *Theory, Culture, and Society* 15.2 (May 1998): 67–88.

———. *Understanding Popular Culture.* New York: Routledge, 1989.

Foucault, Michel. *Discipline and Punish: The Birth of the Prison.* 1977. New York: Vintage, 1995.

———. *The History of Sexuality.* Vol. 1, *An Introduction.* 1976. New York: Vintage, 1990.

———. "Nietzsche, Genealogy, History." *Language, Counter-Memory, Practice: Selected Essays and Interviews.* Ed. Donald F. Bouchard. Trans. Donald F. Bouchard and Sherry Simon. Ithaca: Cornell UP, 1977. 139–64.

Franklin, H. Bruce. *Prison Literature in America: The Victim as Criminal and Artist.* Expanded ed. New York: Oxford UP, 1989.

Fredrickson, George M. *The Black Image in the White Mind: The Debate on Afro-American Character and Destiny, 1817–1914.* New York: New York: Harper and Row, 1971.

"The Game Within: Latrell Sprewell v. P. J. Carlesimo." *National Post* 18 Nov. 1999: B12.

Gates, Henry Louis, Jr. *Figures in Black: Words, Signs, and the "Racial" Self.* New York: Oxford UP, 1987.

———. *The Signifying Monkey: A Theory of African-American Literary Criticism.* New York: Oxford UP, 1988.

General Electric. Advertisement. *Ebony* Feb. 2001: 53.

George, Nelson. *Elevating the Game: Black Men and Basketball.* New York: HarperCollins, 1992.

Gilmore, Mikal. "Easy Target: Why Tupac Should Be Heard before He's Buried." *Rolling Stone* 31 Oct. 1996: 49–51+.

Gilroy, Paul. Introduction. *Eight Men* by Richard Wright. 1961. New York: HarperPerennial, 1989. xi–xxi.

Glaude, Eddie S., Jr. *Exodus: Religion, Race, and Nation in Early Nineteenth-Century Black America.* Chicago: U of Chicago P, 2000.

Gloster, Rob. "Sprewell Admits He Made a Mistake." *Edmonton Journal* 10 Dec. 1997: D4.

GM Certified Used Vehicles. Advertisement. *Sports Illustrated* 8 Sept. 2003: 75.

Greenfield, Jeff. "The Black and White Truth about Basketball." 1975. *Signifyin(g), Sanctifyin', and Slam Dunking: A Reader in African American Expressive Culture.* Ed. Gena Dagel Caponi. Amherst: U of Massachusetts P, 1999. 373–78.

Gubar, Susan. *Racechanges: White Skin, Black Face in American Culture.* New York: Oxford UP, 1997.

Guerrero, Ed. "The Black Man on Our Screens and the Empty Space in Representation." *Black Male: Representations of Masculinity in Contemporary American Art.* Ed. Thelma Golden. New York: Abrams, 1994. 181–89.

———. *Framing Blackness: The African American Image in Film.* Philadelphia: Temple UP, 1993.

Halberstam, David. *Playing for Keeps: Michael Jordan and the World He Made.* New York: Random House, 1999.

Hale, Grace Elizabeth. *Making Whiteness: The Culture of Segregation in the South, 1890–1940.* New York: Pantheon, 1998.

Hanes. "Boxers or Briefs?" 29 Sept. 2005 <<http://www.advertisementave.com/tv/ad.asp?adid=360>>.

Harper, Phillip Brian. *Are We Not Men?: Masculine Anxiety and the Problem of African-American Identity.* New York: Oxford UP, 1998.

Harris, Cheryl. "Whiteness as Property." *Black on White: Black Writers on What It Means to Be White.* Ed. David R. Roediger. New York: Schocken, 1998. 103–18.

Harris-Lacewell, Melissa Victoria. *Barbershops, Bibles, and BET: Everyday Talk and Black Political Thought.* Princeton: Princeton UP, 2004.

Higginbotham, A. Leon, Jr. *Shades of Freedom: Racial Politics and Presumptions of the American Legal Process.* New York: Oxford UP, 1996.

Hoberman, John. *Darwin's Athletes: How Sport Has Damaged Black America and Preserved the Myth of Race.* New York: Houghton Mifflin, 1997.

Holland, Sharon P. "Bill T. Jones, Tupac Shakur, and the (Queer) Art of Death." *Callaloo* 23.1 (2000): 384–93.

Holloway, Karla F. C. *Moorings and Metaphors: Figures of Culture and Gender in Black Women's Literature.* New Brunswick: Rutgers UP, 1992.

Hooks, bell. *Black Looks: Race and Representation.* Toronto: Between the Lines, 1992.

———. "Representations of Whiteness in the Black Imagination." *Black on White: Black Writers on What It Means to Be White.* Ed. David R. Roediger. New York: Schocken, 1998. 38–53.

————. *We Real Cool: Black Men and Masculinity*. New York: Routledge, 2004.

Houck, Davis W. "Attacking the Rim: The Cultural Politics of Dunking." *Basketball Jones: America above the Rim*. Ed. Todd Boyd and Kenneth L. Shropshire. New York: New York UP, 2000. 151–69.

Hurston, Zora Neale. *Mules and Men*. 1935. New York: Harper and Row, 1990.

Jacobson-Hardy, Michael. "Behind the Razor Wire." *Behind the Razor Wire: Portrait of a Contemporary American Prison System*. New York: New York UP, 1999. 1–12.

Johnson, Charles, and John McCuskery. *Black Men Speaking*. Bloomington: Indiana UP, 1997.

Johnson, James Weldon, and J. Rosamond Johnson. *The Books of American Negro Spirituals*. 1926. New York: Da Capo, 1969.

Jones, Chris. "Tall versus Big at the Negotiating Table." *National Post* 28 Oct. 1998: B10.

Jones, Gayl. *Liberating Voices: Oral Tradition in African American Literature*. Cambridge: Harvard UP, 1991.

Jordan, Joseph F. "Without Sanctuary." 31 Jan. 2003. <<http://www.nps.gov/WithoutSanctuary/message_curator.htm>>.

Kelley, Robin D. G. *Freedom Dreams: The Black Radical Imagination*. Boston: Beacon, 2002.

————. *Yo' Mama's Disfunktional: Fighting the Culture Wars in Urban America*. Boston: Beacon, 1997.

Kennedy, Randall. *Race, Crime, and the Law*. New York; Pantheon, 1997.

The Last Blackface. Dir. Aaron Blandon. Videocassette. Independent, 2002.

Levine, Lawrence W. *Black Culture and Black Consciousness: Afro-American Folk Thought from Slavery to Freedom*. New York: Oxford UP, 1977.

Lhamon, W. T., Jr. *Raising Cain: Blackface Performance from Jim Crow to Hip Hop*. Cambridge: Harvard UP, 1998.

Lipsitz, George. "The Greatest Story Ever Told: Marketing and the O. J. Simpson Trial." *Birth of a Nation'hood: Gaze, Script, and Spectacle in the O. J. Simpson Case*. Ed. Toni Morrison and Claudia Brodsky Lacour. New York: Random House, 1997. 3–29.

Little Bill. Advertisement. *Essence* Dec. 2003: 210.

Litwack, Leon F. "Hellhounds." *Without Sanctuary: Lynching Photography in America*. Ed. James Allen et al. Santa Fe: Twin Palms, 2000. 8–37.

Lott, Eric. *Love and Theft: Blackface Minstrelsy and the American Working Class*. New York: Oxford UP, 1993.

Lubiano, Wahneema. Introduction. *The House That Race Built: Black Americans, U.S. Terrain*. Ed. Wahneema Lubiano. New York: Pantheon, 1997. vii–ix.

Malveaux, Julianne. "Gladiators, Gazelles, and Groupies: Basketball Love and Loathing." *Basketball Jones: America above the Rim*. Ed. Todd Boyd and Kenneth L. Shropshire. New York: New York UP, 2000. 51–58.

Marriott, David. *On Black Men*. New York: Columbia UP, 2000.

Mauer, Marc, and Tracy Huling. *Young Black Americans and the Criminal Justice System: Five Years Later*. Washington: Sentencing Project, 1995.

McCall, Nathan. *Makes Me Wanna Holler: A Young Black Man in America*. New York: Vintage, 1994.

McClintock, Anne. *Imperial Leather: Race, Gender, and Sexuality in the Colonial Contest*. New York: Routledge, 1995.

Merck. Advertisement. *Ebony* June 2001: 12–13.

Metzger, Bruce M., and Michael D. Coogan, eds. *The Oxford Companion to the Bible*. New York: Oxford UP, 1993.

Miller Brewing Company. Advertisement. *Ebony* June 2001: 119.

Miller, J. K. "From the Press Box: A Survey of the Media's Sports Coverage." *The Source Sports* Apr. 1999: 39–40.

Miller, Jerome G. *Search and Destroy: African-American Males in the Criminal Justice System.* New York: Cambridge UP, 1996.

Mitchell-Bray, Marsha. "A Two-Pack of Tupac." *Tough Love: Cultural Criticism and Familial Observations on The Life and Death of Tupac Shakur.* Ed. Michael Datcher and Kwame Alexander. Alexandria: Alexander, 1996. 101–4.

Moore, Steve. "In the Bleachers." Cartoon. *Edmonton Journal* 2 Jan. 1998: D4.

Morrison, Toni. "Home." *The House That Race Built: Black Americans, U.S. Terrain.* Ed. Wahneema Lubiano. New York: Pantheon, 1997. 3–12.

———. "The Official Story: Dead Man Golfing." *Birth of a Nation'hood: Gaze, Script, and Spectacle in the O. J. Simpson Case.* Ed. Toni Morrison and Claudia Brodsky Lacour. New York: Random House, 1997. vii–xxviii.

Moses, Wilson Jeremiah. *Black Messiahs and Uncle Toms: Social and Literary Manipulations of a Religious Myth.* University Park: Pennsylvania State UP, 1993.

"National Basketball Association Loses Employees due to Lockout." *National Post* 15 Dec. 1998: B11.

Nationwide Insurance and Financial Services. Advertisement. *Essence* Sept. 2003: 119.

Nike. "The Fun Police: Find the Ref." Advertisement. 1998.

———. "The Fun Police: Kid Never Passes the Ball." Advertisement. 1998.

———. "Pro Vent Top." Advertisement. *Sports Illustrated.* 3 Nov. 2003: 71–72.

Noel, Peter. "Driving while Black: Fear and Loathing on the New Jersey Turnpike." *Village Voice* 9 June 1998: 39+.

Office Max. "Rubberband Man." Advertisement. 2004.

Ogren, Kathy J. *The Jazz Revolution: Twenties America and the Meaning of Jazz.* New York: Oxford UP, 1989.

Olguín, B. V. "Tattoos, Abjection, and the Political Unconscious: Towards a Semiotics of the *Pinto* Visual Vernacular." *Cultural Critique* 37 (Autumn 1997): 159–213.

O'Malley, Michael. "A Blood Red Record: The 1890s and American Apartheid." 27 Jan. 2003 <<http://www.ferris.edu/news/jimcrow/links/misclink/1890s/>>.

Patterson, Orlando. *Rituals of Blood: Consequences of Slavery in Two American Centuries.* New York: Basic Civitas, 1998.

Payloader. Advertisement. *U.S. News and World Report.* 1 Feb. 1957.

Perry, Imani. *Prophets of the Hood: Politics and Poetics in Hip Hop.* Durham: Duke UP, 2004.

Powell, Kevin. "Bury Me Like a G." *Rolling Stone* 31 Oct. 1996: 38–46.

Puma. Advertisement. *FHM* May 2002: 54, 56.

Quinn, Eithne. *Nuthin' but a "G" Thang: The Culture and Commerce of Gangsta Rap.* New York: Columbia UP, 2005.

Quinn, Michael. "'Never Shoulda Been Let out the Penitentiary': Gangsta Rap and the Struggle of Racial Identity." *Cultural Critique* 34 (Autumn 1996): 65–89.

Raab, Scott. "Dennis Rodman, in the Pink." *GQ* Feb. 1997: 136–41.

Reddy, T. J. "A Poem for Black Rhythmeticians." *Prison Literature in America: The Victim as Criminal and Artist.* Ed. H. Bruce Franklin. Expanded ed. New York: Oxford UP, 1989. 251.

Reed, Ishmael. "Another Day at the Front." *Police Brutality.* Ed. Jill Nelson. New York: Norton, 2000. 189–205.

Reid, Mark. *Black Lenses, Black Voices: African American Film Now*. Lanham: Rowman and Littlefield 2005.

———. *Postnegritude Visual and Literary Culture*. Albany: SUNY P, 1997.

"Reveal Jim Crow Policy in U.S. Advertising; 'Menial' Negroes Only Are Shown in Ads" [April 1950]. Clipping Files: Advertising Industry—Negroes. Schomburg Center for Research in Black Culture, New York Public Library, New York.

Rodman, Dennis, and Tim Keown. *Bad as I Wanna Be*. New York: Delacorte, 1996.

Rodman, Dennis, and Michael Silver. *Walk on the Wild Side*. Ed. Michael Silver. New York: Delacorte, 1997.

Rodríguez, Dylan. *Forced Passages: Imprisoned Radical Intellectuals and the U.S. Prison Regime*. Minneapolis: U of Minnesota P, 2006.

Roediger, David R. Introduction. *Black on White: Black Writers on What It Means to Be White*. Ed. David R. Roediger. New York: Schocken, 1998. 1–26.

"Romijn Dressing." *GQ* Feb. 1997: 142–51.

Rose, Tricia. *Black Noise: Rap Music and Black Culture in Contemporary America*. Hanover: UP of New England, 1994.

Russell, Thaddeus. "Is Rap Tomorrow's Jazz?" H-NET Discussion List for African American Studies. 22 Aug. 2005 <<H-AFRO-AM@H-NET.MSU.EDU>>.

Scott, James C. *Domination and the Arts of Resistance: Hidden Transcripts*. New Haven: Yale UP, 1990.

Shaw, William. "Rhyme and Punishment." *Details* Apr. 1996: 154–58, 173.

Shields, David. *Black Planet: Facing Race during an NBA Season*. New York: Crown, 1999.

Shropshire, Kenneth L. "Deconstructing the NBA." *Basketball Jones: America above the Rim*. Ed. Todd Boyd and Kenneth L. Shropshire. New York: New York UP, 2000. 75–89.

Smith, Craig V. "Darkness Visible: The Politics of Being Seen from Ellison to Zebrahead." *Canadian Review of American Studies* 26:1 (1996): 111–22.

Smith, Danyel, Rob Marriott, et al. "Tupac Shakur, 1971–1996." *Vibe* Nov. 1996: T1–T8.

Smith, Theophus H. *Conjuring Culture: Biblical Formations of Black America*. New York: Oxford UP, 1994.

Smitherman, Geneva. *Talkin and Testifyin: The Language of Black America*. Detroit: Wayne State UP, 1977.

Solotaroff, Ivan. "Gangsta Life, Gangster Death." *Esquire* Dec. 1996: 77–86.

Spillers, Hortense. "Mama's Baby, Papa's Maybe: An American Grammar Book." *Within the Circle: An Anthology of African American Literary Criticism from the Harlem Renaissance to the Present*. Ed. Angelyn Mitchell. Durham: Duke UP, 1994. 454–81.

Steiner, Christopher B. "Body Personal and Body Politic: Adornment and Leadership in Cross-Cultural Perspective." *Anthropos* 85.4–6 (1990): 431–45.

Sundquist, Eric. *To Wake the Nations: Race in the Making of American Literature*. Cambridge: Belknap Press of Harvard UP, 1993.

Tate, Greg. "He Is Truly Free Who Is Free from the Need to Be Free: A Survey and Consideration of Black Male Genius." *Black Male: Representations of Masculinity in Contemporary American Art*. Ed. Thelma Golden. New York: Abrams, 1994. 111–18.

———. "Introduction: Nigs R Us, or How Blackfolk Became Fetish Objects." *Everything but the Burden: What White People Are Taking from Black Culture*. Ed. Greg Tate. New York: Broadway, 2003. 1–14.

Taylor, Clyde. "The Game." *Black Male: Representations of Masculinity in Contemporary American Art*. Ed. Thelma Golden. New York: Abrams, 1994. 167–74.

Taylor, Phil. "Phil Taylor's NBA Insider." *Sports Illustrated: Pro Basketball* '97@–98 13 Oct. 1997: 6–11.

Toyota Tundra. Advertisement. *Sports Illustrated* 3 Feb. 2003: 59.

Tupac Shakur. Ed. Alan Light. New York: Crown, 1997.

Voisin, Ailene. "Allegations of NBA Racism Not Surprising." *National Post* 17 Dec. 1998: B11.

Walcott, Rinaldo. "Images of the Middle Passage: History, Memory, and the Changing Present." Black Speakers Series Lecture. Southern Arkansas University, Magnolia, 14 Feb. 2005.

———. "Pedagogy and Trauma: The Middle Passage, Slavery, and the Problem of Creolization." *Between Hope and Despair: Pedagogy and the Remembrance of Historical Trauma.* Ed. Roger Simon et al. Lanham: Rowman and Littlefield, 2000. 135–51.

———. "The Struggle for Happiness: Commodified Black Masculinities, Vernacular Culture, and Homoerotic Desires." *Pedagogies of Difference: Rethinking Education for Social Change.* Ed. Peter Pericles Trifonas. New York: Routledge, 2003. 137–54.

Walker, Alice. "In Search of Our Mothers' Gardens." *In Search of Our Mothers' Gardens.* New York: Harcourt Brace Jovanovich, 1984. 231–43.

———. "The Unglamorous but Worthwhile Duties of the Black Revolutionary Artist, or of the Black Writer Who Simply Works and Writes." *In Search of Our Mothers' Gardens.* New York: Harcourt Brace Jovanovich, 1984. 130–38.

Washington, Patricia A., and Lynda Dixon Shaver. "The Language Culture of Rap Music Videos." *Language, Rhythm, and Sound: Black Popular Cultures into the Twenty-first Century.* Ed. Joseph K. Adjaye and Adrianne R. Andrews. Pittsburgh: U of Pittsburgh P, 1997. 164–77.

Watkins, Craig S. *Representing: Hip Hop Culture and the Production of Black Cinema.* Chicago: U of Chicago P, 1998.

Webber, Thomas L. *Deep Like the Rivers: Education in the Slave Quarter Community, 1831–1865.* New York: Norton, 1978.

Wells, Melanie. "Nike's 'Fun Police' Ads a Hit among Young Urban Viewers." *USA Today* 6 July 1998: 14B.

White, Armond. *Rebel for the Hell of It: The Life of Tupac Shakur.* New York: Thunder's Mouth, 1997.

White, Shane, and Graham White. *Stylin': African American Expressive Culture from Its Beginning to the Zoot Suit.* Ithaca: Cornell UP, 1998.

Wideman, John Edgar. "All Stories Are True." *All Stories Are True.* New York: Vintage, 1992. 3–17.

———. *Brothers and Keepers.* New York: Penguin, 1984.

———. "Doing Time, Marking Race." *Behind the Razor Wire: Portrait of a Contemporary American Prison System.* Ed. Michael Jacobson-Hardy. New York: New York UP, 1999. 11–17.

———. *Hiding Place.* 1981. New York: Vintage, 1988.

———. Introduction. *The Souls of Black Folk* by W. E. B. Du Bois. 1903. New York: Vintage, 1990. xi–xvi.

———. "The Language of Home." *New York Times* 13 Jan. 1985 <<www.nytimes.com/books/98/10/04/specials/wideman-language.html>>.

———. *The Lynchers.* New York: Holt, 1973.

———. *Philadelphia Fire.* 1990. New York: Vintage, 1991.

———. *Reuben.* New York: Penguin, 1987.

Wiegman, Robyn. *American Anatomies: Theorizing Race and Gender.* Durham: Duke UP, 1995.

Williams, Frank. "The Living End." *Source* Nov. 1996: 103–4.

Williams, Patricia J. *The Alchemy of Race and Rights.* Cambridge: Harvard UP, 1991.

Wilson, Robert Rawdon. "Graffiti Become Terror: The Idea of Resistance." *Canadian Review of Comparative Literature* 22.2(1995): 267–75.

———. "Tattoos: Play and Interpretation." *Textual Studies in Canada* 3 (1993): 63–85.

Wood, Amy Louise. "Lynching Photography and the 'Black Beast Rapist' in the Southern White Masculine Imagination." *Masculinity: Bodies, Movies, Culture.* Ed. Peter Lehman. New York: Routledge, 2001: 193–211.

Wright, Richard. "The Man Who Lived Underground." 1961. *Eight Men.* New York: HarperPerennial, 1989. 19–84.

DISCOGRAPHY

2Pac. *2Pacalypse Now.* Interscope, 1991.

————. *Makaveli: The Donkilluminati: The 7 Day Theory.* Death Row/Interscope, 1996.

————. *Me against the World.* Interscope, 1995.

————. *RU Still Down? (Remember Me).* Interscope, 1997.

————. *Strictly for My N.I.G.G.A.Z.* Interscope, 1993.

Ice Cube. *The Predator.* Priority, 1992.

Public Enemy. *It Takes a Nation of Millions to Hold Us Back.* Def Jam, 1988.

INDEX